CONCERNING BEAUTY

LONDON: HUMPHREY MILFORD
OXFORD UNIVERSITY PRESS

Michelangelo. Studies for the Libyan Sibyl

Metropolitan Museum, New York

CONCERNING BEAUTY

BY

FRANK JEWETT MATHER, Jr.

MARQUAND PROFESSOR
OF ART AND ARCHAEOLOGY, EMERITUS
IN PRINCETON UNIVERSITY

PUBLISHED ON
THE LOUIS CLARK VANUXEM FOUNDATION

PRINCETON
PRINCETON UNIVERSITY PRESS
1935

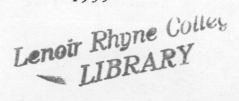

PRINTED AT PRINCETON UNIVERSITY PRESS
PRINCETON, NEW JERSEY, U.S.A.

To

WILLIAM RANKIN

GOOD COMRADE
IN THIS QUEST

PREFACE

THE *only thing noteworthy about this new and per-*
haps superfluous book on esthetics is that for over
forty years of active esthetic experience I have refrained
from writing it. The crystallizing shock came in the form
of an appointment to the Vanuxem Lectureship at Prince-
ton University, and though the book was not written in
lecture form, most of its substance was given as lectures
in the late winter of 1935. While for over thirty years I had
done much desultory reading in esthetics, I intentionally
postponed systematic reading until the manuscript was
complete, preferring to build the book rather upon my own
esthetic experience than upon the theories of others. This
procedure has involved some slight rewriting and some
residuum of inconsistency and trial and error. It is custom-
ary to edit such a treatise into complete consistency, but I
think it may actually be advantageous to a serious reader
to follow some of those hesitating processes that inevitably
underlie all broad generalizations. On the whole, while in
the theory of correspondences of rhythm, I believe I have
presented a relative novelty, I have wanted the book to be
less a systematization than a thorough ventilation of its
theme. Esthetics is a subject that easily becomes at once
gaunt and stuffy through elimination of what is too pe-
dantically labelled as the non-esthetic. This error, I hope, a
long empirical experience has enabled me to avoid. My
considerable debt to earlier estheticians is sufficiently
acknowledged in the text and bibliography, except in the

case of John Dewey's Art as Experience, *to which as handsomely confirming and fixing my own still nebulous point of view I am under peculiar obligations.*

F. J. M., Jʀ.

Three Brooks
Washington Crossing, Pennsylvania
February 1935.

CONTENTS

Contents

CHAPTER VI

THE ARTIST

Contents

ILLUSTRATIONS

lyric. It wants to be sung. In theory the poet should compose not merely in words but also in melody. Since the Middle Ages and the troubadours this has rarely happened. That engaging Irish troubadour of our great-grandfathers' time, Tom Moore, is highly exceptional. But the moment a lyric is set to music by an artist not the poet, a new form is interwoven with the old, and a form conceived in a new medium. For the purist we now have a new work of art, but whose? Is Schubert's *Erlkönig* predominantly Schubert or predominantly Goethe? The latter, I think, but of course I cannot prove it. And Schubert's *Erlkönig* is again existent only in an infinity of individual interpretations by as many singers. Indeed every reading aloud of a lyric is different, implying a difference of response in each reader— that is, a different form of each reader's experience of beauty.

Even a painting or statue, which we are inclined to reject if it is not completely autographic, may by no means be so in reality. For most of the work of his last six years Raphael merely supplied working drawings and supervision. The work of his assistants was imperfectly under his control. For their energy of conception, Vasari admired as the greatest Raphaels such frescoes as "Heliodorus expelled from the Temple," "St. Peter liberated from Prison," and the "Burning City." We differ from Vasari, preferring to these sensational narratives, which are still predominantly Raphael, the "Parnassus," the "Dispute concerning the Sacrament," the "School of Athens," and the "Mass of Bolsena." But these frescoes too are by no means completely autographic. There is much work of assistants in them. Yet no person of taste would prefer to them the simpler and less able Madonnas of Raphael's earlier years, though these are entirely of his own craftsmanship, completely controlled by him.

This is not to deny the delight of exquisite and entirely integral workmanship—such ultimate refinements as we have in the few nocturnes of Whistler that are well preserved, or in the handful of lovely pictures by Jan Vermeer. But these are not typical cases in the art of painting. Most of the Whistler nocturnes have changed disastrously, most old pictures we see through a veil of repaint. The Titians were very bright. Even the few that still seem bright, such as the amazing "Bacchus and Ariadne," at London, and its companion pieces at Madrid, have darkened appreciably. Yet these greatly changed and much impaired masterpieces are still the joy of the art lover. Much as there is in them that Titian never wanted or would have approved, they are still predominantly Titian.

That the case is the same in sculpture, I need hardly maintain. All of Rodin's marbles are copies mechanically but very skilfully made by minor artists from the master's clay models. Only the bronzes are relatively autographic. This is the general case with stone sculpture, and has been for centuries; the nominal sculptor only designs the work, he may not even model it to scale. It is cut in stone by some artisan assistant.

This practice has been treated very scornfully by the purist critic, Wilenski, who insists that the sculptor should be what the word literally implies, a stonecutter, while maintaining that all modelling is an inferior art akin to painting. While a good case can be made for this position, and an admirer of Rodin might well prefer the "John the

Baptist," and the "Age of Iron," to "The Kiss" and "The Fountain," I cannot see that the marbles are really less Rodin than the bronzes. In whatever material and at whatever remove from his own craftsmanship he speaks the same language.

Again most sculpture is made for a particular environment for which its form is carefully calculated. Change the environment, move the statue to another climate, another light, an alien setting, and it yields an appearance which the artist never intended. Enough, if its character remains predominantly that of its creator.

That a work of architecture, any fine building, is from beginning to end a variable need hardly be argued. The architect may design his building, but he cannot build it himself. Its ultimate appearance, its artistic form, depends upon a hundred and one persons and considerations. His control over the actual construction is at best remote. He must in the main accept such an interpretation of his intention as his foreman and workmen are capable of giving or willing to give. One who has ever built will marvel that anything comes off as the architect intended.

Moreover the building is constantly subject to repairs and alterations which were never in the architect's mind. Indeed many of the grandest buildings, notably the great medieval cathedrals, were built over long periods of time with much change of plan, and the loosest control of details of decoration. Every great cathedral is a curious composite of many minds working after all in a similar direction. And paradoxically these eminently composite works of art which no man really controlled often give not merely the richest but also the most integral effect of beauty. The work of art then is not fragile but tough and even somewhat elastic. It can bear rude handling.

So we came by a devious route to the consoling conclusion, that if we must get along without constancy in the work of art, and accept it as a variable, yet the work of art retains all its benign potency. It is these variables that evoke sufficiently the most stable experience that human kind knows—that of beauty.

If considered analytically and merely in its formal aspect the work of art is not a constant but a variable, so it is a variable when studied in its only reality, as an object that produces an effect upon an observer. The work of art has existence only in opinion, the Italian philosopher Gentile has justly remarked. Let us imagine that an artist carries through to successful completion a masterpiece. It embodies all the meaning with which he meant to invest it. It attains perfectly the form he had glimpsed through long endeavor. On finishing it, the artist dies, and thereafter nobody ever sees, let us say, his statue. So long as he cared about it and worked at it, it was alive, produced an effect upon him while he wrought it, but now it is dead, produces no effect upon anybody. Let us suppose that his statue is heedlessly destroyed; then it is dead irrevocably. Imagine rather that it is stored obscurely. It still has potential life. It will come alive whenever somebody regards it with love and admiration.

In short the best analogy *per se* for a work of art is a sweetheart. The loveliest girl imaginable is not intrinsically a sweetheart, though she clearly is such potentially. She is a sweetheart only while some man holds her such. So no work of art nor scene in nature has beauty as its own attribute or integument. It is beautiful only when and so long as it evokes an experience of beauty in somebody. Beauty then is a quality of a human experience, and not of any object. The search for beauty involves therefore a study of such experience, a most difficult but still a feasible investigation. The accurate statement of any experience of beauty is never: this is a beautiful object, and I am enjoying its beauty, but rather I am enjoying an experience of beauty apropos of this object. Concerning all this, Lord Listowel has written eloquently and truly:

"The beautiful, in its most essential features, is a special attitude of the human soul in the face of things, an experience that transpires in the person of the artist or artistic spectator, strictly speaking beauty only exists in the universe at the actual moment of creative activity or appreciative delight."

Later we must face and if possible solve the paradox that that beauty which is only in our own psychical experience we inevitably regard as exterior to ourselves and resident physically in some arrangement of colors, shapes or sounds—a work of art, an appearance in nature. For the present I wish only to note that since the work of art lives only in opinion, its effect is even less a constant than is its form. A much loved masterpiece lives only in an infinity of appreciations, no two of which are precisely alike, and many of which are radically different.

The case may best be illustrated from a great masterpiece of painting which has continuously evoked delectation in hundreds of thousands of men and women for over five centuries—Titian's "Sacred and Profane Love." The title is not his, but that of some gallery director. Ambiguous in meaning, the picture has undergone many conflicting interpretations and has given contradictory delights. Idealizing lovers of Titian's symbolical idyll have always held that the clothed matronly figure symbolizes sophisticated, that is, profane love, while the nude maiden holding up a burning lamp impersonates artless, that is, sacred love. This is probably the standard and popular interpretation today. Others have reversed the meaning of the figures, correctly I think. For, consulting the picture itself, Titian has given the poetical clue in the respective backgrounds. In the distance beyond the nude figure are running rabbits, proverbially most sexually incontinent of beasts, and, as well, a man and woman in the ultimate embrace. The nude figure then glorifies the simple passion of the human animal.

And in the pastoral distance behind the clothed figure are people at work and a man returning home. If the matronly figure means anything about love at all, she impersonates disciplined or socialized love. This, as consecrated to uses and ends beyond its own immediate gratification, may reasonably be regarded as Sacred Love. Such an interpretation is reinforced by the brazier which the matron touches, in which the fire, which flames freely from the lamp upheld by the nude figure, is carefully contained and preserved.

This general interpretation, passion in anticipation versus love in social experience, was made by an old friend of mine, the late William P. Andrews of Capri. He published it in the *Nation* and I have merely added the corroborative features from the background.

TIZIANO VECELLIO 1477 · 1576

Titian. Sacred and Profane Love

Borghese, Rome

the merely visual effect of the picture, all sensitive art lovers make a very similar response.

Since sculpture is at once a more generalized and forthright art than painting, its appreciation is perhaps less variable. Yet even here over a course of time there is variation enough. For about three centuries after its discovery, the Apollo Belvedere passed for a consummately great statue. Then the Pheidian marbles were brought to London and thoroughly studied; the pediments and metopes of Olympia were excavated, and then the Hermes of Praxiteles. Meanwhile the Maidens of the Acropolis were dug up and the bronze charioteer at Delphi and the Ludovisi throne. As each of these marvels of Greek sculpture came alive after centuries of suspended animation, the life of the Apollo dwindled. Today, perhaps too condescendingly, the trained art lover regards it chiefly as a document of the mannered elegance of the Hellenistic decadence. It has ceased to be a great work of art because no competent person now thinks it so.

The experience of any free standing statue is of course a composite made up chiefly of aspects which are not in sight but remembered. No two observers make the composite response in the same way.

The best lyrics have so much the crispness of flowers in a dewy morning, carry so fully their whole meaning, that they might seem immune from misunderstanding. Everybody would feel the same about—

"Drink to me only with thine eyes"
"O Fons Bandusiae, splendidior vitro"
"She dwelt among the untrodden ways"
"Du bist wie eine Blume"

"Quand vous serez bien vielle, le soir à la
    chandelle."
"Five fathoms deep thy father lies"
"Guido vorrei che tu e Lapo ed io"
"When in disgrace with fortune and men's eyes."

I have recalled by their first lines eight famous lyrical
poems as they have occurred to me. No attentive reader,
I feel, could possibly miss the main meaning of any of them.
But in every case of appreciation the total meaning, its
density and richness, its quality in short, depends on overtones which are not the same in any two individuals and
produce different shades of meaning, varying timbres.
Horace's invocation to his Bandusian fount, means more
to one who has experienced the rarity of a clear spring
in Central Italy than it does to one who knows springs
only in their abundance in New England. And Ronsard's
prophetic vision of the faded beauty of his Helène means
more to one who has glimpsed the former beauty of a
loved one across the ravages of time—means more to such
a reader than it can to the most sensitive person who has
not had such an experience. Thus while in general the
appreciation of lyrical poetry differs between individuals
chiefly in the matter of overtones; it differs also in each
individual experience as changing conditions and character impede or further understanding. There is no constant
or standard experience of any great lyric that can be submitted to analysis. The life of the lyric like that of every
work of art, indeed like life itself, is a variable. The advantage of the lyrical form is simply that when we assert
that what we feel is predominantly Dante, Shakespeare,
Ronsard, Wordsworth, Ben Jonson, Horace, Heine, we

may use the word predominantly with unusual confidence, for the variation is less than in other forms.

That the same piece of music is most variously appreciated need hardly be argued. Some hearers are hearers only. I imagine they are the best appreciators. Others have generalized, spatial feelings, being under a vast dome and the like. Still others see particular images and actions as the music develops. In short, the appreciation of music is quite as various and unstable as is musical form itself. All this may be read at large, and very interesting to a psychologist the material is, in the books of Anstruther-Thomson and Vernon Lee.

This frank avowal of the relativity both of artistic form and esthetic opinion, should convince us that while esthetics is assuredly a worthy field of study, as assuredly it is not a science. To treat it as such would be to seek to find the common element among such variables, and this would be merely to set up a hollow abstraction—a form that never was in any work of art, an opinion that no art lover ever held. Short of such falsifying generalizations, there is much that may be profitably investigated.

From Plato and Aristotle through the centuries, whoever has discussed beauty and its creation has stressed in the creative act either feeling or judgment. Plato regarded the creative and appreciative state as one of ecstasy, of divine madness, and since such feeling, as resisting the restraints of reason, is purely personal and antisocial, he banned the artist from his ideal republic. This view that a fine frenzy is the fountainhead of all art and beauty has on the whole prevailed. Kant in his *Esthetics* has given it its classic formulation.

Aristotle grounded art on reason and judgment in his famous theory that art is a free imitation of nature and limited by probability. Here an act of understanding and judgment is implied. The imitator must know the thing imitated, and when in artistic imitation he takes liberties with the object he is representing, discretion, an intellectual not an emotional faculty, must be his mentor. Aristotle's theory of free but selective imitation has never lacked followers, though many have not realized its intellectualistic implications.

Plotinus appears to hover between Plato and Aristotle, when he rests beauty on an ecstatic understanding of the rational order of the universe—of the *Logos*. The Hindoo psychologists without exception regard beauty as a high act of intellection and free from ordinary emotional content. Artists in particular, until the eccentric movements of our own day, have almost invariably regarded themselves as imitators of nature. One of the greatest of them, Leonardo da Vinci, reiterates constantly the Aristotelian dogma, illustrates selective imitation concretely by classifying what may or may not be imitated by the painter, and rests the creative faculty of the artist or person of taste in judgment—*giudizio,* occurring hundreds of times, is the favorite word in his *Treatise on Painting.*

Croce's intuition as the basis of art may possibly be meant to mediate in Plotinian fashion between the view of art as emotion and that of art as a special sort of knowledge, but unluckily Croce's intuition has never been satisfactorily analyzed or defined. Thus the issue expressed in the couplet—

"Tell me where is fancy bred,
In the heart or in the head?"

has never been settled to everyone's satisfaction, and perhaps never will be. It requires some presumption on my part to reopen a discussion apparently predestined to remain inconclusive. Yet sometimes one gets more light on a fight by moving around the edges of it than by engaging in it directly. In such a course lies my only hope of contributing anything new to this well worn controversy.

And let me say at the outset that the contradiction seemingly involved in the two positions is not necessarily a sharp one. Plato, who grounded art in ecstasy, by no means denied the judgment required to make a work of art. Rather he stressed it and deplored it as misused. And Aristotle in setting around artistic imitation such limits as the improbable and the intolerable appeals quite as much to the emotions as to the reason. Moreover in his famous doctrine of purification (*Katharsis*) of the emotions he assumes that the emotions have been profoundly perturbed.

Generally speaking, when the best men of letters who have written about beauty have regarded it as a sort of feeling, while almost all the articulate artists have regarded it as a kind of understanding and judgment, the sensible layman must conclude that neither group can be wholly right or wholly wrong. Both views must contain much truth, neither can contain it all. It is not thinkable that the finest critics and philosophers humanity has produced can be completely deceived in regard to their own experience of beauty, nor is it to be admitted that almost without exception the artists who have been self-conscious enough to study their creative processes have given an entirely false report of them. In such a situation, on the most general principles, there should be some way of bringing nearer together positions which, we have seen, already overlap.

Now if we examine these contrasting views more narrowly, we shall see that nobody denies that into the experience of beauty, whether creative or receptive, both head and heart enter. The issue is simply that of the order of entrance—is an emotion the starting point or merely some especially modulated perception? Here we should not fail to note that the issue is perhaps clouded by an obsolete and ill-defined terminology. The old triad—feeling, thinking, willing—which I studied many years ago in Mark Hopkins's admirably clear writings, may still have its convenience, but it has not withstood the analysis of the new psychology. We do not just feel, think, or will separately, in a void. We cannot will anything which we have not first felt to be desirable, nor can we attain our desire without taking thought. Apart from mere emotional explosions, which have little to do with esthetic experience, to assert the desirability of anything involves in itself an act of judgment. Fancy is perhaps bred in the heart but it is nourished from the head. Similarly it is difficult to imagine any understanding without a prior will to understand. So if we base beauty on feeling, we mean a feeling energized by will and expressed largely through judgment, while if we base beauty on thinking, on an act of judgment, we mean a thought that to achieve expression must promptly enlist the will and thus acquire a tinge of feeling.

Now beauty does not consist in the exercise of any single faculty. There is no inherent beauty in feeling, none in willing, none in thinking. Beauty exacts a vital alliance of all three in an orderly act of creation or appreciation. The real issue, then, is which is senior partner in the alliance? Where does the active process that is the experience of beauty, whether creative or receptive, begin? There is no beauty without some sort of ecstasy, none without some sort of judgment. Both Plato and Leonardo are right, however much they may seem to disagree. The link between the two views may lie in their common relation to the will, an attitude which we may grasp only through inference, since Plato and Leonardo pretty much left the will out, presumably taking its presence for granted.

But recent psychology and esthetics agree in giving the will a peculiar prominence in the old psychical triad. Indeed empirically it seems no longer a by-product of feeling or the minister to thinking, but probably the master faculty, subsuming in its operations the other two. Since Schopenhauer, the place of the will in the activities of the soul has been constantly, and I believe correctly, exalted. The Biblical aphorism "As a man thinketh so is he," today hardly makes sense, unless it is considered as including "As a man willeth, so he is." And this predominance of the will, may, if not necessarily, indicate its priority in all active experiences. At least it makes it very unlikely that in all esthetic experiences some other faculty than the will is always prior.

Nor should we ignore the possibility that similar experiences are reached from different routes and points of departure. An American will say "I married my wife because I loved her," while a Frenchman will say with equal truthfulness "I love my wife because I married her." Obviously the Frenchman and the American are thinking of a somewhat different nuance of love, but this does not affect the priority of emotion in one case and judgment in the other. The modern interpretation of the experience of beauty, and of the work of art, as an activity, excellently expressed by Mr. Henry Osborn Taylor as quoted above— this dynamic conception of the matter makes the will the principal factor in the esthetic process, and if it be the principal factor, is it not also the prior factor? Generally I think this is true. Would anyone begin an elaborate constructive process without a will to construct, or an appreciative process without a will to appreciate? It seems to me this wanting to make something and this wanting to enjoy something made is generally the first movement towards beauty. But I cannot deny that there are possible alternatives. It seems to me that a master of the nude like Ingres painted the nude because he loved it, while an equally great master, Degas, if he loved the nude at all, did so only because he painted it. Naturally, as in the example taken from marriage, the verb love means something rather different in the two cases, but the essential contrast seems to hold: any emotion may evoke the will to embody it, or the will to embody something may evoke a corresponding emotion.

In short all dogmatizing about priorities in the experience or creation of beauty seems to me vain. In theory it may begin with an emotion which enlists will and thought; with a thought which by enlisting the will receives an emotional color; with a discursive act of will focusing in an emotion which is defined and embodied with the aid of the judgment. All these seem to me possible, while I think it very difficult to find any of them concretely and surely in any given experience of creation or reception.

Moreover, these priorities may not matter except to the minute analyst. Suppose you are plaiting a braid out of strands in Rubens's triad of azure, rose and corn yellow. You may begin by crossing any two tints and starting the plait with the third, and it will be very much the same sort of braid whatever tint starts it off. But it does matter if you double or triple strand one of the tints, and it matters substantially whether an artist's creative activity is governed by much or little feeling, by more or less judgment, by a will resolute or the contrary. Thus the purely psychological problem of priority really has meaning for esthetics only in terms of the general psychical orientation, in simpler terms, the predisposition of individuals. The *idée maîtresse* of Taine may really be an *émotion maîtresse,* or a *volonté maîtresse,* and according to the dominance of one disposition or another we have the broad difference between a Shakespeare and a Racine, a Goethe and a Victor Hugo, a Thackeray and a Balzac, a Monticelli and a Delacroix, a Tschaikovsky and a Brahms. Not that the dominant tendency by any means explains everything in so complicated an activity as that of artistic creation. It merely gives the general lines of an interpretation which in the very nature of the case remains incomplete.

To sum up, while I believe that in most esthetic experience the will to create and the corresponding will to appreciate are at the head of the process, it may often take its start either from a feeling or a judgment. In this I differ from Theodor Lipps who denies to judgment any esthetic quality, making it merely auxiliary to feeling. Here I cannot labor so subtle an issue. Let me rather observe that no esthetic experience originates within the esthetic field. An experience becomes esthetic as it assumes a certain form, is invested with a special mood, and conditioned by a particular aim. The issue is, then, is the initial judgment a part of the esthetic experience, or does the esthetic experience begin only when the initial judgment shall have added to itself, say, an emotion? It is, I think, impossible to answer such a question, nor is it for me important that it be answered.

What matters, to return to our metaphor of the braid, is the broader coloration of the varicolored fabric. Matthew Arnold defined religion as "Morality tinged with emotion." Until we know the depth of the tinge, the definition tells us almost nothing about any particular form of religion. It may consist in morality highly rationalized and very slightly tinged with emotion—say Unitarianism; or we may have to reverse the terms of the definition, and say, in the case of many of our Negro Methodists, that religion is an emotionalism very slightly tinged with morality.

One more observation on the beginnings of creative activity. Many works of art, pictures, musical compositions, even poems would not exist except for orders or conditions, which very definitely dictate the subject matter. Most sculptures and practically all fine buildings are made to order. Excellent novels have been evoked by the prospect of a prize. In all these cases we may say either that these conditions are merely antecedent to making the work of art, and for the esthetician no part of its making, or we may argue that the act of will and judgment combined in undertaking such commissions is actually the first step in the creative process. Such purists as Theodor Lipps will strongly maintain the former view; common sense will plead for the latter. So long as the artist is ultimately wholly absorbed in his subject matter it seems of little importance whether he has chosen it passionately for himself, or whether he has judiciously accepted a subject matter chosen for him, in which case he is merely in the position of our Frenchman who loves his wife because he has married her. To treat as inferior all works of art which, being commissioned, have grown out of an act of the artist's judgment would be absurd. And since without such limiting conditions at the outset, many of the greatest works of art simply would not exist at all, common sense will surmise that such conditions have been rather conducive than obstructive to the production of great art. Notoriously the painters from Giotto to Velasquez— worked almost exclusively to order. And this is admittedly the greatest period of painting.

In view of such facts it does not interest me to argue whether an antecedent *sine qua non* should be regarded as part of an apparently continuous process or as prior to and outside of the process. What seems important is that in creation and appreciation the feelings, thoughts and desires are all engaged in one activity, in such order and proportions as the conditions favor or permit. There is no reason to suppose a uniform procedure in the case of any individual artist. Delacroix painted "Liberty leading the People" and "Sardanapalus" as free inventions of his own, and "Jacob wrestling with the Angel" and "Heliodorus expelled from the Temple" on an order for the church of St. Sulpice, and these church decorations are his greatest works. In this matter it may reasonably be argued that a commission with specification of subject matter is normally an incentive to a painter of power and imagination, and a deterrent only to a painter of low vitality and narrow interests.

If I shall have brought any sidelight to bear on the problem of the priority of thought or emotion in esthetic activity, and on the place of judgment in creation, I will contentedly waive closer analysis which, however interesting in itself, seems to me to have very little practical bearing whether on the production or on the enjoyment and understanding of the work of art.

That the sense of beauty is entirely disinterested and destroyed by the slightest tinge of self-seeking has been maintained stoutly by the austerer sort of estheticians from Kant to Theodor Lipps. Schopenhauer crystallized the doctrine when he defined the state of esthetic contemplation as "selfless and willess." The weakness of this definition we have already shown. Nietzsche on the contrary asserted a great esthetic value in experiences colored or even dominated by our ambitions and passions—a Dionysian beauty as contrasted with an Apollonian.

That the sense of beauty requires a considerable detachment from our ordinary concerns and a high degree of disinterestedness nobody who has experienced it will deny. The issue is merely whether a tinge of everyday interest destroys the esthetic state.

Before dealing with the problem of disinterestedness at large, we should observe that any strict application of the doctrine in all its austerity would plunge us deep into the absurd. Normally the artist lives by selling his works. While this consideration should not be vividly present during the creative activity—were it present, it would unquestionably impair if not destroy that activity—yet the fact that the artist means and hopes to sell the work he has in hand must at times come to mind. To assert that the mere existence of this bread-winning consideration seriously impairs the creative activity, hence the work of art, would be to insist that only artists who have independent incomes or have achieved success beyond financial worry can produce first-class works.

Similarly it might be maintained that no collector could experience the beauty of a work of art he desired to own. Again, obviously if his mind were on the details of purchase, on the prestige which such ownership would bring, on the profit that might result from resale, his receptive activity would be interrupted, impaired, probably annulled. His mere desire through ownership to experience the beauty of the work of art more often and more conveniently, far from impairing his immediate pleasure might actually, by adding pleasures in anticipation, enhance it. In any case, what is important is not the theoretical purity of any esthetic experience, but its dominating quality. The completely integral and detached psychic state is nonexistent for the psychologist and existent for the esthetician only as a Platonic form or, perhaps better, a doubtfully beneficent illusion.

We shall do well to face this issue more concretely in its most acute form—the relation of sexual desire to the experience of beauty. The answer of Theodor Lipps is sharp—where there is interest of sex, there is no interest of art. In an extreme case no one will deny the dictum. I look, say at a nude Hellenistic Venus, a Danae by Correggio, or at the Antiope of Titian, and my sexual desire is sharply aroused. No experience of beauty is possible under these conditions. An immediate urge has destroyed or prevented, as the case may be, anything like contemplation. The work of art has been misread as a real woman or has evoked imaginations of women desirable in actual life, whereas the work of art is merely a represented woman who has nothing to do with ordinary life whatever, but exists only as contemplated.

Nobody would, I think, contest this, nor yet deny that many fine or even great works of art are very subject to such misreading, may easily be thus misused especially by young and inexperienced persons who cannot assume the relative or complete detachment with which the artist has envisaged his theme. Thus very great artists such a Lucretius, Boccaccio, Shakespeare, Lafontaine, Stendhal, Flaubert, Byron, any great sculptor or painter who has generally found his themes in the nude, may be so misread through no fault either of the artist or defect of the work of art.

Though it is no part of my subject, let me say that I think practically no bemused young person ever got moral harm from a book, a picture, or a statue, that would not have come, probably under worse auspices, in the course of his or her ordinary living. Accordingly I think it is a mistake to try to keep great books out of the hands of adolescents because the erotic tinge which is strong in many great books may conceivably be exaggerated, with moral harm to the reader. Here I may merely say that the person who is morally damaged only by great works of art is lucky indeed, for there are many worse ways of being damaged. And I may end this digression by recalling a well meaning and exemplary Princeton senior, who in the interest of his own morality and that of his classmates confessed to me that the Danae of Correggio was seriously playing upon his erotic imagination. I believe I treated a situation of some distress sensibly when I simply told my young friend that he must be tough enough to bear it. I recall him chiefly to show that his experience of a masterpiece of painting had clearly passed entirely out of the esthetic field. And so I return to my proper subject.

And here I think we may best proceed concretely. Let us take the painting of François Boucher. Is it art? Can it evoke an experience of beauty?

Boucher was a frank voluptuary; his Irish mistress was his model. It is impossible that he should while painting not keep some sense of her allurements, of pleasure past or to come. Clear is it also that this erotic interest was subordinate while Boucher painted. It did not compromise or perturb his very intelligent and resolute execution, but it qualified the product. As for Boucher's pictures, they not merely have a distinctive erotic allure, due to the coming and going of amorous desire or recollection, while the pictures were in progress, but they were meant to have it. Indeed this teasing and enticing quality of Boucher's art was and is the ground of his popularity. Thus he was in a degree a pander, and as his admirers, the brothers Goncourt, candidly admit, vulgar—*canaille.*

Now, the issue is this: must we deny that the paintings of Boucher are works of art? Shall we class the enjoyment of these paintings as simple pleasures, and so as outside of esthetic experience? I do not think that even a Theodor Lipps would go so far, though his doctrine would require him to do so. The better view might seem to be; yes, the Bouchers are works of art, for whatever erotic allure they have is in a painted and conventionally organized, and not in a flesh and blood world. Enough contemplation went into these works to make a world of their own, but the creative impulse was adulterated by Boucher's libertinism. In short, we have to do with a mixed and inferior order of art, and with an inferior esthetic experience both in Boucher himself and in his observer.

In fairness it should be said that this inferiority is relative, and that any implied comparison of Boucher with artists like Rubens, or, worse, Poussin, is uncalled for and absurd. Within his own category—the art that teases and entices on the border line between contemplation and actual living, François Boucher is not inferior at all, but a rather important painter.

It would seem then that there are experiences of beauty, not the highest, which admit of a considerable admixture of our everyday interests and desires. Such experiences, according to their preponderating quality, may be called esthetic experiences tending to become mere pleasures; or pleasures tending to become esthetic experiences.

We need such definitions to cover works of art, by common consent such, which include and to a certain extent depend on our usual interests. Surely the highly erotic lyrics of a Lorenzo de' Medici cannot be excluded from the art of poetry, nor the old French *pastourelles* nor the stories of Boccaccio or Chaucer. As evidently, we may not reasonably deny beauty to a woman, because that beauty has in it someting provocative.

Even if the artist wishes to deal with us on terms of ordinary living, which I feel is rarely the case, the conventions through which he must express himself in the work of art establish between us and the matter represented a certain distance. All this was admirably worked out by Charles Lamb, in his famous essay on the "Old Artificial Comedy," when he showed that what would matter tremendously in the real world, simply mattered not at all in the highly artificial world constructed by Wycherly and Congreve. Lamb's apology has naturally been contested by moralists, but they are right only if they have authority to forbid us what William James called "moral holidays," and no plebiscite has ever given the moralist such a prohibitory function in the world of the arts.

This principle that the world of the arts is necessarily a fictitious one pretty well covers our whole problem. It justifies the heroic bawdiness of a Rabelais and the minor bawdiness of a James Joyce. Even the egregious eroticism of a Casanova is to be distinguished from pornography because the scene is a consistently preposterous world— one in which nothing really matters except one's latest bedfellow of the other sex. And even a Casanova keeps a certain distance from the actual physiology involved in his narrative, may be said to maintain a sort of ideal of himself as a great lover. In the case of Rabelais and Joyce the distance is greater. They are outside of and above the obscenities in which they deal. Such an attitude is always antiseptic.

The existence of such mixed experiences of beauty evidently has a bearing on the theory of the complete isolation of the esthetic experience and its stimulus, the work of art. Here I agree with Volkelt that such isolation is never complete, and disagree with Lipps. The contribution of associational values both to the creative act, hence to the work of art, and to the experience of beauty which it evokes, however far such associations be assimilated and sublimated—the mere mass of such associational convergence means that some associations remain marginal and never become of the esthetic essence. Also the fact that the range of such associations is not the same in the artist and in any hearer or beholder of his work forbids us the customary too facile distinction of primary associations—those which inherently belong to the work of art, from secondary associations—those which more or less arbitrarily hook themselves on to the esthetic experience. Such a distinction can be made and has to be made by every trained art lover in some rough practical way in his own case, but even in his own case it never is completely accurate.

Briefly, though the psychologist must deny the complete isolation of the esthetic from ordinary experience, the esthetician may reasonably assert it as a truth, in William James's words, "good for so much." That is, these penumbral associations and interests usually lie in the unconsciousness and only peer beyond its threshold. The esthetic experience, at least in its higher ranges, seems one of isolation from everyday concerns, and for the esthetician whatever unquestionably seems to be, is. But there are also mixed esthetic experiences where the marginal associations come into the consciousness, and these too are experiences of beauty, evoked by many unchallenged masterpieces in art.

To conclude a discussion essential but perhaps unduly prolonged, the complete isolation of the experience of beauty required by a Schopenhauer or a Lipps is valid only relatively, and then only for the greater experiences of beauty. Nietzsche's free inrush of the ambitions and passions into the esthetic state merely means that his Dionysian beauty is not beauty at all as a separate entity. His Dionysian beauty is merely a highly dynamized modulation of his Apollonian beauty. Of beauty there are infinite modalities, but not two beauties. Between the casual Titanism of Nietzsche and the purism of Schopenhauer and Lipps lie many mixed experiences of beauty which we know but cannot successfully put in hierarchical order nor yet verbally define.

Clearly, if the experience of beauty admits some traffic with so formidable and alien a rival as the erotic, it may deal also with morals, politics and the like. But it deals with them at its peril, unless it deals on its own terms. It will hardly be denied that *Bleak House, Les Misérables* and *Madame Bovary* are exceptionally fine novels, though they deal respectively with judicial abuses, social injustice, and the error of romantic sentimentalism—are all novels of tendency. But one should not fail to note that Dickens and Victor Hugo, working overtly in the sense of the reformer, did not in these novels make works of art of the first class, while Flaubert working by indirection and example, and suppressing his sympathies and antipathies, created a masterpiece of the novel of manners, produced also, I think, a deeper moral effect. He was not disinterested, for he personally hated and despised Mme. Bovary and her kind, but he kept his esthetic distance, dealing with his distasteful theme only in terms of the work of art.

Such an example of sublimation and esthetic assimilation of a refractory moral attitude in the artist may serve to illustrate Friedrich Vischer's genial paradox: "In the realm of the beautiful there exists an earnestness which is not earnest, and an interestedness which is disinterested."

On the practical side esthetic distance and disinterestedness are potent in determining the form of the work of art. Most of the valid conventions are traceable ultimately to the need of isolating the work of art from everyday reality. These conventions will be studied in the chapter on the work of art.

Just a word of summary and anticipatory explanation. Art is no isolated or static thing. It is a force which affects people. Like electricity or light, it moves towards results. In the words of the wisest artist I have ever had the advantage of knowing, John La Farge, it is a transaction between a maker and a spectator through a medium, the work of art. When I use the word spectator, I betray the fact that this survey will deal chiefly with the visual arts, those most familiar to me, but I shall not refrain from seeking analogies from such auditory arts as music and poetry. This limitation of my scope is indicated not only by my own experience and by the appalling vastness of the field, but also by the fact that the effects of the visual arts are restricted in time and relatively clear, by the fact also that these arts offer more abundant evidence as to their creative processes than do the auditory and mixed arts, and, finally, by the fact that they lend themselves to easy and repeated experiments. Even in these radiographic days you cannot at will hear the Ninth Symphony, while the high points of the acted drama are today only so much literature. But you can go to New York should you wish to see Jan Vermeer's "Woman at the Casement," or El Greco's "Toledo." And you may from photographs quicken your memories of masterpieces seen long ago in distant places.

For these reasons I believe that the limitations imposed by my own experience may really work in a clarifying way, even as regards the broader field of esthetics. Beyond this, let me merely say that I shall try to avoid abstractions and minute classifications for their own sake, preferring to deal less with art as an entity than with those in the troubled rapture of its creation or with those in the more serene rapture of appreciation. Apart from these persons in a peculiar spiritual orientation, the work of art has no meaning whatever. Accordingly I shall, except in the chapter devoted thereto, avoid formal analysis of the work of art save where it can be clearly related to the experience of an actual artist or spectator. Art then, always being a personal experience, a real esthetic would build up a contemporary *dramatis personae,* including pretty nearly everybody who is deeply concerned with the creation or fostering of esthetic experience. For this reason I shall not hesitate to include the collector, though his love of art is qualified by the desire of possession, and the dealer, though his love of art is tempered by the need of profits. After all, as things stand, the art that most engages me, that of painting, would without the dealer be numbered among the dead or merely residual arts.

Collateral problems, some of them highly important, such as the origins of art, a possible esthetic of the so-called lower senses of touch, taste, smell, temperature lie apart from my theme. So does any elaborate treatment of the decorative and applied arts. We are to study together the processes of creation and appreciation in gifted and somewhat complicated persons, the artist so far as history and observation reveal his creative processes, and the contemporary lover of art who knows the field broadly in the past and in the art of today. This approach is chosen, not from any condescension towards the cruder and more rudimentary forms of appreciation, which are in themselves well worthy of study, but from a conviction that they are really contained in the richer and more complicated experiences of cultured people. It is eternally true that

> "The Colonel's lady and Judy O'Grady
> Are sisters under their skins,"

but it is also true that the wise psychologist will begin his study with the Colonel's lady. For if he can interpret her, he has the key to the simpler problem of Judy.

Returning to our main theme, art is a process or a transaction, a becoming—a state of mind in the artist becomes a picture; the picture in turn becomes a similar state of mind in the spectator. These states of mind are our proper study. Esthetics is merely a special branch of psychology. The work of art in itself concerns esthetics only insofar as the work of art symbolizes and thus conveys something akin to the artist's state of mind in creation. From the work of art we must work forward to the spectator or backward to the artist. Since what we know about the creative experience of the artist is largely inference from his work, formal study of the work of art may seem of first importance. But this is really not so. We have no reason whatever to suppose that our formal analysis of any work of art corresponds to the artist's state of mind in creation. Our hope of finding the artist lies in finding him in ourselves. Humility, concentration and love may recreate in us his creative passion, not precisely, but in its essentials; there is no other way.

The analysis and definition of the appreciative and creative experience in competent spectators and artists is then the main business of esthetics. The quest has many difficulties which should at the outset be frankly admitted. The artist's creative experience we can study only by indirection—inference from the work of art, inference from various appreciations of his work, inference from the rare writing of artists or from reported sayings of theirs. Companionship with living artists may yield something. But in all such investigations we meet the obstacle that the artist is seldom wholly conscious of his own processes, while he is rarely articulate save in the medium of his own art. On the other hand, the artist frequently has a rare divination of the processes of his fellow artists. The best documents for the artist's mind are the writings of practising artists who have the critical gift and that of literary expression. Leonardo, Sir Joshua Reynolds, Delacroix, Fromentin, Roger Fry, John La Farge, Kenyon Cox, Sir Charles Holmes, are notable examples of trustworthy spokesmen for their craft. That the artist necessarily feels

and thinks in terms of technique is often held to dis-
qualify the layman as an interpreter. But here it may be
said that no great artist thinks solely in terms of technique,
while a layman by simple observation may learn to think
in terms of all the technique that the artist ever intended
him to see.

Yet, when all is said, the problem of the psychology of
the artist probably admits of solution only in very general
terms. Paradoxically, for without the artist there would
hardly be esthetics, the problem of the artist is really of
secondary importance. The important thing is that the
work of art continues to evoke certain exalted experiences.
In short, appreciation, the end of the artistic transaction,
is the real object of study. It is also the safest object of study.
Subject to the disadvantages of all introspective investigation, it has the means of minimizing these disadvantages.
Admittedly a state of mind can be defined and analyzed
not while actually experienced, but only as remembered.
But the analysis can be made repeatedly, at various ages
under many conditions, can be checked up for aberrations.
Between my twenty-fifth and forty-fourth years, for example, I saw Botticelli's "Primavera" perhaps a hundred times,
at intervals of a few months, a few years, a few days, in
vigorous health and in invalidism, with various degrees of
historical and literary preparation. Meanwhile I may have
looked at the photograph of it a thousand times at rather
short intervals. The more or less composite account of all
these experiences in my essay on Botticelli ought to be a
truthful account of the enduring characteristics of my
personal reaction to this lovely picture.

Apart from introspection of his own experience, which is necessarily the chief study of the esthetician, he has valuable means of control in the abundance of written testimony by art lovers of many ages. The esthetic experiences of his friends are accessible to him, either in the presence of the work of art or in exchange of views about it.

To distinguish the pleasures which are esthetic from those which are not, would, were it possible, require a book rather than a few paragraphs. Yet the general line of demarcation has been approximately drawn by recent estheticians. The late Henry Rutgers Marshall has written, "Beauty is relatively stable, or real, pleasure." This expresses the truth that the ordinary pleasures are soon exhausted. Porena and Santayana virtually agree in regarding "objectivized pleasure," pleasure regarded as a quality of a thing, as the pleasure proper to the sense of beauty. Obviously, as Porena remarks, such pleasure may be unrelated and absolute, or related and comparative. The physiological esthetician, Grant Allen, finds that the esthetic pleasures involve a maximum nervous stimulus with a minimum of nervous wear and tear, "in processes not directly connected with vital functions," which seems merely a rather elaborate way of saying that the esthetic pleasures are those of the imagination. Wordsworth's famous phrase that beauty consists in "emotion recollected in tranquillity" comes to very much the same thing, though he might well have added "emotion in anticipation." All these definitions imply in esthetic pleasure a detached and contemplative quality. Such pleasure does not possess us utterly; we are conscious both of it and of ourselves as experiencing it. This sense of being at once in and outside of the pleasure at least severs it from that which is associated with the ordinary bodily functions, and probably a closer discrimination is impossible. We may think of ordinary pleasures tending to become esthetic as they are sublimated through contemplation; and of esthetic pleasures tending to become ordinary pleasures as the contemplative state weakens. There would remain a debatable ground where the discrimination between the two orders of pleasure would be impossible.

This conclusion would leave the esthetic pleasures confused with other pleasures of contemplation—such as those of morality and religion. Here Plato's common-sense observation in the *Hippias,* that beauty is a mode of seeing and hearing, may be helpful. Esthetic pleasure seems to be evoked only by something visible or audible, whereas the other contemplative pleasures imply neither visual nor auditory experience.

A word may be due on the physiological esthetics of Guyau and his school. For him esthetic pleasure rests on the enhancement of our ordinary processes of sensation, perception and volition, and on the sudden awareness of such enhancement. Here it need only be noted that in alleging perception and awareness Guyau slips out of physiology into psychology. Moreover the very small physical energy engaged in experiencing beauty makes it unlikely that the sudden awareness of such slight physiological tensions should produce so great a psychical effect. Much more energy is expended in digesting a chop than in hearing "Tristan and Isolde." A sudden kick in the shin will give more pain than the sight of the dreariest daub will bring to the most sensitive esthete. In short, the weakness of the whole physiological esthetic seems to lie in regarding a highly qualitative activity as merely quantitative.

I agree with Professor John Dewey that in the experience of beauty we are not dealing with something completely sundered from our ordinary living. He holds that any well organized and satisfactory experience has an esthetic tinge, and that the purely esthetic activity is such only because it reaches out of ourselves toward an object, and is not achieved within ourselves or within the field of our narrowly individual interests. Anticipating Professor Dewey's attitude, Mr. I. R. Richards called the esthetic experience an "experience completed," as compared with those everyday experiences which are only approximated and usually remain incomplete.

Common experience bears out this view. You have carried through a difficult negotiation with complete success. Yet if you be a person of any vivacity of imagination, for hours your mind will be teeming with emendations. This you might have said earlier or better or with a different emphasis. Such revision implies that apart from its purpose the negotiation had an ideal form of its own without attaining which it failed of being a "complete experience." Your supererogatory criticism presupposes a purely esthetic standard, for practical bearing it has none whatever. If this be so, we must expect to find a shading off between esthetic and merely well organized experience—such a shading off as we have noted in the case of mere pleasures and those that are esthetic.

I may add that Professor Dewey's description of a real or satisfactory experience puts into concrete form

Theodor Lipps's analysis of the human soul as naturally endowed with the capacity to arrange the data of the senses and the perceptions in a hierarchical order of emphasis and subordination. Upon this eminently judicial capacity of the soul Lipps founds his entire system—a system which, not quite consistently, he proceeds to elaborate on the basis of the priority of the emotions.

In concluding this introductory chapter, let me recall words which I wrote years ago in an esssay on El Greco which I repeat only because I cannot now say them better and because my accomplished friend, the late Henry Rutgers Marshall, approved them. They may suggest the eminently active and balanced character of all esthetic experience:

"For me the sense of beauty admits all manner of excitement, but always an excitement contained within an enfolding serenity. Within limits many degrees of keen emotional experience are possible. But the moment the sheer excitement perturbs the serenity, the impression of art is tottering; the moment it prevails, the sensation is no longer of art at all. Contrariwise, when the excitement departs, the serenity becomes void of content, a complacency splendidly null. If this be true, the sense of beauty is akin to the feelings that we have at moments of greatest physical and mental efficiency. The orator riding the storm against hostile hearers knows the calm of throbbing nerves, and that, I take it, is the serenity of art. Thus every expression of art must end well in the sense of leaving us calmed and fortified—the meaning, I take it, of the much discussed term of Aristotle—*Katharsis*."

Naturally this somewhat oversimplified treatment of esthetic appreciation can be only a starting point. The experience of beauty is far more rich and complicated than the bringing of an excitement into balance with a serenity. Obviously too, while appreciative activity is reasonably comprised within such a formula, creative activity is not. The major problem of esthetics is the creation and appreciation of beauty considered as a consecutive process or transaction in which the work of art mediates between its creator and its appreciator. We necessarily approach the problem in several ways, the way of the artist, the way of the work of art, the way of the art lover, but we never should forget that we are actually dealing with the transmission of a highly organized energy through the work of art as a conductor, or, more genially, as the rendezvous where the spirit of the artist and that of art lover may commune.

CHAPTER II

THE ESTHETIC TRANSACTION

IN ALL cases the esthetic activity is in the nature of a transaction, and the esthetic transaction—a phrase which I learned with much else from the gifted painter John La Farge—is the most accurate and useful term at our disposal. We must study then the esthetic transaction with some elaborateness in its generalized aspects and must also investigate it in more concrete terms in the various arts. In this analysis I naturally draw much from my own experience as a minor artist in letters, but I have tried to check what may be idiosyncratic in my own case from the experiences of artists and art lovers as told to me directly or communicated through books.

The esthetic transaction seems to me to begin always with a person who has a predisposition to make something beautiful, an artist, a maker to use more broadly that excellent Scottish word for poet. In the mind of the true maker float constantly, form and dissolve, images or schemes of things that might be made. They emerge out of a richly varied chaos which the artist has more or less consciously built up in the spirit of the gardener preparing his fertilized soil. Professor John Livingston Lowes in that remarkable study of Coleridge's imagination, *The Road to Xanadu,* has admirably illustrated from Coleridge's notebooks and reading this preliminary process of apparently random accumulation. These images or schemes appear to originate in the unconscious, at any rate they usually come into the consciousness unasked. Such images and schemes normally have only approximate form, they may be thought of as asking the artist to find a fit form for them, and the maker may be thought of as judging such requests as weighty or the contrary—to be granted or denied.

That able but unfortunate writer, my friend the late Edwin Lucas White, author of many excellent poems and in *El Supremo* and *Andivius Hedulio* of two of the finest historical novels of our time, once showed me, years ago in our Johns Hopkins days, a note-book containing hundreds of themes for poems. Such themes simply came to him and usually without hint of the metrical form in which they should be embodied. They were, to repeat our trope, asking him to find a fit form for them, and for many of them he did. Others never got beyond the note-book. We have to do with a stream of consciousness which constantly tosses up subjects inviting organization and formulation in a particular material. A work of art is begun when an artist accepts one of these invitations. Such an acceptance implies an emotion and a judgment. I like the subject matter, or it appeals to me—either statement is correct—but I like it because I feel I can make something good out of it. One may begin the esthetic transaction with an act of will: among the various subject matters drifting in my consciousness I instinctively choose one, which means I choose as well to embody it in a given material and a fit form. Such choice again immediately draws in feelings and judgments. If on the contrary I choose a theme deliberately, it is because I find it attractive, and when I choose to embody a theme, I judge what I can do with it, and I anticipate the joys of the struggle needed to transform the as yet virtually formless theme into a work of art.

Often, however, the artist has no sense of choosing a theme; rather it chooses him, obsesses him until he heed its claim to be embodied. In my own case the theme of a short story or an essay often simply presents itself as irresistibly alluring; there is no scrutiny of an eligible list, such as that in the note-book of my friend Edwin Lucas White, no act of elimination. Probably the happiest creative activity begins in this way. Generally, I think, the painter, author, sculptor, musician feels as if his subjects rather came to him than were sought after or chosen. In short, the usual direction of creative activity seems to be from subject matter to form.

But in many instances of successful artistic activity the subject matter is prescribed while something like the ultimate form is suggested. All buildings are normally designed to order under conditions which profoundly affect the form. Until a century and a half ago most paintings and sculptures were commissioned and the subject matter at least roughly indicated by the patron. Occasional poetry takes its theme often from necessity, and not from choice. Frequently the playwright must accept a subject matter as fitting the talent of the actors and actresses available. A mass may be composed to order, and so may an opera. The song writer must find his theme in a lyric poem which he may or may not have selected. Obviously the translator or the copyist often has his original chosen for him. Nevertheless among translations and copies there are notable works of art. Many critical essays are book reviews written to order. This has often been my case. I receive a book from an editor who wishes an essay review. My freedom is merely whether to write the review or not.

Or I may ask to review a book because its subject or author already interest me.

If I have recalled the various ways in which a subject matter may come to an artist, it is to show that it really is of little importance how it comes to him. What is essential is that he should accept it whole-heartedly and that it should completely possess him. And here we should note that such whole-hearted acceptance is not a single act and necessarily anterior to the constructive activity of the artist. He may be wholly possessed by his theme only after, one may guess as a result of having begun to work it into a form. What matters is merely that early in the making of his work of art he have full confidence in the value and validity of his theme.

But we may reverse the situation with which the artistic transaction normally begins, and say that the artist may begin by choosing a form which seems to seek a fit subject matter. He may be in the general position of wishing to make a play, an ode, a sonnet, a sonata, a symphonic poem. Indeed the young artist during his tutelage is normally and quite properly in this situation. Such conscious rehearsals of artistic activity may be but seldom are notable works of art. Perhaps the chances of success along these lines could best be measured by perusing a series of Newdigate Prize Poems by Oxford undergraduates. The showing would not be brilliant.

While in theory it is possible for the artist to proceed from form to substance—the late Roger Fry among others has ingeniously argued the possibility—I think the possibility exists even theoretically only through a very ambiguous use of the word form. The form which may be

said to seek a subject matter is of course never the form
that the work of art is finally to assume. In short, as regards
the particular work of art, it really is not a form at all, not
its form, and obviously a work of art can have one form
only. The form which can be regarded as seeking a subject
matter is embryonic or generic—a sonnet, an ode, an
arrangement in rose and silver, a play, a novel, a symphonic poem. But these generic forms exist only as conveniences of thought, and in thought. No work of art has
a generic form. Its form is proper to itself and unique. In
critical discourse we may speak of the sonnet; in poetry
there are only sonnets, and all are different.

We now have the artist in one way or another possessed
of his theme and in the early stages of his constructive
activity or about to begin it. The actual making of any
work of art is so various that the process can be suggested
only in very general terms. It is a very concentrated but also
a most varied activity which involves tensions and releases,
doing and undergoing, elations and despairs, acceptances
and rejections. There is a constant balancing of the claims
of subject matter, of those of the tentative form, of those
of the material employed. The thing is a give and take, the
subject matter now yielding to the form, now modifying
the form as yet provisional, both subject matter and incipient form dominating or yielding to the material. Instinct and judgment blend or act separately in this intense
activity of adjustment and readjustment. It is highly
charged with emotion, and involves a resolute and unremitting act of will, while both feeling and will are reinforced by the cooperative approval of the judgment. It was
the element of judgment in the process that Delacroix had

in mind when he wrote that genius lies "in being reasonable in a superior fashion." The direction of the creative effort is from a form more or less vaguely sensed and approximated towards a form that is definitive and satisfactory.

It is customary to think of the creative activity as freely exercised. As a matter of fact it is always conditioned and limited by the artist's established habits and preferences. He cannot renounce his own funded experience. To a large extent he must do what he has already done. Furthermore, as the work progresses, it develops its own necessities. The choice of an initial motive, whether formal or of substance, immediately forces the exclusion of a host of motives perhaps in themselves attractive, but incongruous. As the work is elaborated, freedom correspondingly diminishes. A set of established rhythms and proportions can admit only what is proper to the establishment. In the last stages every good work of art proceeds under a strict law or logic of its own, permitting no freedom of choice to the artist. This law of diminishing freedom again I learned from the lips of John La Farge.

In one aspect the creative activity may be thought of as a series of opportune sacrifices, of subject matter to form, or vice versa, or both, to the law of the material, but this negative expression of the process really disguises its essentially positive character. We must think of all such sacrifices as adjustments that far from diminishing the meaning of subject matter and form actually enhance the meaning of both and so blend them that a complete unity is finally achieved—a unity which may be expressed either as a substance that has achieved form, or as a form that embodies and freely expresses a substance.

However random and disorderly this process may seem, it really follows and obeys a deeper rhythm and order which are those of the artist's bodily and mental activities. And this dynamic rhythm and order pass into the work of art, which, though a sort of symbolism, produces analogous activities of an orderly and rhythmical sort in a fit hearer or beholder.

But I am going too far and too fast. Let me return to the artist just starting his making of the work of art. We have seen that he is generally committed to an arduous process of trial and error. Few poems have, like *Kubla Khan,* been perfected in an effortless dream. Now this process of trial and error is in part directed by the consciousness and in part determined from the unconscious. According to one or the other, the conducting of the creative activity will be orderly and systematic, or, contrariwise, a Topsy-like growing. In either case the work of art itself will be orderly, for the creative activity, whether consciously or not, is, considered as a whole, orderly.

The practical difference involved in the two procedures will be that when there is conscious and systematic planning, the form will usually be attained in the abstract or in some provisional material before it is worked out in its ultimate material. And the final form will differ very little from the form merely ideated or provisionally embodied in other than the final material, because the exactions of the final material have been more or less calculated in advance. But where there is no systematic planning, the form can be worked out only in its own material, and since the exactions of the material have not been foreseen and in a degree provided for, these exactions are likely to be more exorbitant and more determinant of the form.

Let me atone for this perhaps harsh and involved statement of the case by simple and I hope clarifying illustrations. When Mr. Sinclair Lewis constructs a novel, everything is thought out in advance of writing. All the topography is actually charted, to plans of houses and towns. To aid visualization, important features are sketched graphically. The *dramatis personae* are fixed in number, in character, and in their relations. What is to be dialogue and what narrative is settled, likewise the chapter divisions and the general movement and scale of the whole novel. Christian Gauss has very interestingly described this eminently orderly and systematic procedure in an essay on Mr. Sinclair Lewis to which I refer the reader for further particulars. So far, we have a very complete and elaborate scheme or scenario. Though in words, it is not yet in the ultimate form, which of course is literary form. When it is written out, there will be only such changes from the scenario as are effected by emphasis and a sort of embellishment. The addition will be chiefly of overtones to actions and ideas already formulated. Of trial and error there will be rather little in the writing out, and that little will be chiefly concerned with phraseology. The greater construction is fixed once for all in the scenario.

For lack of a better contrast, let me confess my own slovenly and unsystematic way of composing an essay or a short story. The theme or motive usually comes to me unsought and with no more initial suggestion of form than that it is to be a piece of approximately such a length. There ensues a curious period of fermentation. Phrases, situations, ideas, people bubble up unexpectedly. They may or may not be available for the story or essay, and oddly there is no conscious censorship of them as available or not. They simply come out of my unconsciousness, assert themselves in passing, and return to it. They never emerge as bare schemes or ideas, but are always conveyed in a more or less literary form. This form is often considerably revised and criticized mentally. Nothing as yet is written out, but much has been thought out in an entirely fragmentary and disconnected way. There is as yet no idea of the general structure. Ordinarily weeks or months intervene between fully committing myself to the theme and writing anything down. The activity is intermittent and not continuous.

Some day a feeling of uncomfortable repletion forces me to write, to get rid of the perilous stuff that has been so long fermenting. If possible, I write uninterruptedly, very rapidly and under pressure, still with no clear notion of the structure of the piece, but working out its form entirely in the material—words and phrases, sentences and paragraphs. The order of ideas seems to be settled from the unconsciousness. I have no feeling of directing. Over the diction I maintain a constant censorship at all times. When the thing is written out, its larger structure is what it is, and cannot be changed without destroying the form. As I write out a short story, unexpected people pop up freely and almost embarrassingly; in an essay, unexpected ideas and opinions. Generally such self-asserting persons and opinions have to be received. They usually belong in the action or argument. At times they are rejected by a conscious act of criticism.

Paradoxically the story or essay that has been produced in so casual and apparently disorderly a way will under analysis prove to be well organized, and in its own fashion entirely orderly. It cannot be reconstructed, or at least I cannot reconstruct it. I should have to begin all over again. All this merely goes to show that the creative operations of the human mind, whether conscious or unconscious, are intrinsically orderly. Only through such common psychic orderliness is there possibility of communication between the artist and him who appreciates the work of art. But this orderly creative procedure may be more or less directed by the consciousness. One may make an orderly work of art as M. Jourdain spoke prose—*sans le savoir.*

At the risk of repetition, I will note that the differences between entire schools of art depend upon the above considerations and procedures. A Florentine painter in prolonged trial and error through a series of sketches fixed the pattern and details of his drawing in a working drawing. This was enlarged almost mechanically into a cartoon of the exact scale of the picture, enlarged often not by the artist but by an assistant; the cartoon was again traced upon the panel or canvas. The actual painting was in the nature of superficially embellishing a construction already completely ideated, was almost a mechanical process, of however delicate a kind, which was often entrusted wholly or in part to an assistant.

The Venetians or a Velasquez, after a few preliminary sketches, began to paint the picture, working it out in the material, prepared to make corrections as they painted, and with only an approximate notion of the ultimate pictorial form when they took the brush in hand.

The results of the two procedures are broadly speaking what might be expected. No Venetian picture has the richness of mental overtones that any good Florentine picture normally offers; no Florentine picture has the material richness and purely sensuous appeal of the average Venetian picture. No more in art than in life can we have it both ways. We are bound by our decisions, which invariably involve sacrifices.

In certain arts, one procedure or the other seems indicated. One can hardly think of an architect letting a building be built except upon his completed working plans. Yet up to and through the Renaissance, the architect presented to the builder only a model on a miniature scale. Perhaps the greater charm of medieval and Renaissance buildings rests precisely on the fact that both the architect and the builder worked them out three-dimensionally in a material suitable for building and without too much preliminary study on paper. Evidently the procedure gave to the master-builder much greater freedom and responsibility than he has today. His rôle rather than that of rendering a paper design in the material was that of a cooperation in a degree creative.

By a romantic idealization, the creative activity is often regarded as continuous and urgent. In briefer lyrical expression it may be so. But a great artist may apply himself intermittently to any particular work of art. Titian habitually had at once a score of paintings in progress, and worked at many in a single morning. Ariosto wrote comedies while he was composing the *Orlando Furioso*. Some apology may be needed for remarks so obvious, but the case is often and even usually misrepresented by writers on esthetics who consider works of art in the abstract and not under the actual conditions of their production.

It should be added that that stream of activities which pauses in the work of art, as a river broadens into a lake, is constantly fed and enlarged by affluents from association. As the artist paints, or carves or models, designs a building, writes, imagines a musical composition or strums it tentatively on the pianoforte, all his previous activities of a cognate sort rush in upon him; so do kindred activities of other artists; so do more far-fetched and capricious associations of every sort. Now these inrushing, multitudinous associations may be contributory to the work of art or confusing and obstructive. Accordingly they must be controlled by some sort of discriminating censorship. I believe such censorship is generally instinctive and at the unconscious level. Were it not so, any activity of creation, or for that matter of appreciation, would promptly be smothered by an associational avalanche. Many of these associations have to be handled by a conscious critique. Twice Leonardo da Vinci, while making composition sketches for the "Last Supper," put Judas alone on the near side of the table—an associational choice based on a long artistic tradition. When he worked out his final form, Judas had to be one of a sub-group of three, and had to move to the table's far side. And this involved also a considerable change in motive. The apostles who in earlier Last Suppers had been paired, now could be distributed more effectively in groups of threes. In all this it is to be assumed that Leonardo knew what he was about.

We have now arrived at the work of art. To its creation have gone the acceptance of a theme or subject matter, the working of this into a form in a given material through a complicated process of trial and error which may be more or less directed by the consciousness. To this progressive activity associations of all sort rally, and have to be incorporated or repelled. Throughout the creative activity a will to make is the constant energizer, a sense of the value of a beauty present in his natural exemplar and prospective in the finished work of art is the sustaining emotion. Finally the whole activity involves the most lively interactions between a theme or motive and the requirements of a form and the even stricter exactions of a material. This three-way give and take is again harmonized partly by a conscious criticism, more I think by an instinctive adjustment below the level of consciousness. All that is positive in this process is worked into the work of art so that its appearance or sound is organized micro-cosmically after the pattern of the creative activity.

At this stage, having put everything he can into his work, the artist relatively loses interest in it. He has his next work vividly in mind, and he means to put more into it than he could put into the work already finished.[1] By a paradox, the work which now only slightly interests its creator may awaken among chosen spirits for generations an interest of the most intense order, if, in the words of Delacroix, they are wise enough to look for beauty where the artist has put it.

[1] When an artist does return to his own work it is often with disapproval. Here the extensive rewriting in the definitive editions of George Meredith, Henry James, and Joseph Conrad is most instructive. No editor ever treated the copy of a novice with more severity than did these fastidious stylists their own famous novels.

Motor activities, generally real but sometimes imagined, enter into the making of the work of art. One wields a brush or pencil, a mallet and chisel; one models, writes with a pen or typewriter, whispers or speaks aloud, hums, fingers a piano, etc. In the early stage of composition or construction, such activities may of course be merely imagined. One thinks of such motor activities as completely directed by the creative impulse and will. But since the doing may be hard or easy, an obstruction or a facility, the motor activities may influence, to a certain extent change the form of the work of art. And since every good artist contains a good craftsman who likes to work at his craft, one may rightly suppose cases in which the tool and medium or material actually assume an initiative. A sketch is made because a painter casually took up his brush, a story is written because the author sat down at his typewriter. At least there are cases where without such an act, the corresponding work of art would never have been made. Such considerations may seem to be merely an aspect of that law of the material which we have already studied, and the material is obviously deeply involved in such cases. But the material works chiefly negatively, by resistances, whereas these activities are positive assents to the bidding of the creative impulse.

Here is not the place to study elaborately the nature of the work of art. We are now concerned with it merely as a factor in the esthetic transaction, as the transmitter of the essentials of a creative activity to a hearer or beholder. To the questions how and why does the work of art communicate its maker's experience, it is not easy to give an answer, though the fact that such communication takes place and with singular accuracy is undisputed. Evidently, considered merely as an embodied deed, the work of art is shaped by the doing and reveals much of this doing to any attentive observer. Take a very simple instance, the conventionalized ivy band roughly scratched around a late Roman jar. One sees exactly how the pattern was made and incised, can easily imagine himself doing it. This is the "inner imitation" of Karl Groos. In far more complicated instances, an attentive observer might easily repeat mentally the main processes that went to the making of the work of art. In this regard it is not unlike any other made object which tells the story of its making.

But the work of art tells also much concerning the state of mind of its maker while engaged in the creative process. The nature of such revelation has been very variously interpreted. Those who see the cause in inner imitation would argue that just as a particular mental state was intertwined with an executive act in making any work of art, so to repeat in imagination the executive act will evoke a mental state analogous to that of the artist in creation. The word mental is here used in the broadest sense as synonymous with psychic. The relation of this explanation to the famous Lange-James paradox—I pray because I have knelt—is obvious, and the explanation has its weight. But I much doubt that the mere sight or hearing of a work of art necessarily produces inner imitation and repetition of the mental state that attended its making—that the work of art evokes such a motor and psychic experience under any conditions and with every or all hearers or beholders.

We must, I think, seek a simpler and more straightforward explanation in the fact that the work of art is a part of a widely accepted symbolism or language which has been built up gradually by silent consent through the ages. The artist has to learn to write in this language and the beholder or hearer has to learn to read it. It is idle to suppose that any untrained person can appreciate more than superficially any rich and complicated work of art—an *Antigone* or *King Lear*; an *Aeneid* or *Divine Comedy*; a "School of Athens," or a Sistine Ceiling; a Parthenon or a Chartres; a "Fifth Symphony" or a "Tristan and Isolde." Unquestionably an untrained person may get pleasure from, may feel awe before such masterpieces. But that will be an exceptional untrained person born with what Dante calls a "gentle soul." At best the pleasure will be vague and unfocused, and the awe without understanding, while to most untrained persons such masterpieces will say nothing whatever, or will reveal only unrelated fragments of their meaningful totality. Just as no illiterate person can get the meaning of a printed page, or probably the full meaning out of any thoughtfully composed utterance, just as a literate person can get the meaning of a printed passage only if he take the pains to read and if necessary to study it, so the language of art is readable only by persons who have learned it in general and bring to any particular perusal an active will to understand.

If it be true, and I think it is, that the communicative efficacy of the work of art is that art like speech is a universal symbolism to which by convention and consent certain meanings have been attached, then we must conclude that "inner imitation" works only occasionally, and probably only in the more elementary kinds of art, and that while it may easily further and enhance esthetic appreciation, it is not the vital and causative factor in such appreciation.

We have arrived, by a route perhaps too devious, at that stage in the esthetic transaction at which the hearer or beholder is in the presence of the work of art and strongly predisposed to understand and appreciate it. His appreciative activity significantly parallels the creative activity of the artist. It is grounded in an habitual will to understand, entirely analogous to the artist's habitual and generalized will to make. It is conditioned by all earlier relevant experience, by established preferences and prejudices. There ensues a vague sort of apprehension and acceptance of the subject matter accompanied by a general but not precise comprehension of the form in which it is embodied. This stage of appreciation is evidently entirely analogous to the artist's choice or acceptance of a subject matter which either comes to him with or promptly receives a tentative form.

Next comes, through an abridged process of trial and error, a fuller grasping of the meaning of the subject as expressed through a form the rich organization and fitness of which gradually reveal themselves until substance and form become an integral thing outside ourselves with a meaning that is in one sense evocative of, in another, evolved by a high and passionate activity of understanding. Only at such a stage do we, through achieving a sort of mystic oneness or rapport with the work of art, fully experience its beauty. Evidently this ardent endeavor to perceive and live ourselves into the unity of substance and form in the work of art is entirely analogous to that long effort of trial and error by which the artist brings subject matter, form and material into perfect accord in the ulti-

mate form. In short, the appreciative activity in its final
stage as throughout is so closely analogous to the creative
activity that Goethe's maxim, "To enjoy is to create anew"
—*Geniessen ist nachschaffen,* seems fully justified. And the
creating anew by the art lover has even this advantage
over the original creative activity of the artist, that in its
trial and error there is very little of the momentary failure
and obstruction which the artist had to cope with and over-
come painfully. And finally, as long as the work of art
lasts, the raptures of appreciation may be repeated by
successive multitudes *in saecula saeculorum* with infinite
modalities, while the personal rapture of creation perishes
with the artist and, as regards any particular work of art,
usually perishes with its completion.

Let me add that just as many confluents of an associative
sort rush into the stream of creative activity, as perturbing
or contributory factors, so the associations crowd enrich-
ingly or confusingly upon him who treads the path of
appreciation. Some are proper to appreciation, some lead
away from it. Thus, like the artist, the art lover has to
exercise some sort of censorship over the associations, a
censorship that may be established on the conscious or
unconscious level, but will always have a certain if limited jurisdiction in the consciousness.

Since a perfect appreciative activity would repeat precisely the corresponding creative activity, a perfect handling of the band of associations demanding to be admitted,
would be to identify all that the artist admitted, receive
only them and exclude the rest. But this is obviously impossible. Every individual has his own range of associations,
and it is not the same in any two persons. Thus, so far as

appreciation is concerned, every response is different from every other, and all are different from the artist's creative activity. Each appreciation lacks some associations that the artist entertained and incorporated in his work, and is tinged by some associations that never came into the artist's mind. The practical bearing of all this, and it is one of the most practical issues in appreciation, being one of its few modalities which is relatively within our control— the practical bearing is this: by appropriate preparation we may recover many of the associations, perhaps the more important that have enriched the creative activity and the resultant work of art. Of the other associations, the task is to admit only such as seem relevant to the work of art, such as we may imagine the artist as approving had they come to him. A critic often finds meanings in a work of art which surprise the artist, and sometimes the artist welcomes and validates meanings of which in creation he was not conscious. That rough consensus of opinion which constitutes the solid social and historical fact of taste shows that a practically successful sifting of associational values is possible. Were it not so, every appreciation would be merely a cluster of different associations; there would be no consensus, no taste of a social and historic sort.

We have seen that motor activities, imagined and real, always accompany the making of the work of art. Do they also, as we should expect, accompany its appreciation? The brief answer to a question which must be more fully answered elsewhere is that imagined motor activities probably always accompany appreciation, while actual movements may or may not enter into appreciation, and in any case are relatively unimportant. The movements imagined while we enjoy a work of art seem to me to be of two sorts. In a much abbreviated and purely generic way we repeat the act of the artist, swing his brush, handle his clay. I believe any complete appreciation is likely to include some such vague sense of actual cooperation with the artist. More important are the imagined motor responses to the form of the work of art. In imagination we move about in its space, touch the mass it represents, mimic the swing of its lines, the postures and actions of its figures. Only through such inner imitation does the work of art come alive to us, only in this way does it receive life from us. All this must soon occupy us more fully as we study the doctrine of Esthetic Sympathy.

The relation of the art lover's creating anew to the artist's creating has often been described as a generalized or generic similarity. This view I feel exaggerates the difference. I like to think of a good appreciation as qualitatively identical with but quantitatively less than the creative experience. One might put it so—that, except for possible untoward associational extensions, every conceivable good appreciative activity is already contained within the corresponding creative activity. In essentials nothing in a valid experience of appreciation is really outside of the original creative experience, being already subsumed therein. The difference is quantitative. Evidently the art lover cannot put into a few minutes or hours of appreciation the energy of thought, will and emotion that the artist put into the work of art through months or years.

I may add that into any complete appreciation of a work of art enters some imaginative sharing of the technical processes by which it was made. Such sharing is at best partial and abridged. Even so it may greatly contribute to understanding. In short, in its fulness the esthetic transaction requires not merely that the beholder or hearer should participate in the artist's states of mind but also in his executive processes.

Before investigating the appreciative activities more searchingly—they are the central problem of esthetics—we should consider the esthetic transaction implied in the enjoyment of beauty in nature. It is apparently a twofold transaction, between some appearance in nature—including man—and a beholder. Inherently it would seem to be a less coherent and rich experience than that of the beauty of art since the shaping of it really rests wholly with the spectator, with no expert guide, such as the artist, in charge of the activity. Of course nature lovers would indignantly deny this inferiority of natural beauty, as art lovers would generally affirm it. Here it may be remarked that neither is usually in a position to dogmatize, being prejudiced in one direction or the other. Even a John Ruskin, a nature lover *par excellence* but also a great lover of art, loved art with distinct reservations.

In a case of a devout person, one may say that the esthetic transaction which includes nature is tripartite, God being the Supreme Artificer who has created natural appearances for our delectation. But such a statement would be subject to restrictions and reservations which practically annul it. A devout person would hardly presume to say that the activities through which he appreciates the beauty of nature are identical with or even closely analogous to the Divine activities in creation. In short, such enjoyment is not a creating anew.

We return then to the conception that beauty in nature involves only a twofold relation, between a natural appearance and a spectator. And we may well insist that nature unobserved by man has no inherent beauty at all, that it yields beauty only as transformed and reorganized by man either actually or mentally. Indeed this view is implicit in our major premise that beauty is not an attribute or quality of an object but a quality of human activity in relation to an object. We may believe also that more generally than is suspected the approach to the beauty of nature is mediated through the beauty of art. A cynical Frenchman once remarked that there would be little ideal or romantic love had it not been so egregiously advertised through literature, and it is at least certain that there was no deep or widespread love of nature until the way had been prepared by descriptive poetry and prose, and by landscape painting. If there were in nature an intrinsic beauty, it would be hard to account for the tardy appearance and slow development of its appreciation. There are adumbrations of deep concern with nature, especially with the sea, in Anglo-Saxon poetry, but the range of appreciation is very limited, and centuries intervened before even this partial and limited appreciation was common in England.

As for appreciation of natural appearances in classical literature and what little remains to us of classical painting, there is next to nothing, while that little, the nature of Hesiod and Homer, of Theocritus, Horace and Virgil, is always a nature refashioned by man, artificially subordinated to his uses and pleasures. In this artificial tradition is most of the love of nature expressed in the literature of the Middle Ages and Renaissance. Nature is a park or pleasant garden, and, at that, usually envisaged not directly but in a dream. It is not until the seventeenth century that expressions of the love of wild nature are even sporadic, and not till the eighteenth that the sentiment for nature is prevalent.

To this general fact of retardation China offers a striking exception. For fifteen hundred years China has felt and created a landscape beauty which has little to do with human habitation. And the influence of China kindled Japan to a similar enthusiasm a full century before anything of the sort was felt in the western world. It would lead us far afield to inquire into the causes of China's priority. Why did the Chinese artist seek panoramic vastness when the western artist sought limitation and intimacy? Such a question admits of no brief or simple answer. But I may at least suggest that for a China touched by Indian thought, landscape was not an entity but an aspect of a greater, of a supreme whole, and interpretative of that whole. Of that whole the Chinese artist was also a part or aspect. For him landscape beauty was either an adumbration of a greater whole, or an extension or emanation of his own feeling and thinking about that whole. Consequently the inevitable dilemma of the one and the many was faced and resolved by the Chinese artist centuries before it was vivid, or even present, as a problem to the artists of the west. Such is the principal reason why for nearly a thousand years China produced the greatest idealistic landscape the world has seen. Which may suggest that to concern himself with the problem of the one and the many, a concern quite alien to the western mind, might also for the western artist be a very fruitful activity.

So far as we enjoy nature through transforming it, we are acting as artists, repeating the preliminary activities of the poet or painter up to the point where he deals with the material of his art. Such really creative experiences of the nature lover, are, as Volkelt has rightly pointed out, merely a branch of the esthetics of art. They by no means fully cover the beauty that is felt in nature. I believe that no one who has analyzed deeply his own impressions of natural beauty, no one who has read understandingly the eloquent inventory of natural beauties of John Ruskin, and the sedater and possibly more truthful descriptions of a W. H. Hudson or a John C. Van Dyke—no such observer and reader, I am confident, will fail to admit the difference between experiences of natural beauty that are tinged with art, and those that have no such tinge.

In my own case, being an enthusiastic student of painting, much of my delectation in nature lies simply in my ability to transform the appearance into the sort of picture I would paint if I could. But I do not transform a storm coming down through a mountain gorge, a gale at sea, the majestically floating clouds that I see as I lie in the grass or on the sea sand, the swirling rush of a great river, the white narrowing and crystal broadening of a mountain brook, the shifting pageant tints of ineffable brilliancy at sunset and sunrise—these appearances and many like them I take for what they are without thought of revising them to my taste. Every unspoiled person does so. And, despite the silence of art and literature, I believe such direct unmediated delectation from nature may go very far back in the history of the race. Such experiences, however precious and intense, are common. Poet and painter may easily have taken them for granted. Besides, even with the extraordinary increase in the technical resources of poetry and painting, these greater manifestations of the power and beauty of nature are still refractory subject matter for poet and painter. There are few Joseph Conrads, few Winslow Homers.

Having to put into a few paragraphs what is a theme for a book, I may merely note that those natural appearances —sunset glow, for example—which by common consent are beautiful, often have little formal character. This naturally is equally true of their appreciation. We are dealing with dynamic impressions of a very simple order, however grand in effect, with magic of diffused irradiation of colored light. The fact that we have descriptive prose and poetry and landscape painting proves that we want something that joy in nature does not give us—and that something seems to be a richer and more complicated harmony, more varied supporting rhythms, more distance—in short, psychic experiences of a more elaborately ordered sort than those we get from immediate contemplation of nature itself. From the purely formal point of view, then, beauty of nature is always and inevitably inferior to beauty of art.

That it is inherently a beauty of lower order, or one properly to be measured by formal standards does not follow. The magnitude and intensity of the impressions we receive from nature far transcend those of art. From the finest painting imaginable one never got the rapture from color that he will get from hundreds of sunsets in any year. No suggestion of motion or energy in any work of art, not even I think in music, ever went to the nerves with the impact of a Niagara or a storm at sea. Few impressions of art are so positively life-enhancing as the more ordinary effects of natural beauty. The beauty of art is never unbearable, does not normally move to tears. That of nature often will. The tragic effects of art are rarely so shattering that we feel a kind of greatness in ourselves in being able to endure them. The tragic effects of nature often are of this sort.

Such considerations perhaps bring us near the truth of the matter, that the beauty of nature largely consists in the amplification of ordinary pleasures. One sees more intensely, breathes more deeply, gains a fuller sense of his bodily validity, his capacity to enjoy or endure. Indeed the physiological esthetics of Guyau, which we have seen very inadequately explain the experience of beauty in art, do seem to apply admirably to the experience of beauty in nature, in that in such experience our sense of life is quantitatively enhanced. Nor would I deny that such quantitative enhancement may amount to a qualitative difference. I can find little common quality in bravely enduring a toothache and witnessing a dangerous storm with a rapture of fortitude. But the difference is never moving towards the experience of beauty in art, but rather away from it, to a state that is not multiform but simple, a state in which pleasure and fortitude are not subordinated to larger issues, but rather increasingly indulged for their own sake.

It may seem then that the experience of beauty in nature is less humanly significant, if more intense and elemental, as implying a far simpler and less elaborate activity. For the esthetician weighing the apparently unlimited beauty of nature against the quite limited beauty of art there is perhaps a profound parable in the vision of Elijah on the mount. There was a great wind, an earthquake and a fire, but in none of these was God. Then a still small voice, and God was manifested to His prophet.

This leads us back, if circuitously, to our central problem of landscape beauty. If, as it seems, no prior experience of beauty has been embodied in nature, no artist, one may say, has put beauty there, how does a spectator derive beauty from nature as contemplated? The answer of modern psychology is, he himself puts into nature the beauty he attributes to it, acts to it much as the artist acts towards the work of art. Obviously the spectator does not make the natural appearances that delight him, though he does contribute not a little to their making. Reshape and refashion these appearances he does, according to the laws of his own choicest activities. This remaking amounts practically to a making. In short, sensing and perceiving the correlation of the activities of nature with his own, the spectator fuses these activities into a unity of which he regards the natural appearance as the container or symbol.

This is what the German estheticians call a feeling oneself into an object, an act of *Einfühlung*. Empathy, the late Professor Tichener called it. Let us use the less technical if less speaking term Esthetic Sympathy. Since for many modern estheticians beauty and esthetic sympathy are really one and the same, designating merely an activity and the psychic state that accompanies it, esthetic sympathy well deserves and shall have a chapter of its own.

Our analysis of the esthetic transaction has necessarily been made in generalized terms. To bring concreteness into the discussion let me imagine the course of the two esthetic transactions, namely, between myself and a scene I know intimately and love—the view of the North Conway Intervale looking towards Mount Washington; and between myself and a most familiar and widely loved masterpiece of painting, Botticelli's "Allegory of Spring." For the sake of simplicity I will begin with the view of the Intervale.

It yields a sense of a much expanded self, yields this soothing and exalted feeling after a preliminary self-surrender. I go out into the gracious vale closed by the blue barrier of the Presidential Range; I am less bounded by my own body; I breathe more deeply and tranquilly. Next I become conscious of an order and proportionateness in the converging, opposing, repeating contours and masses of color. I glimpse a system, a congruity of quite a complicated sort. I begin to read the parts of this proportionateness. Here it is important for further discussion to note that what is really static I read as dynamic. The contours of the slopes that interlock up the valley are read most variously. They are drooping, festooning elements; they press with force on the intervale, they rise strongly from it to the wooded summits. The level river valley thrusts between the impinging declivities like a wedge, meets the push of the mountain shoulders and does not merely bear it as dead weight. Similarly the relation of green intervale, darker green wooded mountain areas, and the ineffable blue of the big mountain is conceived not merely as a lovely pattern of color areas but as a rhythmical stepping back in space.

These are merely examples of many readings of the organization of the scene, readings that hover at the verge of the conscious and the unconscious, readings that impute motion to what is motionless, in short—and this is highly important for our later study—convert proportions into rhythms. All this reading has taken time, perhaps only a few seconds, surely not many minutes, and it seems as if this time element were read into the scene as motion. The climax of the activity which has been very partially sketched is a sense of complete awareness and understanding, of heightened consciousness and power. You have given yourself to nature, and nature has given back the surrendered self, enhanced, ennobled, glowing with the joy of unexpected capacity.

In my own case the reading of this lovely scene would be much conditioned by what I know of landscape painting. By my twelfth year I was turning over the plates of the Turner Gallery, and from not much later I remember the first exhibition of great landscapes by Inness and Blakelock. Accordingly, as I read the contours of the scene, I should imagine myself following them with brush or pencil. And this imagined act would imply an activity related to the contours themselves, would increase the dynamic character of my reading.

The reading of a naïve nature lover unversed in painting would differ chiefly in lacking all reference to drawing or painting the scene, in a less conscious apprehension of its organization, in a smaller imputation of dynamic quality to the masses and contours. But in all psychological essentials the course of the appreciative activity would be the same—a giving oneself as smaller to the gracious vastness of the prospect; a receiving oneself back enlarged, tranquillized, endued with the importance of the scene itself. In every case the process is one of abnegation, losing a smaller habitual self in order to gain an exceptional self of a greater order.

In the year 1477, Lorenzo di Pierfrancesco de' Medici having bought a villa at Castello, on the Prato road, commissioned a young Florentine painter, Sandro Botticelli, to paint a decorative panel for his villa. The dimensions, about seven by ten feet, and the subject, the "Coming of Spring," were prescribed. Lorenzo, not to be confused with his cousin and more illustrious namesake, was himself a minor poet and in touch with the great humanist poet Angelo Poliziano. Thus he was a patron of a kind to feel the loveliness of a Tuscan springtime. Botticelli accepted the theme with enthusiasm and cast about for its embodiment.

Instantaneously the general decorative arrangement flashes into Botticelli's mind, for a pattern is already there, waiting for a subject. He has admired the great new engraving of ten fighting men by one of his masters, Antonio Pollaiolo—a fine arabesque of tensely constructed white bodies effectively contrasting with the formal verticals of a grove in the background. Sometime Sandro meant to use the motive more exquisitely. This is his opportunity. His figures shall show a greater variety in drapery and semi-nudity.

It was perhaps at this stage some humanist friend called Sandro's attention to the beautiful lines in which Lucretius described the coming of spring.

> "It ver et Venus, et Veneris praenuntius ante
> Pennatus graditur, zephyri vestigia propter
> Flora quibus mater praespargens ante viai
> Cuncta coloribus egregiis et odoribus opplet."

A. Pollaiolo. Ten Nudes. Engraving

Botticelli. Primavera

Uffizi, Florence

"Spring and Venus move by, and the winged herald of Venus goes before; and close upon the track of the West Wind Flora, their mother, strews flowers ahead, covering all the paths with fairest colors and odors."

A group of five figures begins to order itself in Botticelli's mind; the composition now has found its main theme, but he consciously transforms the processional order of Lucretius. Spring no longer leads with Venus, but is blown and chased in by Zephyr at the rear of the line. And the trees shall bend as Zephyr passes, admitting his gentle power. As for Zephyr, Poliziano, in the *"Stanze"* is better than Lucretius. He represents Zephyr as lustful and flying behind Flora. Such shall be his relation to Spring. Flora does not follow Zephyr, but treads daintily ahead of him, behind Venus. Cupid's place as herald is above Venus and a little before her, and since he has wings, shall he not fly rather than walk? In its essentials the group at the right-hand side of the panel, the group that carries the meaning, is now established.

The carpet of spring flowers is obvious. Does not Lucretius suggest it? The flowers shall be so truthful that you could pluck them. They will contrast effectively with the formality of the paling of orange trees which he will pick out decoratively and conventionally with gold. But he will not stand on the somewhat monotonous verticalities of Pollaiolo's paling of trees. His paling shall be interspersed with olive branches delicately sharp against the sky. Everything shall be as fine and precise as any goldsmith's work.

So far everything has gone swimmingly. Presumably sketches have been made of the five figures, the group has taken on organization, at least mentally. Enrichments and refinements have occurred. Out of Spring's lovely mouth roses shall grow; the flowers woven in Flora's frock shall proclaim her function; Venus shall be gravid and heavily draped, for contrast with the semi-nude figures and because spring is the birthday of the year. But now comes an unforeseen difficulty; on the small scale customary at the time, the five figures will never make out a composition for the big, oblong panel. Some filling figures of a congruous kind are indispensable. What figures?

Sandro is reasonably educated, but no scholar. He consults a humanist friend who has the ready answer. Of course Mercury and the Three Graces are the fitting attendants for Venus. Did not Horace, Book I, Ode xxx, when he bid Venus visit the home of his mistress Glycera, summon also the Graces with girdles loosed and Mercury, who withal is a minor cloud-dispeller? Witness *Aeneid,* IV, 245. As for the Graces, Sandro's own fellow Florentine, Leonbattista Alberti, in his treatise *Della Pittura,* which Sandro has doubtless duly read, tells us that their hands should be intertwined, and they themselves clothed in ungirt and transparent veils—quoting Seneca, "implexis inter se manibus, ridentes solutaque, perlucida veste ornatas." So the humanist counsellor.

Sandro thinks it over. Here are the needed filling figures, and excellent figures for the purpose. Mercury shall be fanning the mists from an orange tree with his caduceus. That will carry the processional rhythm across the picture up to a high finish. He shall then be the terminal figure of the group. But the Graces shall be treading a solemn measure and not smiling. Only the hoyden Spring with the rose in her mouth shall be joyous.

The rest shall be pensive, or, like Flora, enigmatically detached, for if spring is the beginning of new life in the world, is it not also the beginning of new death? The flowers and love itself are but for a moment between budding and withering.

Something like this in Sandro's mind as he sketches the four new figures and considers the organization of the two groups into one. Here the general cadence is clear. The onrush of Zephyr and Spring shall be retarded into the dainty treading of Flora, shall come to a monetary full pause in the heavily clad figure of gravid Venus, shall be resumed in a moderated and more subtle fashion in the dance of the Graces, shall end with the resolutely poised figure of Mercury with his back turned while his hand and magic wand make on high a closing repetend of the right to left motion.

The composition of the picture is now mentally complete. Remains a task of some days to set it down in all its details in a working drawing—a drawing unhappily lost, for which any sensible collector would mortgage his house to the limit. Remained still a task of many months to paint it through on the panel. Rapturous work, work under highest tension, nothing lost of the freshness of the primal vision, much added by way of fit enrichment; fastidiousness in choice of shapes and tints never relaxing, never overasserting itself; a marvel of taste, a miracle of executive prowess.

When it was set in the wall at Castello, Botticelli, unless he was entirely unlike any other painters, relatively lost interest in it. He was now at work on his nobly tragic "St. Augustine" for Ognissanti in competition with the formidably popular Ghirlandaio's "St. Jerome," he was already thinking of great frescoes to be made in Pope Sixtus's new chapel at Rome. Botticelli's part of the esthetic transaction connected with the "Allegory of Spring" was completed and well completed. That the transaction should continue was now the responsibility of others.

The painting is now ready to play its part in the esthetic transaction. Let me imagine myself before it. First at a distance I perceive the general design—a very varied processional advance of clothed and lightly draped forms from right to left across a quite formal paling of orange trees. Here I have repeated the primal vision of Botticelli as elaborated by trial and error. Of this trial and error virtually nothing comes to my attention, though I may note that the four figures on the left are out of the main action, may divine that they were an afterthought.

On nearer approach I grasp the exquisiteness of the detail without losing the sense of the whole picture. This detail, the ripe oranges on the trees, the iris, larkspurs, daisies, wild orchid, wood-strawberry daintily balancing in the grass tell me that it is early springtime. Herewith comes the meaning of the figures. Gravid Venus is identified by her winged son. The fantastic figure with a beflowered frock, and strewing flowers must be Flora. An associational item confirms and extends the identifications. I have read Herbert Horne's happy citation of the lines from Lucretius which names all five figures for me. This literary association is legitimately part of my appreciation, for it guided

Botticelli in creation. Since it was important for him, it is important for me.

As I identify the main figures I sense their fastidiously distinguished character and the loveliness of the postures, actions and details which represent and delicately emphasize their functions. What a cadence it is, rising from the solemn boisterousness of Zephyr, through the adorable awkward twist of escaping Spring, to the mincing elegance of Flora's measured stride, and the full stop where Venus stands in undulating repose. It is also an undulation in depth, coming forward with Flora and the Graces at the ends, receding with Venus at the center. My sense of the whole picture is being constantly deepened and enriched as I make these explorations of details, and continue then through the flowery sward, the grove, the group of Mercury and the Graces. Here in appreciation I am perceiving that infinite delicate elaboration and richness which arising in Botticelli's imagination commanded his nervous and fastidious hand. These observations gradually tell me of the language in which Botticelli's meaning is expressed. While there is a lovely accompaniment of muted color, it is primarily a language of line—line that races, slows, darts, turns, stops, resumes, always giving assurance of form in implied motion. My soul has echoed the controlled sweep of Botticelli's hand. The sense of the pervading wistful, tranquil melancholy that surrounds and almost denies the high spirits of romping Spring grows deeper as I look.

The experiences which words can only enumerate as successive, have actually overlapped, interwoven, blended, and have uninterruptedly built up that psychical volume which is my appreciation of this lively picture, my virtual if also approximate repetition of what was essential in Botticelli's creative processes—my complete *Geniessen,* my partial but sufficient *nachschaffen.*

But the psychical volume is unstable. Deforming associations emerge. Is the condition of the picture as fine as Herbert Horne says? Is that horrible legend of the British copyist who saw the tempera surface sponged with water, and colors wrung out of the sponge—is it true? The association, though inherently interesting and even important, is out of place and to be dismissed. The picture is what its fate has made it, what it is today. At best the association may help me to imagine a more brilliant original coloring, but my imagination would be too vague to be of esthetic service.

Another association pops up. Does not Venus look like a girl I used to skate with in Berlin years ago? Betty must be gently kept out of the picture. Botticelli could not have seen her prophetically. The association, however pleasant to me, is intrusive.

In censoring these inutile associations again I am repeating Botticelli's creative processes by a sort of parallelism. He too indulged momentarily associations which had to be kept out of the picture.

Through all these activities in which the sense of the whole has been growing through inspection of the parts, explorations constantly intermitted for renewed contemplation of the whole, the lovely form and the lovely poetic content have been fusing into an ineffable unity. In an ecstasy which is both breathlessly tense and deliciously tranquillizing, I share according to my capacity Botticelli's elegiac vision of the transient yet passionate assertion of new life in every spring, of a new life already condemned to death; share the vision as pattern, line and color, as rhythm of design in space, as cadence of motion, muted harmony of unearthly tints—share the vision in my mind and in my heart.

This culminating act of sympathetic understanding will be brief—only a measured minute or two. No one can really look at any picture for more than five minutes. The concentration required is too intense. So it is time to leave Primavera and rest up by looking at something less taxing.

In this imaginary course of activities from the making to the enjoying of a great picture I have wished to emphasize the analogies between the creative and the appreciative experience. Of course I cannot put the energy, passion and refinement that Botticelli expended on his masterpiece into my appreciation of it. But I must have in my soul something kindred to Botticelli's if I am to understand his vision at all. I hope that this perhaps too obvious recounting of a particular esthetic transaction may help to clarify the whole problem—may at least illustrate concretely the profound truth in Goethe's aphorism— *Geniessen ist nachschaffen.*

This illustration should disabuse the reader of the misconception that the esthetic activity is unitary at high tension. On the contrary, whether in creation or in response, it is highly modulated, passing readily from level to level. At some point, a climax, there is great intensity. Elsewhere the activity may sink momentarily to a sort of neutral estate. What is valuable is the activity as a whole. It should not be necessary to write that there is no specific unitary taste of the Primavera, as there is of yellow Chartreuse or green, but the over-simplified character of much artistic criticism forces us to remind ourselves to the point of obviousness of the very complicated character of such experiences of beauty as are connected with works of art.

CHAPTER III

ESTHETIC SYMPATHY

SO FAR, for convenience, we have treated the esthetic transaction as if it moved in a single direction from the artist through the work of art to beholder or hearer. But our study of the beauty of nature strongly suggests that in that case the direction is not from the object in nature to the beholder, but rather from the beholder to the object. On any other basis it is hard to explain the experience of beauty in nature. The work of art we may imagine as charged, like a storage battery, with the essential creative experience of the artist in its making, and thus as capable of transmitting such experience. But it is begging an entire teleological question to consider nature in any such way. What nature gives us is the possibility of impressions of sense, nothing whatever beyond that. Whatever more nature seems to give us we really give to her. The organizing activities of isolation, subordination, selection, enrichment from association are human activities—our activities. If we seem to find them in nature, they are there as our largesse. We have put them there, and generously forgotten our gift. We have felt beauty from ourselves into nature by what is technically called an act of *Einfühlung*. Nearly a century before Robert Vischer coined that term, Coleridge expressed the reality of it in the lines,

"O Lady! we receive but what we give,
And in our life alone doth nature live."

Now if we receive beauty from nature only as we have first given it, is it not at least probable that only on the

same terms we receive beauty from a work of art? May
not the beauty which seems to us inherent in the work of
art be really an activity of our own? Admitting the theoretical possibility, the direction of the esthetic transaction
would no longer be in one direction but in two directions,
converging from the artist and the art lover upon the work
of art. It could then be regarded as a sort of magnet, attracting prospectively the artist to his activity of creation
and attracting retrospectively the beholder or hearer to his
activity of appreciation. Both movements toward the work
of art may seem to arise in esthetic sympathy, *Einfühlung*—
the desire to project a fine human experience into an object.

A theme which can be thus simply expressed has been
subjected to the most elaborate and suggestive analysis by
Lipps and Volkelt. Since the reader may gather the gist
of their researches from any recent book on esthetics—I
can warmly recommend the excellent summary by Lord
Listowel—it seems unnecessary in such a sketch as I am
undertaking, to go into the subject at length. As an
example, when we admire a great tree, we feel ourselves
stretching up and outwards, and twisting and bearing
down with the tree, but we feel these activities as in the
tree and not in ourselves. Yet these activities are not in the
tree as a bare phenomenon. They are in the tree only after
we have read them into the sensory impressions through
an act of perception. They are, then, in the tree only as we
have thought or felt them into it.

Coming to the work of art as similarly animated and
made beautiful by esthetic sympathy, let me choose the
simple case so elaborately followed through by Lipps, that
of a Doric column. With an irreverence entirely friendly

I can never think of that thrilling chapter except under the caption, The Capers of a Column. To Professor Lipps's sympathetic eye, the column goes through the most various and exciting activities—stands firm, rises up, bears down, carries weight, swells, contracts, thrusts upwards and downwards from the middle, pushes out its base and capital into a bulge, but a bulge which meets a stabilizing contraction. In short, as perceived by esthetic sympathy, the equilibrium of the column is not static, as it is or virtually is in reality, but highly dynamic. All this may be read by those who dread to undertake Lipps's clear and attractive German, at length and with admirable commentary in *Beauty and Ugliness,* by Anstruther-Thomson and Vernon Lee. My part is merely to convey the general notion.

Now clearly of the manifold activities suggested above the column really exercises at most two, and these are perhaps only one—that of supporting so much weight and exerting so much vertical pressure. And this it does passively. All the active functions of the column as it capers are imputed functions, activities not of the column but of its beholder. While it must be admitted that few beholders feel themselves into a Doric column with the vivacity of a Theodor Lipps, or a Vernon Lee, whoever does experience beauty in a Doric column, does it, if more tranquilly, in a kindred way. For the column simply as a datum of the visual sense has no beauty at all. Its beauty may then depend on borrowed activities and perceived relations tinged dynamically by the perceiver. A column lying down, or suspended in the sling from a derrick would not seem beautiful, but it is the same column that seems beautiful in a Greek temple.

Again it should be clear that as in nature so in art beauty may be traced to an activity of a beholder or hearer which is transferred to an object, and felt as belonging to the object. We identify ourselves with the object, endue it with our own experience. What we have projected from ourselves we give to the object unreservedly, so to speak, leave it there and regard it as no longer ours, but as a quality or attribute of the object.

The only difference between experiencing beauty, in nature and in art, is that in art there has been a purposeful act of creative activity, esthetic sympathy directed towards doing, which we may readily repeat in an analogous activity of appreciation. Since the work of art was made to be appreciated, its appreciation is much facilitated. But in feeling beauty of nature, the way is not thus prepared for us. We must be both the artist and the beholder, must transform the natural appearances into a work of art and then experience its beauty. For such reasons I entirely agree with Theodor Lipps that the highest esthetic activities are those concerned with art and not those concerned with nature. The mere difficulty of maintaining the double rôle of artist and beholder would seem to make experience of natural beauty less definite and satisfactory. What are often regarded as major esthetic experiences of nature— the expansive serenity of a sunset, the virginal quiet and hush of sunrise—are probably to be regarded as elementary pleasures of an uncommonly intense order, and not as esthetic experiences in the fullest sense. The mind and the will enter into such experiences very slightly if at all. All genuine esthetic experience draws heavily upon judgment and will.

Now the apparent trouble with esthetic sympathy as a complete explanation of the experience of beauty is two-fold: esthetic sympathy is involved in all acts of perception, and not merely in the experience of beauty; without it there is no understanding of a person or a thing; while to find beauty in a process of projecting our own activities into an object of which they never are a property or an attribute, is to rest all esthetic experience on illusion.

The rôle of sympathy in all perception is so much a commonplace of modern psychology that it may almost be taken for granted here. We understand a person only by first putting ourselves in his place, living in him ourselves through the imagination. Without this act of sympathy, we have no means of access to the experiences of another soul. We may infer feelings and motives from behavior, but the behavior itself is meaningless save as we feel how we ourselves should have behaved under the same circumstances. The meanings which we find in others are inevitably our meanings.

No one, I think, will deny that sympathy is the path of understanding towards animated creatures—our fellow beings, animals, perhaps even plants—but the part of sympathy in understanding inanimate objects may not seem so clear. We may understand a watercourse by regarding it as a result of erosion and alluvial action, of growth and decay of vegetation. But the watercourse tells nothing of this merely as an appearance. Erosion, alluvial action, growth, decay are all mental concepts transmitted to us from the past thinking of the race. We read these concepts into the appearance of the watercourse, animate it from the activities of our own soul. The relation of sympathy and perception to all understanding is hard for common sense to grasp and admit. Why is not the watercourse inherently an eroded, deposited and overgrown thing? Why can we not read its characteristics directly from the appearance, instead of inferring them indirectly through our own experience? To answer these questions fully would require what is impracticable here, a treatise on the theory of knowledge. We may simply recall the Kantian position that our faculties and capacities shape and reshape the data of sense after their own image. We understand what our physical and mental organization fits us to understand. Within certain velocities of light vibrations, our eye and brain are fitted to interpret them as color; above and below this range of vibrations we can still think and even experiment in terms of vibrations, but we can no longer see them as color. In short, color is something which we do to the light vibrations reflected from objects. It is neither in the objects nor in the vibrations; it is quite literally only in our eye, if we include therein the entire apparatus of vision. If there were no eyes in the world, there would be no colors.

This simple example may serve as a reminder that the senses give us no knowledge, but merely the raw material from which knowledge may be made. Knowledge about things is first perceived or, as it may be, conceived by us, then returned to the thing and assumed to belong to it. For practical purposes we consider the thing as actually corresponding to our feelings and ideas about it. Philosophy can neither affirm nor deny this correspondence, indeed philosophy has difficulties even in admitting, certainly in proving the very existence of things outside of ourselves.

But in esthetics what clearly and convincingly seems to be is, and the metaphysical problems indicated above do not arise. It is enough if this brief survey has satisfied the reader that we understand anything only through sympathy with it, through enduing it with our activities, through lending it our experience. As Theodor Lipps tersely puts it: "Humanly understandable for us is only the human being and what is thought of as similar thereto."

This leaves us with the difficulty of distinguishing that sympathy which is the way of all understanding from that esthetic sympathy which is the way to beauty. The problem parallels that of pleasure—what pleasures are truly esthetic, what non-esthetic? While we shall find an answer more readily in the case of pleasures, it is probable that these lines of demarcation can never be sharply drawn, and do not need to be. I think Professor Dewey is right in feeling that our ordinary well organized and satisfactory experiences have a tinge of the esthetic and shade off imperceptibly into experiences that are distinctly esthetic. Indeed, all such experiences should be thought of as in active balance and tending to shift in one direction or another. There is probably no such thing as a purely esthetic experience, meaning an experience the balance of which has no tendency to dip towards the great world of the non-esthetic. And there are probably few satisfactory experiences on the plane of ordinary living which do not tend to increase their incipient esthetic value.

In the cases, however, which are really important and worthy of analysis we are in no doubt as to their location with regard to the frontier of esthetics. They are well inside of it or outside of it. And if the frontier itself be not a dotted line but a debatable land, that is what frontiers have often been in human history. So while strict bounds may matter greatly to the esthetician as psychologist, to the artist and art lover they really matter very little. Suppose as artist or art lover I am out of bounds, it is of no importance unless my straying be unhappily reflected in imperfection of the work of art or dissatisfaction in its appreciation. Such imperfection or dissatisfaction will be felt immediately and will not be arrived at through analytical processes. In short, the warden of the marches lying between the esthetic and the non-esthetic is not the dialectic of the esthetician but the individual judgment of the artist and art lover.

If the experience of beauty really depends upon our finding beauty where we have put it ourselves, and where it is not in fact, then all esthetic activity is clearly based on a delusion—and worse yet for the believer in *Einfühlung,* on a delusion that is known to be such. Here we meet also the paradox that the highest certitude we enjoy, the supreme affirmation of our nature, seems to rest simply on an error in psychological analysis. Putting the case more colloquially —do we merely fool ourselves into finding certain objects beautiful?

Theodor Lipps and others meet this paradox by asserting that in esthetic sympathy we fully identify ourselves with a work of art or scene in nature. If so, we may say indifferently beauty is a quality of our feeling, or a quality of an object. Both statements would be true. Here I may take certain subtleties of Lipps too literally, but I am sure there is no state of ecstasy, much less of mere esthetic satisfaction, in which we lose awareness of the difference between ourselves and the object which we feel to be beautiful. In legend this has happened—in the case of the Chinese painter, Wu-tai-Tse, who walked into his picture and disappeared, and the legend has value as a parable of the self-abnegation involved in the contemplation of any great work of art, but in real life I have never heard of anybody who has even momentarily felt he was a poem, a picture, a statue, a symphony. We may concede to the champions of *Einfühlung* an electric instant of fusion in which, being one with the work of art, we may, as it were, deposit our experience of beauty and leave it there to be contemplated by us when we shall have dissevered ourselves from the momentary union. But this is a painfully matter-of-fact way of considering our most poetic experiences. And we are always left in the plight that to benefit by the projective activity of *Einfühlung* we must always misinterpret it as receptive.

I imagine the answer to this dilemma may be that the esthetic activity and its analysis are in entirely different worlds, neither of which is bound by the terms of the other. If in esthetic activity beauty seems to be in objects outside of ourselves, it is actually there while we are experiencing beauty. This is a truth of a world of esthetic contemplation. That it may be not a truth but an error or illusion in quite another world, that of psychological ratiocination, is perhaps of no consequence practically. Nobody analyzes beauty while experiencing it, nor experiences it through analysis. In esthetic experience things are what they seem to be, no questions are asked, no challenges made. It is a realm of complete certitude. No one enters in without making, in Coleridge's pregnant words, "that willing suspension of disbelief for the moment which constitutes poetic faith." That in another realm all sorts of questions are asked and challenges made has no bearings on esthetic experience. As art lover, Theodor Lipps forgets esthetic sympathy while he exercises it; as esthetician and psychologist he analyzes it in this way or that. In whatever way it be analyzed, the experience of beauty is the same. In short, while the theory of esthetic sympathy may give us a persuasive analysis of our esthetic experiences, it does not define them or in any sense express them.

We may admit, then, that measured by the perhaps irrelevant standards of our reasoned living beauty is a pure illusion. In its own realm there is no measure that will prove it an illusion or not, for its world is one of seeming to be, one in which what seems to be effectually and indisputably is. In the same way in which the activity of beauty reconciles the many and the one, it fuses appearance with reality, illusion with complete certitude.

Doubtless the rôle of illusion in esthetic experience needs further study. Eduard von Hartmann found that esthetic activity lies in a sort of give and take, a pendulum movement, between illusion and ordinary reality. We yield to the illusion, come out of it and perceive its illusory nature, return to it, and so indefinitely. Ingenious as the theory is, I feel that the oscillation supposed by Hartmann must be a mixed experience and not fully esthetic—a state very like the coming and going between sleep and waking at the end of a troubled night. I cannot find in such states that integrity and ultimate serenity which are of the essence of all esthetic experience. Moreover I am sure there is no fully esthetic state which does not exclude such intermittent reference to common reality. But everyday experiences may have a tendency to become esthetic, those connected with the more stable pleasures, the organized and satisfactory experiences described by Professor Dewey. Many of the slighter esthetic experiences are undoubtedly of this mixed order. But the integral esthetic experiences traffic with ordinary living only on penalty of self-destruction. Such traffic ordinarily does not produce even a mixed esthetic experience, but an entirely different experience, on the plane of our practical living.

Before leaving the subject of Esthetic Sympathy, another thought for what it may seem worth. Considered empirically, and even on careful analysis, our souls, our bodies, external nature, the work of art all seem to reveal common patterns of existence and activity. These correlations and analogies are not mystically imputed. Experiment of the psychologist, physicist, biologist, chemist, geologist seems to confirm them as facts. Now suppose such facts of analogy and correlation to be realized not in deliberate thought, but immediately, through intuition, in feeling. We should thus find ourselves in our fellow men, in the artist, in the work of art and in nature. And this discovery with its accompanying rapture might constitute or at least start the experience of beauty. Instead then of speaking or projecting ourselves we should speak of finding ourselves. It would still be an act of esthetic sympathy, but receptive rather than projective. And such a characterization of the activity of beauty would correspond more closely than does the postulate of *Einfühlung* to our feelings about the esthetic transaction while we are part of it, and to our analysis when we merely summon it in memory for consideration and definition.

To such a conception of esthetic experience a philosophy of universal vitalism and a cosmology of pantheism would obviously correspond. It is perhaps the advantage of esthetics over other studies that it calls neither for a philosophy nor for a cosmology. If within itself esthetic experience be coherent and satisfactory, the character of the universe within which, but also apart from which it takes place does not matter. Or, perhaps, matters only to this extent— that esthetic experience might seem even more rewarding and satisfactory when contrasted with a world of doing and being which seems eminently unstable, hazardous, incoherent and unrationalized. If the experience of beauty consists in illusion, it is an illusion superior to the alleged realities.

CHAPTER IV

THEORY OF CORRESPONDENCES OF RHYTHM

LET US pursue further that theory of correspondences sketched in the last page. Since Heraclitus asserted the universal flux, since Plato divined music in the courses of the stars and asserted a cyclical departure and return, this notion of a cosmic vibration or undulation has ever haunted the minds of the great sages. Indian thought is full of it, often carries the notion to extremes in which grotesqueness and sublimity singularly blend. A Zen adept who merely loses his temper remarks, "an ignorant man has killed his mother." The imprisoned poet senator, Boethius, wished that men might be guided by that active principle of love which moves the stars, and Dante borrowed the thought for the last line of his *Divine Comedy*—

"Amor che move il sol e l'altre stelle."

It is unnecessary to follow out this idea through widening paths that will lead to many hilltops of vision, and, alas! also to many Serbonian bogs of delusion. Suffice it to say that ordinary experience goes far to confirm these mystical apprehensions. Our own rhythm of birth, growth, fructification, decline, death we share with all living things. The differences are merely those of tempo: a flower or a butterfly completes the cycle in a few weeks; the cycle of an elephant is three times ours; that of an oak twice that of an elephant; that of a giant redwood twenty times that of an oak. But, more or less accelerated or retarded, it is always the same rhythm. Looking inward, our daily living is one of levels fluctuating rhythmically like a sea.

Our circulation, digestion, respiration, excretion, nervous vibration take place rhythmically. Sleep and waking are our greater tidal experiences. All conscious effort follows a curve of intermittent intensity and relaxation. Even the experience of beauty in art, as Clive Bell shows in his book *Enjoying Pictures,* is never long maintained at a level of ecstasy. It swings from level to level between mystic concentration and a diffused happiness. The biologist and physicist tell us that the undulations which characterize our physiology and conscious living rule also in the cell and its nucleus, in the molecule and the atom.

Through geology and cosmology holds the same principle of rhythmical change and recurrences. Planets are shrunk out of star dust, live, die. The shaping of a continent through upheaval, erosion, sedimentation, glacial sculpture, evaporation, precipitation, growth and decay of plants and animals, habitation and practical domination of men—all this may reasonably be regarded as a majestically retarded phrase in a cosmic fugue.

Our ordinary words when we speak of inanimate nature are a recognition of this universal dynamism. We do not say that a mountain is high, we say it rises; a tree top is not merely broad, it spreads; a cataract plunges; a river broadens. And these are not metaphors of studied speech, they are common speech's recognition of the world as it manifests itself in ordinary experience.

Now we ourselves are always in this rhythm, completely a part of it, and a very small part. Yet through consciousness we can provisionally withdraw ourselves from this ordered flux, observe it, contemplate it as outsiders. Only on such terms of detachment can we perceive the flux at all and ourselves as both in it and separate from it. Our separateness, an entire illusion in itself, is the condition on which we attain to any kind of reality. Indeed, our surest moments of self-realization, of our own autonomy and dignity, are precisely those in which the mind insists that we are merely strands in the cosmic weaving, while the soul denies that it is so. Paradoxically this contradiction troubles neither the mind nor the soul; they seem to agree to disagree. Rather they agree on some supralogical plane in mutually admitting the coexistence of the many and the one.

Now the bearing of all this on the esthetics of nature should be obvious. Nature seems beautiful to us in the measure that she reveals her formative processes. The inherently beautiful scene is orderly and unconfused in the larger sense. Such a scene meets our need of rhythmical and orderly experience, contributes to such experience. Such a scene exists only as a mental picture. No natural appearance is stable. Sunlight and shadow, clouds, mist, rain, noontide glare, and evening dusk transform it hour by hour and almost minute by minute. Of course a similar variability of effect holds in the case of a building or a statue in the open air. But, though each variation is the possible occasion of a separate work of art, we do not feel there are several buildings or statues. Relatively the architecture of the Conway Intervale, or of the view down the Tiber from Perugia is as stable as that of Rouen cathedral, is as stable to the mind's eye. We may look at it either in terms of transience or permanence—with Monet or with Cézanne. One may concentrate on the architectonics of a natural scene—and I believe the highest esthetic pleasure from nature lies in this direction—or one may rather follow passively the adventitious epidermal splendors constantly given and taken away by the circumambient light and air.

Now the mere intellectual apprehension of these universal cosmic rhythms would not constitute an esthetic experience; it would merely be a concept. But suppose such apprehension to be also highly charged emotionally, suppose we accept this universal rhythm passionately and with admiration, feel the orderly ongoing of the whole to be far greater than ourselves, and yet feel ourselves as participating in its transcendent greatness—might not such feelings go far towards explaining the experience of beauty in nature? Of course I am aware that in our sense of natural beauty such feelings do not emerge with the precision of a formula. That they are always present in some vague but vital way I am convinced. The forest sages of India, a Saint Francis, a Wordsworth, a Goethe, all have hinted at, nay often specifically described this state in which we are at the same time beatifically conscious of our oneness with the universe, and yet aware of ourselves as different and outside and contemplating the rhythms that move the sun and the other stars.

For a choice example of this sense of appearances as revealing activities and rhythms let me quote the late Father Tabb's poem "Wood Grain." Sometime Father Tabb looked contemplatively at the grain of a board, and this is how he interpreted it.

> "This is the way that the sap-river ran
> From the root to the top of the tree—
> Silent and dark,
> Under the bark,

Working a wonderful plan
That the leaves never know
And the branches that grow
On the brink of the tide never see."

Does not the creative process here correspond to the first canon of painting by the Chinese sage Hsieh Ho, which was published in the fifth century A.D.? I use Mr. Coomaraswamy's wholly literal translation

"(1) Operation or revolution, or concord or reverberation of the spirit in life movement,"

which for our purposes may be briefly paraphrased as participation in the universal rhythm.

Father Tabb's exquisite gnomic lyric again obeys the law of the *Upanishads* (once more I draw on Mr. Coomaraswamy's excellent book *The Transformation of Nature in Art*), namely that—

"the song should be sung according to the course of the Spirit and the Waters."

If such an analysis of our activity of beauty have any persuasiveness, *Einfühlung* would take therein merely a secondary if essential place as the basis of all perception. Obviously we perceive a person or a thing only on condition of putting ourselves in his or its place, and at the beginning of every esthetic experience unquestionably lies a perception. But under this analysis, *Einfühlung* would not be the specific constituent of the experience of beauty, much less the capital activity of that experience.

This perhaps hazardous hypothesis of a universal rhythm has the advantage that it does not rest the sense of beauty on our mislaying our own feelings in an object and treating our own feelings as no longer ours, but as properties of the object in which we have deposited them. Thus it bases the experience of beauty not on an error or an illusion, but on something which is verifiable—namely: the infinite correspondences and analogies that are actually discernible between the particular modes of the universal rhythm.

In the esthetics of art it is highly probable that *Einfühlung* plays a large but by no means an exclusive rôle. We feel in the work of art not merely its formal rhythm. We know that somebody created that formal rhythm in order that we should feel it. Our sharing the creative activity of the artist—and we may and do share it—is a high and precious act of esthetic sympathy. Yet even in the field of art we should, I feel, beware of exaggerating the importance and necessity of this variety of *Einfühlung*. If vividly present, it undoubtedly enhances the sense of beauty. But often any intuition of the creative activity is either absent or only dimly present when we experience the beauty of a work of art. When the overpowering richness, dignity, and graciousness of Chartres come over me, how far am I at all aware of the activities of the scores of architects, sculptors, and glass designers who contributed to the eminently composite glory of that great shrine of the Virgin? Unless I be a designer in architecture, sculpture, or stained glass myself, I shall have little such awareness. I accept the thing made, and take the making for granted. Similarly when I live rapturously in the little heavens that the mosaic makers of Ravenna have created in tomb or baptistery, what sharing have I in the executive activities of these nameless great artists? None whatever, I think, unless I be myself a designer in mosaic, and then my technical lore is quite as likely to impair as to enhance my sense of a consummate beauty.

And in this connection we should beware of overstressing the various isolationist theories of the work of art. That the consummate work of art exists in a world well apart from that of our everyday practical activities is of course indisputably true. Most works of art, on the contrary, are deeply bound up with our ordinary living. It is a grave defect of much recent esthetics that it has pretty much confined its attention to the sublime. And it is not at all true that the creative activity inherent and revealed in every work of art in its substance and formal rhythm, is in a world outside of the universal rhythm. It is, on the contrary a part of it; its particular rhythms are pregnant with analogies and correspondences with the all-including order of the universe. The feelingful apprehension of such correspondences and analogies seem to me to play a larger part in the experience of beauty from a work of art than any activity of esthetic sympathy.

Again this view relieves the sense of beauty of the embarrassment of seeming to rest upon a sort of error in psychology. We feel what is there and where it is—particular formal rhythms in the work of art which correspond at once to many rhythms of our own activity and to many of the universe at large. And this view has also the advantage of extracting the modicum of truth from the old formal esthetic, which found beauty in objective rhythms and proportions. For us beauty will lie rather in the psychical activities which relate these particular proportions to a universal proportionateness and to our own experience.

Every alert reader will have noted that I have been using rhythm and proportion as completely synonymous. Such a reader will contend that while the rhythms of prose, poetry, music, acting, dancing are in time and correctly spoken of as rhythms, the proportions of painting, sculpture, and architecture are relations in space with no time element. Is this the case?

As perceived, certainly as experienced esthetically, I believe all proportions are to be regarded as rhythms. They are perceived only by a rhythmical activity of the intelligence in time. The time element and rhythm of their apprehension becomes their time element and rhythm. As proportions are animated and brought into time, proportions become rhythms. Here perhaps is the quite limited rôle of *Einfühlung* in esthetic activity. It animates proportions, makes rhythms of them. Where there is actually no rhythmical motion, *Einfühlung* seems an indispensable if minor part of esthetic experience. Where there is actual rhythmical motion, *Einfühlung* may seem an optional and adventitious feature of the appreciative activity. If present, it will probably enhance the activity; if absent, the activity will still be esthetic. Far more important is the experience of a particular rhythmical orderliness in the work of art which gives us hope of a universal order, and momentarily pushes back that disorder in which we habitually live. To this extent I am at one with Plotinus in feeling that he who has fully experienced beauty has sensed the *Logos*.

The varying tensions and durations of esthetic experiences from the several arts has often been remarked, but, so far as I know, never satisfactorily explained. The theory of correspondences, I believe, goes far towards providing the explanation, which in an indirect way tends to validate the hypothesis, for those arts of which the rhythms are most familiar to us, hence most readily perceived, seem to be the most accessible.

In one of his most winsome sonnets, Pierre Ronsard declared his intention of shutting himself up and reading the *Iliads* of Homer in three days. Doubtless he did it, and since he read in Greek, the three days were broken by few intermissions. I who write have sat up all night in order to complete a reading of the *Ring and the Book* within fifteen hours or so, and I have several times read deep into the small hours to finish a novel of Henry James. Now I am sure no one could give any such unremittent attention for as much as three hours to any play, opera, dance, musical composition, much less to the contemplation of any sculpture, painting, building or scene of natural beauty.

If as it seems, poetry and tensely wrought prose move us more deeply, immediately, and for a longer period of delectation than do any of the other arts, the reason must be that literary art deals in rhythms wholly familiar to us, to which in ordinary living we are constantly attuned—namely: the finer rhythms of speech. These rhythms all of us at times practise ourselves. They arise in our most intimate thinking and feeling, they are shaped by our whole physiology, are measured by the ingoing and outgoing of our breath, by the beat of our pulse, by the resistance or conductivity of our nerves. Accordingly when we pass from a merely good and adequate rhythm of workaday speech to the finer rhythms of the poet or master of cadenced prose, we make the transition without effort and almost without awareness. Naturally, then, poetry or impassioned prose move us more readily, more deeply and for a longer space of unflagging enjoyment than any of the other arts. The sensitive individual is always nearly in tune with the art of speech; for the other arts he has to put himself in tune.

The mixed arts of which speech is an important element, the play, the opera, the song, are nearly as accessible as the literary arts, but give satisfaction for a shorter time. There is, except perhaps in the case of the clearly recited song, a greater effort of adjustment. Between ourselves and a great poem or novel there is a minimum of distance, and little or no problem of maintaining a distance that is favorable to appreciation. The closer we get, broadly speaking, the better. But in the play and the opera there is a constant delicate adjustment to preserve a favorable distance. We must arbitrate between the actor as a man and as a person of the drama, between his speech as real or rightly artificial, between his actions and feelings as in our everyday world or in the arranged and fictitious world of the playwright. With regard to the stage, there is the same give and take, between reality and illusion. Is the back drop just so much painted canvas or is it a spreading vale seen between groves? To use the scenery aright we must realize that while for the purposes of this play it really is a far-spreading vale, it also is just so much canvas smeared with distemper paint.

These and many similar adjustments require of the theater or opera goer a greater effort than is required of the sympathetic reader. The relation to the rhythms of ordinary living is more remote and ambiguous. Hence no play could keep the most enthusiastic beholder-auditor fully attentive for many hours on end.

A Greek play went off in a matter of two hours; the great comedies of Molière are played in only a little more time. Few Elizabethan or Jacobean plays, as put on at the time with little change of scenery, required of the playgoer more than two hours and a half of attention, and within this space smoking and traffic with the pretty orange girls were permitted. Pragmatically, we may say that no one without benefit of intermissions can give untroubled esthetic sympathy to a play or an opera for more than two hours or two hours and a half. No human being could sit even contentedly, not to say rapturously, through the five hours when *Parsifal* is on stage, without the usual merciful provision for walking about, beer and cheese sandwiches. As an act of piety, the whole or nearly the whole of Goethe's *Faust* is occasionally given in Germany. It lasts, with many intermissions, from about two o'clock in the afternoon till past midnight. Without the *entr'actes* it would have put an intolerable burden on my appreciation, and even with the intermissions the performance made less for my esthetic rapture than for my literary edification.

Music again, save in its higher ranges, is one of the more accessible arts. Its physical rhythms are akin to our physiological rhythms. The beat corresponds to our breathing and our walking. Even the abstractness that characterizes the material of music—the scale, the basic harmonies—is en-

tirely familiar to us through use and wont, and is accepted
without conscious effort of adjustment. Yet this abstractness
and conventionality of material keeps almost automatically
the necessary distance between the auditor and the musical
piece. I have heard of a spectator shooting the villain,
which may seem the maximum infraction of distance,
in a melodrama, but never in an opera. It is perhaps because
music is at once so near us and so far from us that it is
increasingly the favorite art, and of all perhaps most fully
alive today.

Thus music can engross us for a longer span than the
visual arts, yet its span of satisfaction is strictly limited.
Long experience has fixed the time of an elaborately con-
certed piece at a half an hour or a little more. Beethoven's
Ninth Symphony needs about an hour for its performance,
and, with hesitation I suggest such an irreverence, I think
it is too long, that its purely musical character would not
carry it off were it not for adventitious aids, that a rendition
is an event and a solemn ceremony, were it not that the
somewhat arbitrary climax in the great choral carried the
orchestration where the orchestration might fail to impose
itself upon hearers already too heavily taxed and fatigued.
However that be, experience seems to show that the span of
unremitting musical attention is not much more than half
an hour, while the reasonable duration of musical enjoyment with saving intermissions and refreshment is probably not much more than three hours, about that of a play.
The reason for this may well be that while music is one of
the most accessible arts, it is also one of the most tyran-
nically engrossing, and one can yield an undivided devotion
to anything only for so long.

Of the visual arts undoubtedly architecture admits of the most prolonged enjoyment. This is partly due to the entire familiarity of its materials, to the fact that its mathematical proportions again are well within our common experience.

Again the beauty of architecture in a particular building is felt over a considerable period of time and at many modulations and levels. There may be a favorable aspect of a building, but there are also many other revealing aspects. The appreciation of any great building involves its exploration, seeing the parts while keeping or, perhaps, rather progressively creating a mental picture of the whole. Its appreciation is serial, involves a considerable time element, and in this the appreciation of a noble building is truly akin to that of a stately music, as following a planned course to an end only in which is the glory and integrity of the composition fully revealed. Again, the appreciation of a temple, or cathedral or palace, is more like the enjoyment of a long poem or a novel—a progressive understanding of many parts within a sense of the whole in the making.

It is only the brief, intense spans of appreciation of architecture from a single point of view that can properly be compared with the appreciation of a statue or a painting, which is a brief, intense and, as regards levels, relatively unmodulated activity. I can well imagine prowling around Chartres, or San Zeno, at Verona, or Durham, or St. Francis's basilica at Assisi for a full day and regretting the coming of nightfall, but in such a day there would be only a few moments of intense esthetic sympathy; below this there would be many grades of interest, pleasure, and curiosity. The question how long may a single state of intense esthetic sympathy be maintained in architecture, may seem purely academic. From my own experience and observation I should say for longer than in the case of painting and sculpture, and for less than in the case of music and poetry.

Concretely I have for half an hour felt fully conscious of the lively nobility of that sublimest of interiors, that of Santa Sophia. I would gladly have stayed on indefinitely, but had I done so, I should have been no longer in a state of esthetic sympathy, but in a pleasantly bemused condition into which the forms of Santa Sophia entered only partially, and perhaps faintly. On any object, even the most engrossing, one may keep his eye only so long. Incidentally, this state of agreeable confusion of spirit is of course much cultivated, and often mistaken for esthetic appreciation. It is really a move away from that center which is the substance-form of any work of art into the penumbral mood which every work of art evokes as a kind of irrelevant circumambience. This circumambience is a pleasant place in which to drift about, but such drifting about has at best only a tinge of truly esthetic character.

Since architecture is redolent with human associations of every sort, anything like a pure contemplation of architecture is difficult, and implies a degree of professional interest or training. It may be a signal ingratitude, but the sense of the artist is weak in the experience of great architecture. Great buildings seem to become a part of the natural order, so that who planned them does not seem to matter. It is perhaps the glory of the great architect that he tends to disappear in his work, like that legendary Chinese painter who walked into his own picture and vanished. Finally the relatively long duration of pleasure from architecture may be due precisely to the fact that we do not try to divine the artist through his work, are spared an effort that is considerable, nay crucial, in any real appreciation of sculpture and painting.

Of all the arts painting and sculpture are the least accessible. Today, for one person who deeply enjoys these arts there must be thousands who love literature, music or the theater. It has not always been so. In Athens in her prime we may safely imagine that painting and sculpture vied with poetry and the theater on equal terms, and so it was in Florence of the Renaissance. The reasons for the gain of the other arts against painting and sculpture can here only be hinted at. In a sense painting and sculpture seem to have exhausted their resources and reached their approximate limits earlier, with a consequent shifting of interest to the arts that continually offered novelties. No one since Rembrandt has painted finer imaginative portraits; no one finer realistic portraits since Velasquez. Landscapes of a different sort than those of Claude, Poussin, Ruysdael and Corot have been painted in abundance; it is doubtful if better landscapes than the best by these artists have been or can be painted. In sculpture the case is the same. Now I do not insist that these arts have actually approached a limit, and admit of no further advance. I do not prophesy, but merely emphasize a prevalent state of mind.

What really concerns us is the inherent inaccessibility of these arts, the difficulty of making a fit public for them. Outside of China and Japan, it has happened only for five or six centuries within the four thousand years of recorded history, and under highly exceptional conditions of a succession of three or four generations of men who were strongly eye-minded. It is our task simply to explain why, apart from their inaccessibility, painting and sculpture also afford the briefest pleasure of all the arts.

Concretely, while all my life I have mainly found my joy in art through sculpture and painting, I doubt if I have ever really looked at, actually contemplated a picture or a statue for more than five minutes at a time, and what is more, I doubt if anybody has ever done so. I hear people say they have enjoyed a great picture or statue for hours. I do not believe them. They have doubtless enjoyed something, presumably themselves, before a painting or statue in the pleasurably bemused condition which has been earlier described. But enjoying one's own confused revery even while slackly looking at a work of art, is something far different from enjoying the work of art itself. At best it is a subesthetic experience.

Now sculpture and painting offer difficulties to appreciation for opposite reasons: sculpture is too near ordinary experience; painting too far. Since sculpture deals with the masses, proportions, and rhythms which are ever before us, we are likely to feel a statue as a bronze man or a marble woman, and thus to indulge an absurdity which completely obscures the esthetic situation. In other words, it takes a somewhat arduous and complicated process of elimination and abstraction to feel the actual forms of sculpture as not real but represented, and thus to give the statue its necessary esthetic distance.

The corollary of this is that of all great artists great sculptors are the rarest. All history hardly gives us a score.

There are for one great sculptor a hundred great poets or painters. On the practical and creative side this means that almost anybody can make himself a fair sculptor, as popular repute goes, and that many can make themselves pretty good sculptors, which only beclouds the situation in the rare event that a great sculptor actually emerges. To the untrained eye his difference from a sculptor merely pretty good always seems less than that between a great and pretty good painter.

If we habitually get too near to sculpture, to painting we rarely get near enough. Since it offers us not real but represented objects, we merely identify them and fail to grasp their esthetic reality. Even with the raw materials of the painter we have the most inadequate acquaintance. As an approximate concept we know what a man looks like, what he looks like relatively to a peculiar lighting and colored ambience we have no idea. But to know this is the specific problem of the figure painter, even if he disregard the appearance. We have some mental scheme that corresponds roughly to a given landscape. The actual look of the landscape as so many color areas with so many intimations of form, mass, space, distance, absorption and reflection of light, we rarely grasp at all.

To add to the difficulty, the good artist never gives us the actual look of things as he sees them. The limitations of his pigments forbid such reproduction even to a painter wholly without imagination. Then, the good artist invariably transforms what he sees, and in such transformations he employs rhythms and emphases which are entirely outside of our ordinary experience. Again, the rhythms so essential to great painting are not rhythms in the ordinary sense, actual movements, measures you can beat with a finger. They are merely implicit or suggested rhythms of an ordinary object that is actually motionless. And again, the proportions of any picture, though highly important, cannot be measured and are not easy to perceive. While the highly complicated relations of the color masses, as pushing objects forward or holding them back, as enhancing or muting each other through contrast or modulation—all this A.B.C. of the practising artist is so much Greek even to the cultivated layman.

All these barriers between us and a painting of any richness of elaboration keep it far away from us in a hopelessly fictitious world. It requires resolution, lucidity, and much love to break through these barriers and enter into that psychical reality which is not merely a great, but any well made picture. It is simply because of the difficulty of winning through to the reality of the painter's vision, that we cannot maintain the mood of appreciation for long. It is a state of very delicate balance which can easily be disturbed in one direction or another. We can recover the rightly balanced state, but usually only after a considerable interval.

As against the psychical inaccessibility of painting and sculpture we may set their physical accessibility. The fact that their enjoyment is brief, does not prevent, nay prompts to, its frequent repetition. *Hamlet* is not played every day by a good actor. The Ninth Symphony is not often given, and we may not be able to devote an evening to hearing it. We may not often have the three days in which to read the *Iliads* of Homer. But we can without great pains find an hour for say the Metropolitan Museum, and that marvellous Greek horse in bronze, and the Vermeers, the Rembrandts, the Grecos. Indeed the very brevity of the enjoyment of painting and sculpture means that we can pack into an hour in any good art museum more variety and intensity of esthetic experience than we can gain from many hours spent with any other art.

Indeed if we are in any way prosperous, we may own good paintings and to a lesser extent sculptures. And even if we are not prosperous, we can have in half-a-dozen portfolios of photographs authentic if attenuated echoes of all the paintings and statues that are today worth looking at, while in the graphic arts we may have facsimiles that really are such and may even own fine originals. Such are some of the very practical compensations for the brief duration of the experience of beauty from sculpture and painting.

Our provisional theory of correspondences, in other words of a universal analogy of rhythm, will rightly seem to a sceptical reader to rest on the mere assumption that such correspondences exist. Here I can only say that wherever we have explored any large field we find such analogies. Whoever has studied vertebrate anatomy from the skate and dogfish to man cannot fail to note a similar structure throughout—the same general disposition of the skeleton, of the digestive, circulatory, nervous, and reproductive systems. And that means that the functions of these systems, the physiology and even the psychology of the vertebrates, their vital activities, all follow a similar rhythm. That is, within the vertebrate field these homologies objectively hold. In lower forms of life the precise homologies fail but the broader analogies still are valid.

Hundreds of patterns of plant growth have been studied, and found to correspond to the logarithmic spiral. It is reasonable to suppose that the vital activities which produce these mathematical forms are themselves of an orderly and rhythmical nature and analogous to the measured proportions.

Our problem is not whether within the larger fields there are formal and dynamic correspondences. This is a matter of ordinary observation which scientific research unfailingly confirms. There is no logical hazard in asserting a community of activities physiological, and within limits even psychological, between a man and any other mammal. Every dog or horse owner knows much about that. The difficulty arises when we compare the activities of a man with a lower animal, with a plant, with a geological process, with an atom. And since the field of esthetics is concerned both with animate and inanimate nature, the theory of correspondences has no general validity unless there are such analogies between organisms which act and those which apparently are acted upon. Do the analogies which within great fields are unchallengeable hold between those fields?

Here a fair argument could be drawn from certain interesting analogies between the findings of formal esthetics and those of biometrics. The logarithmic ratios which the late Samuel Colman, in his book *Nature's Harmonic Unity,* found in growing plants, he also found in conventional decorative patterns, in the forms of the Greek capitals, in the disposition of Gothic façades, in the whorls of sea shells. This is a straw which comes down a favoring wind for the believer in universal rhythms. So far as the evidence goes, it points to entirely analogous activities in a man designing a meander, a capital, or a façade; in a plant pushing upward to the light, in a mollusk making its shell.

But I prefer not to rest the case on such slight and partial evidence, but rather to admit frankly that the belief in a universal analogy of rhythm is really an act of faith. Since so far as we can follow them, the analogies hold, let us believe that they also hold where they escape our analysis and vision. The whole thing comes down to an esthetician's bet on an orderly and rhythmical universe, and this is entirely analogous to the scientist's bet on a universe subject to law. Both bets seem pragmatically sound, as giving us a universe more understandable, more habitable, more manageable than a universe approached without such a harmonizing postulate. I may also add that while the positive evidence is avowedly far short of demonstrative, there is singularly little evidence either for a universe of separate and unrelated rhythms or for one in which natural law does not work uniformly.

Quite apart from the metaphysical difficulty, which I have not tried to disguise, there arises in the theory of correspondences a psychological difficulty. The apprehension, or better the experience of correspondences, is rarely on the conscious level. Where it is, as in the charming lyric which I have quoted from Father Tabb, it can be analyzed. But such experiences are normally well below the level of consciousness. No introspection reaches to them, no analysis applies to them. At best we may infer the process from what seems to be its product—a word, an action, a work of art. But such inferences are suggestions of the consciousness and may or may not be true to the activities of the unconscious. Personally I believe that such inferences, if made with care and patience, will have what Schopenhauer called sufficient truthfulness. There is no reason to assume that our unconscious self is so ordered that it habitually deceives our conscious self, nor yet that our conscious thinking inveterately misinterprets our unconscious activities. But when all is said, we are dealing with activities which are refractory to ordinary introspective methods, even more so to laboratory experiment, and plainly can not be rationalized and formulated.

For esthetics as a serious study this may seem a damaging avowal. But in this plight esthetics is simply in the same boat with metaphysics and psychology—no better off, no worse off. When the psychologist will tell me precisely how we organize certain impressions of the senses into perceptions, I will agree to tell him why we feel certain of these perceptions to be beautiful and call them so.

Let me hasten to add that I am not offering the theory of correspondences as a complete explanation of esthetic experience. It is, I feel, merely the starting point, the detonator of a wide-spreading reverberation. I believe this dim but deep sense of analogies and correspondences is what brings us into vital contact with a man or a thing. That contact reverberates, broadens, reaches out and draws in, enriches itself from past experience—and the satisfactory ordering of all these activities of expansion, retraction, accepting, rejecting, divining, associating, judging, is beauty. Perhaps really the value of the experience of beauty lies rather in attaining this capacity for infinite modulation and enrichment, than in what sets the process going. And yet one's conception of the first impulse towards beauty does matter, both logically and practically. If we believe the first act is that of projecting ourself into something else, logically it is hard to distinguish an esthetic experience from an ordinary perception, while practically we reduce the universe to our own measure. If, on the contrary, we conceive the initiatory act to be a vivid sense of a particular activity which is ours as akin to activities which reach everywhere, as more closely akin to a particular activity in something outside ourself, a work of art, a scene in nature—then logically we base the esthetic experience on something that is beyond ordinary perception, while, practically, we take a juster view of ourselves as infinitesimal yet highly privileged parts of a sublime whole.

This discussion has taken me too far afield. It was intended only to confirm from the time element in the enjoyment of the various arts the theory of correspondences. At best it will have done this inadequately and only by suggestion. Yet the digression has enabled me to say something that needed to be said about the conditions determining appreciation in the several arts, and it may perhaps usefully take the place of that customary, and often tedious, classification of the arts which overburdens many excellent books on esthetics.

The well read reader will not have failed to note, perhaps with some impatience, that something like this theory of correspondences was adumbrated nearly fifty years ago by the French symbolists. It appears even earlier, if very vaguely, in Baudelaire's favorite phrase *analogie universelle*. Unhappily these adepts in verse and cadenced prose did not work their theory out. It remained a kind of verbal and private lore of the *cénacle* of Mallarmé and his disciples. More unhappily still, they tended to understand by correspondences not those greater analogies which impose themselves on a sensitive spirit, but too often far-fetched and merely verbal analogies which had to be painfully sought, or were presented not by disciplined feeling but by irresponsible revery. Thus the sound but unanalyzed doctrine of correspondences produced poems of an extraordinary witchery of mood, and, in the music of Debussy, a kindred art of sound. But the doctrine of correspondences as actually worked out in practice also set a subsequent generation of able poets to stretching metaphor to the breaking point. No longer was the good metaphor that which illuminated and applied, but that which came nearest to not applying at all. Thus a valid theory, as has often been the case in the history of art, on the whole produced only a delicate sort of mannerism. From it much very skilful poetry suffers today. However, if we are able to take the theory of correspondences more robustly than the symbolists could or did, we should not deny them a discoverer's credit because, taking their theory effeminately, they achieved not a new style but a new fashion. And after all any priority in the matter goes far back, as we have already noted in passing, to the Hindoo wisdom and to its modulations in China and Japan. It was then and there that the idea arose of a rhythmically unified cosmos, and of an individual soul, if only by illusion and error, steadfastly envisaging it.

The psychological processes involved in the analogy of rhythms I conceive to be these: physical rhythms are ever going on and forming nodes or combinations outside of our intelligence. Diagrammatically we might think of a line constantly turning on itself in loops, such loops being, for example, two parts of hydrogen to one of oxygen, carbon oxidized or the like.· And we may think of the un-conscious mind as following a similar looped line, the loops being filled with such products of experience as water and fire. When loops on the physical and unconscious psychical plane touch or overlap, we have a perception of water or fire, still on the unconscious plane. If the uncon-sciousness works in a generalizing way upon the percep-tion, we have a larger psychical volume which we call an apperception or, as it may be, a conception. If the con-sciousness works upon a perception, not conceptually, but in a concentrating and individualizing fashion by heavier drafts upon previous experience or upon wider data of sense—we have a still larger volume which Mr. Santayana has aptly called an esthetic volume, and this esthetic volume has a tendency to detach itself from the formative rhythms of sense and perception into a separate and, if transient, also thrilling independence of its own.[1] In this sense, and only in this sense, may we reasonably speak of the isolation of the experience of beauty. It is a relative and passing

[1] These pages were in the press before my attention was drawn to the brilliant little book, *The Meaning of Beauty*, by my colleague, Dr. W. T. Stace. With a terminology more precise than mine he had arrived at conclusions very similar to my own. The small difference between us is mostly one of ter-minology. Where I speak of a "concept" only in the sense of a mental generali-zation or category, he distinguishes usefully a special sort of "free concept." An ordinary concept such as house carries with it some sense of a particular house. The "free concept" is a pure abstraction and untied to an image, "perceptual field." Nobility, grandeur, orderliness, gravitation are "free concepts." In Dr. Stace's suggestive word they may be said to "hover" over our general per-ceptual experience seeking images with which they may completely fuse, thus attaining concrete embodiment. The attaining of such fit embodiment is the cause of esthetic pleasure. See Dr. Stace's chapter, "The Essence of Beauty."

isolation, for, as the flower burgeons, it fades, and it never can deny its roots.

Amplifying this bare scheme, the perception of the universal analogy of rhythm is to be conceived of as an active process. It is not to be confused with any Wordsworthian "wise passiveness." The esthetic experience always results in making something new. The artist by transforming rhythms of observation into kindred rhythms of execution, into a rhythmical act of his own, introduces a node which the universal rhythms lacked, and, as Santayana has cogently remarked, if his rhythmical construction be plastic, the artist has actually changed the physical balance of the world. And the lover of art or natural beauty does something similar. His vivid and admiring apprehension of the particular rhythm of a scene in nature or in a work of art becomes a kindred rhythm of his own which draws in appropriate material from his experience and by a curious and ultimately unanalyzable balance of conscious and unconscious activities creates that volume of volitions, feelings and understandings which is the appreciation, in Goethe's words the recreation, of any work of art. Such a psychical volume is of course a new fact and, however conditioned from outside, essentially the creation of the art lover.

What we have to explain is how the artistic representation of an appearance, while a new thing, retains the quality of the appearance, and how the understanding of the representation, though again a new thing, keeps both the quality of the representation and also the character of the thing represented. In short, the problem is, how do such serial new activities keep a sort of solidarity and unity? If it were a physical problem, we should answer unhesitatingly, it is due to some faithful medium of transmission, such as electricity or the Hertzian waves, which will convert, say, vibrations of sound into other vibrations, which in turn may be reconverted into vibrations of sound, which are, barring mechanical defects, identical with the original sound vibrations. Now since esthetic activity is assimilative, constructive, communicative, and interpretive, some universally available medium of transmission is as imperatively called for in esthetics as it is in physics. What may be the case is that those physical vibrations which are in the art lover, the work of art, and in that nature which in any real analysis includes both, are in an entirely parallel relation to the rhythms of thought and feeling, or rather that there is always the possibility of a sort of braiding together of these two always concomitant rhythms into a single psychic strand. Such braiding together always, I think, begins below the level of consciousness, but consciousness may reach down for the braid, take it in hand and elaborate and complete it after its own fashion.

It would be interesting to explore the possibility of universal psychical rhythms which have no physical basis,[2] but evidently such an investigation cannot be undertaken here. Even if such independent psychical rhythms could be proved, I do not see that there would be any immediate

[2] Mr. Shelden Cheney's *Expressionism in Art* was published too late to be used. It maintains a general theory of beauty very similar to my theory of correspondences of rhythm, but with cosmological and theological implications which I do not find essential. In general I feel that Mr. Cheney fails to perceive that the modern vogue of pure expressionism may be rather a dubious fashion than an accomplished revolution. Perforce he ignores the artist's normal desire to communicate with the art lover, which has so long and fruitful a history that its abrogation in our times seems most unlikely. A pure expressionism means a pure anarchy, a mere succession of incoherent idiosyncracies.

bearing on the problems of artistic creation and appreciation. So long as we have, however unexplained, the clear
possibility of the transformation of physical into psychical
vibrations, we seem to have the basis of esthetic communication. It seems well to add that memory, observation,
interpretation, love are constantly enriching the physical
range of rhythms with psychical amplifications, which are
often of a singularly consistent and enduring sort. The great
affirmations and continuities in taste, morals, and religion
really depend upon superior psychical patterns which ever
readily pass into and pervade both the more workaday
psychical rhythms, and those merely physical vibrations
without which there is no vital activity of any kind.

I am of course aware what I have suggested above is a
theory and not a demonstrated fact. Yet I believe the
theory of rhythmical correspondences has something
wholesome in it as removing from the experience of
beauty that artificial penumbra of isolation and preciousness with which esthetics has needlessly dignified it, while
restoring to the experience of beauty its real dignity of
universality. It will be seen that the theory of analogy of
rhythm and of response thereto on the unconscious level
has much in common with Mr. Santayana's constant and
reasonable insistence that we starve and denature beauty
when we deny or forget its origin in animal instinct.

The theory of rhythmical correspondences suggested
above seems to me to agree in essentials with Mr. C. K.
Ogden's doctrine of Synaesthesia—the shepherding into
one organized experience of many activities of a pleasurable sort. The value of esthetic experience would, according
to this view, depend on the variety and richness of the

activities thus organized into a harmony or equilibrium. So far as there can be a measuring stick in the realm of the beautiful, this would seem to be it. Beauty would be a higher or lower sort according to the variety of its component activities, according to the nature of their relations as readily or with difficulty susceptible to organization, according to the complexity and success of the harmonizing effort of the soul.

On this scale, we should not hesitate to say that Raphael's "School of Athens" evoked a fuller experience of beauty than any of his Madonnas and Holy Families; Schubert's "Unfinished Symphony," than any of his Songs; George Meredith's *Richard Feverel*, than any of his Lyrics. But such a measuring stick would have to be applied with a very delicate hand, and with misgivings, for a factor of intensity is involved as well as a factor of complexity and richness. Finally the theory of rhythmical correspondences is not offered as a complete description of any or all esthetic experience, but rather as possibly explaining the inception of such experiences—as a better substitute for the prevailing theory of *Einfühlung*.

To summarize this discussion of the nature of the experience of beauty: I feel that it is primarily a high art of understanding fostered by the will and comprising much emotion. It is the appreciation or perception of an emergent rhythmical organization in its relation to the whole system of universal rhythms. This position evidently approaches that of Plotinus and is even nearer the Hindoo esthetic which rests the experience of beauty upon an ecstatic sort of intellection. Professor Stace's entirely similar position virtually anticipates mine.

CHAPTER V

THE WORK OF ART, ITS FORM

THAT the form of any good work of art is organized, hence orderly, through chosen rhythms or proportions has for over two thousand years been a commonplace of criticism. Where there has been less agreement is as to the cause of such orderliness. Plotinus followed by most romantic estheticians ever since would rest this orderliness on an intuitive perception of some transcendental proportionateness—for him, the *Logos*. Most psychological estheticians down to Theodor Lipps would merely shift the archetypal order from the *Logos* to the human soul, which imposes its own inherent orderliness upon the work of art. This I think is the correct view.

Most of the Greek and Roman philosophers took the view that the orderliness of the work of art was caused by a considered act of the artist—an act of judgment guiding an appropriate act of execution. For the medieval schoolmen this view was standard. "Just as the virtue of prudence is directed to the good of the worker, so art is directed to the good of the work." The greatest of the schoolmen, St. Thomas Aquinas, asserts this most clearly:

"Nihil aliud ars esse videtur, quam certa ordinatio rationis, quomodo per determinata media ad determinatam finem actus humani perveniant."

("Art seems to be nothing other than a certain ordering of the reason, by which human acts through determined means arrive at determined ends.")

This notion St. Thomas's best disciple, John, clinches when he writes, "The perfection of art consists in judging" —*Perfectio artis consistit in judicando*. Nearly three centuries later Leonardo was to confirm this dogma when he reiterated that art must be directed by the judgment (*giudizio*).

When the schoolmen, without really isolating or explaining the work of art, tried to describe its leading characteristics, they arrived at a definition, which being as old as Plato, came near satisfying the problem. Art was primarily a one in a many—according to St. Thomas Aquinas, "a harmony of the various"—*concordantia rerum diversarum*. Such harmony is delectable. Evidently this manifold unity implies proportionateness and fit subordination.

Now analysis of the work of art has the same relation to esthetics properly speaking that dissection of a dead body has to the study of a man. We dissect a dead not a living organism, while we destroy the dead body as we dissect it. Formal analysis of the work of art has, however, this advantage that after taking the work of art to pieces we can put it together again and experience it once more as alive, and with added knowledge.

Refining our definition of the work of art as a unified manifold which is pleasure giving, we must proceed to the seemingly paradoxical activity of subdividing the unity. All investigators agree that it rests on an underlying orderliness which in the temporal arts is called rhythm, in the spatial arts, proportion. We have already noted that, as perceived, all the arts are in time. It is merely a question of time more or less. Hence proportions are always read as rhythms, whether in enjoyment or in analysis. The human mind energizes or activates them, probably by *Einfühlung*.

But what we actually first see or hear in any work of art is simply a formed material—words in verse or prose; musical sounds; wood, stone or brick; clay, marble or bronze; colored pigments. Or we may see simultaneously several formed materials including human beings, as in the dance, the theatre, the opera.

Now what we simply see or hear, apart from meaning or even perception of structure, is called by many modern estheticians the skin of the work of art. I shall use the more general term the surface. In the case of the visual arts the matter needs little elaboration. What we see in the Arena Chapel at Padua is plaster colored in fresco; the mind adds the information that Giotto did the painting, and contributes the meaning of the subjects; what we see in a Titian is a very elaborate and various surface made with oil colors. A Luca della Robbia offers to the eye only a white or tinted enamel made of tin glaze. Nothing is actually seen of Donatello's "Judith" save a curiously modelled surface of weather-stained bronze. The Parthenon, merely to the eye, is just a complex of flat and bulging and concave marble surfaces yellowed by time.

Probably the non-visual arts should be thought of as having a similar surface—a superficial aspect which makes the first impact upon the senses. One may reasonably think of the characteristic sound of prose, poetry, or a musical composition as a sort of patination perceived in advance of perception of structure and meaning. What differences, merely to the ear, let us say, the prose of Mr. Sinclair Lewis from that of Miss Gertrude Stein is the leanness of the patination in Mr. Lewis and its density in Miss Stein. Sometimes I feel her prose is patinated all through, like a very corroded antique bronze which has become completely demetallized. Again we may say that it is the character of the auditory surface that would keep any music lover from confusing a composition of Bach with a somewhat kindred piece of Brahms.

Not to over-labor what may after all be simply a metaphor, I return to the visual arts. Here the existence and the esthetic importance of the surface are undeniable. The character of the esthetic surface has been succinctly studied by Professor DeWitt H. Parker and most elaborately by Theodor Lipps. Both agree that the surface—like the work of art in every aspect, should be a one in a many—a unified manifold. Any close observation of the surface of a fine picture will bear out this statement. For example, the paintings of the early Flemish artists on casual examination seem of one enamel. Yet on closer scrutiny there is much difference of texture. A minute study of the apparently equally burnished surface of any fine bronze statue would show the same differences. It is only bad sculpture, notably the Greco-Roman marbles, that seeks a monotonous slickness.

Toward the necessary unity of the esthetic surface Theodor Lipps takes a characteristically austere attitude, going so far as to condemn all mixture of materials. To accept this dogma in all its austerity would be to condemn out of hand such mixed arts as the theater and opera. Indeed I do not see how, strictly speaking, any clothed woman could be regarded as beautiful unless she wore a mask and gloves. Quite logically Professor Lipps regards the ivory and gold sculpture of Pheidias as an esthetic solecism, though such competent art lovers as the Greeks thought otherwise.

On the practical side, the requirement of unity should not forbid contrast—variety of materials. The problem here is that of right balance. I own a very curious old devotional picture, a "Nativity." The faces, hands, the attendant beasts, the shed are executed in water colors on paper; the draperies are actual silk gummed down, with the folds painted. It is, if not a notable work of art, a very charming and attractive bit of accomplished craftsmanship. In general the principle of unity of surface is useful only as forbidding errors that no good artist is likely to commit—bronze statues that seem to walk about absurdly on a stone base, excellent marble heads made hideous through setting them upon a porphyry bust.

Evidently a beautiful surface is very advantageous to a work of art. It leads one agreeably to the meaning. On the other hand, without any beauty of surface, there may be a fine work of art. Jacques Louis David is a great painter despite his monotonous and unmodulated paint. Many landscapes of Cézanne may be said to be skinless, but they give a very dynamic impression of the relations of weight and stress. Cornelius, though a painter of considerable powers, and in many ways akin to David, is not a great painter, for his surfaces are positively repellant. Those of David are at worst neutral. For a work richly freighted with meaning, a neutral surface—one offering neither direct aid nor impediment to understanding—is sufficient. In short, the surface of any great work of art, whether it have or lack preciousness, is always good enough for its purpose. Finally the magicians of surface making—the Fortunys, Whistlers, William Chases, Alfred Stevenses, Boldinis are rarely great artists. Great craftsmen, accomplished cosmeticians they often are. But the greatness of art lies behind and beyond the epidermis.

Where the variously rich and unified surface is king is in the decorative arts. They are distinguished from the fine arts precisely by the importance of the surface. They offer little else. Hence it is the more needful that their slender offering should be precious. The meaning of, say, a superb Caucasian rug, is just what its skilfully patterned and knotted surface tells of the diligence, taste and love that went into its making—an experience which a fit observer shares. As Mr. Clive Bell has sensibly remarked, the people who made the rug are not to be regarded as artists, but simply as craftsmen who like to do a good job. Now the good esthetic surface is made from the inside out like one's skin or the bark of a tree, and not applied from without. The merely decorative surface is made for its own sake to enhance a particular material. Its latency of meaning is very small. The enjoyment of the decorative arts must, while ranking high among pleasures, rank low among esthetic delectations. These higher pleasures are facilitated less by the character of the surface than by that of the whole pattern and organization of the work of art.

These underlying patterns of rhythm and proportion, as well as the organization in depth and volume, all seem to have a mathematical character. When the patterns seem, falsely I think, to be static, we speak of harmony and symmetry; when they seem dynamic and in time we speak of rhythm or melody. In every case the good work of art seems to try to conform to some ideal scheme of construction. This construction has been ingeniously and rather variously analyzed as corresponding to certain mathematical progressions—the golden section, for example, as developed into the Fibonacci series, in which every term after the second is equal to the sum of the two preceding terms. 1, 2, 3, 5, 8, 13, 21,—is the beginning of a series which may be said to reproduce itself dynamically to infinity. A similar dynamic progression is illustrated by the logarithmic spiral which, as it grows, cuts all vectors at an equal angle—is an excellent example, then, of an unfolding one in a many. We use the principle mechanically, in geared cogwheels of different diameters, and Theodore Andrea Cook, who called these spirals "The Curves of Life" found them in sea-shells, in plant groups and in architectural proportions. The late Mr. Jay Hambidge based his socalled dynamic symmetry on the proportions of the logarithmic spiral in which the product of the extremes of a proportion A is to B as B is to C is always equal to the square of the mean. On these proportions he set up basic rectangles which were supposed to circumscribe any artistic design. The main proportions of the design were determined by diagonals and perpendiculars thereto drawn through the fundamental rectangle or through its orderly sub-divisions.

Mr. Hambidge's dynamic symmetry seemed to work. He first illustrated it from Greek vases and extended it at least plausibly to the Parthenon and other beautiful buildings. Certain painters, notably George Bellows and Sergeant Kendall, to their own satisfaction laid out pictures under these schemes. At least two noted archaeologists, Miss Richter and Dr. Caskey, measured up the Greek vases in respectively the great museums of New York and Boston under this system.

It seemed as if the esthetic murex had at last been fished up. But it occurred to skeptics that the vase measurers were measuring not any vase as seen—the appearance constantly changes in perspective—but the section of the vase as artificially plotted—something no human eye has ever seen, which then can hardly be the pleasure-giving element.

Certain doubters discovered, what Mr. Hambidge, most cautious and modest of scholars, had fully anticipated, that many unbeautiful forms obeyed the laws of dynamic symmetry. My friend, the accomplished landscape architect, Mr. Charles Downing Lay, presented to his astonished clubmates an aluminum frying pan accurately plotted in a root two rectangle, and a gin bottle which was analyzed in the utmost refinements of root five with whirling squares. Neither the frying pan nor the gin bottle could be regarded as a beautiful object. Since there could be present all the proportions which characterize beautiful works of art without evoking any sense of beauty, evidently, while such proportions might be a *sine qua non* of artistic beauty, its activating principle must be sought elsewhere than in formal relations.

This something else which starts the activity called beauty seems to be the meaning of the form—what it meant to the artist in creation and means to ourself in appreciation —something that is not physically present in any work of art, but present only through inference or mental interpretation. A hundred classical estheticians to the contrary, when we have grasped only the form of a work of art, we have grasped nothing of first importance. For it is only as conveying meaning that the form really has existence. What it means is of more concern to us than what it is separately considered. The work of art may be described as a form conveying a meaning or as a meaning expressed through a form. Our perception of one is futile save as we perceive the other. Accordingly as the form expresses chiefly itself, or much more than itself, we may speak of the work of art as form-meaning or as meaning-form. The first of these compound words would apply principally to man- neristic art and such as is purely decorative; the second would apply to such works of art as make a wide human appeal, in short, to the works of art that are greatest. The work of art that is properly described as form-meaning means little more than its creator's zest and pride in his own virtuosity—means not much. The work of art that is rightly described as meaning-form means everything that aroused and captivated a great soul in creative activity— means a whole world.

In either case the severance of form from meaning is entirely artificial—a doubtful convenience of analytical thought. Meaning and form are merely two aspects of the same thing—a form containing and conveying a meaning, a meaning cast in a form in order that it may be expressed. Alone neither makes sense in the experience either of the artist or of the beholder.

By changing the form of a lyric through putting into prose this principle of the unity of form and meaning may be illustrated. For this purpose I choose one of Words- worth's great lyrics to Lucy.

"She dwelt among the untrodden ways
       Beside the springs of Dove,
  A maid whom there were none to praise
       And very few to love."

The theme of loneliness is announced, that Lucy deserved praise and would have liked it is intimated. Try very small changes of form. Substitute for "untrodden" "lonely" thus regularizing the meter—

"She dwelt among the lonely ways"—

Everything has become less concrete and more commonplace. Something of expectancy of the next line has been lost. Form and meaning have changed together.

"A violet by a mossy stone
       Half hidden from the eye!
  Fair as a star, when only one
       Is shining in the sky."

By subtle variation the theme of loneliness rises to a poignant climax in the simile of the solitary shining star.

"She lived unknown, and few could know
       When Lucy ceased to be;
  But she is in her grave, and oh,
       The difference to me!"

The theme of loneliness is reasserted in a very simple unornamented form; the exaltation is modulated towards the ultimate pathos, which again is expressed with a completely telling homeliness.

Now let us try the experiment of putting all the sense of this exquisite poem into prose, as follows:

She lived among the lonely paths at the sources of the Dove. There were none to praise the maid and very few to love her. She was like a half-hidden violet by a mossy stone,

As fair as the first star that shines at dusk.
Lucy lived unknown, and when she died few
Could know of it. But she is in her
Grave, and what a difference it makes to me!

Have not form and meaning perished together? What
we may call the sense of the poem persists in the para-
phrase, but the modulations, the rise to a climax, the subtle
resolution of eulogy into deep personal bereavement—
everything that caused the overwhelming emotional appeal
of the poem is gone, and this emotional appeal is the poem's
meaning.

Nevertheless analysis of the formal relations of the work
of art has its minor utility. One can isolate and describe,
even chart the form. One can teach it. But the total meaning
of the work of art can only be expressed through itself.
It is not convertible into terms of any other art. Any
literary appreciation of a picture, a musical composition,
a statue, a building, even of another literary composition
is at best a remote analogy. If it has interpretative value of
any sort, it is merely because it makes the reader wish to
experience the work of art which is its theme. It is only in
this analogical way that one can in some imperfect sense
teach the meaning of any work of art. Thus one may create
the appetite for the actual experience. It is only to this extent
that formal analysis is defensible. By showing a beginner
that the work of art is elaborately organized, we may arouse
his interest to the point where he will seek the meaning of
the organization. The artist during tutelage or in hesitation
might find forms for himself not through imitation of but
by analyzing and considering the forms through which
choice meanings have in the past been conveyed. In short,

except as a subject of specialized scholarship, or a means of training, the study of artistic form in itself is one of those childish pursuits which, following St. Paul, we shall put aside when we shall have attained esthetic manhood.

Lord Listowel has remarked (I quote him from memory, and approximately) that the work of art may be regarded as a diagram with a meaning that gives pleasure. Since the word diagram has a too static implication, let me substitute therefore the grammatical term, paradigm, which implies an orderly serial development in time. The work of art then may be regarded as a paradigm with a meaning, which gives pleasure. If from this too simple definition we approach the work of art itself, we shall meet the paradox that the verb of art is always an irregular verb. That is, the artist is skilful and the work of art great to the extent that the artist, while keeping the scheme or paradigm ever in mind, takes liberties with it and declines to be bound by its a priori restrictions.

Underlying every work of art is some sort of a traditional paradigm—a metrical form, a dominating rhythm, an orderly progression, a symmetry, a balanced relation of colors, a scheme of proportions. All these I have already tried to show are, so far as the hearer or beholder is concerned, to be regarded as rhythms. Now in certain arts, poetry, music, the dance, the rhythms are palpable and readily shared. In the visual arts, painting, sculpture and architecture, these rhythms are merely implicit and hence obscure, and perceptible only to the trained observer. Similarly the larger rhythmical organization of a great work in prose, or even of a long narrative or epic poem is perceptible only to an experienced reader. But in every case the rhythmical organization is always present—and present in the form of appropriate variations of the underlying paradigm.

Concerning this, the great American illustrator and mural painter, Elihu Vedder, once made to me an enlightening observation. He said that most great decorative painting is built about some sort of precise geometrical symmetry. But the good artist pushes his picture a little off the exact balance, so that it seems to have a tendency to return to equilibrium. The energizing quality, that is the beauty of a work of art depends largely on such apt evasion in the interest of variety and richness, of the mathematical requirements of its paradigm. The meaning also demands and works such modifications of the theoretical form, and similarly the demands of the form may work modifications, which should always be enrichments, of the meaning.

This principle of apt evasion, perhaps deviation is the happier word, may readily be illustrated from the early works of Raphael and from those of his master Perugino. The scaffolding of these pictures is always an exact symmetry, but as Vedder remarked, the scaffolding is pushed a little askew so that it seems to tend to return to balance. To this end there are countless artistic expedients. The swing of a body, the tilt of a head, the pointing of a foot, the over-weighting of a landscape by a few more trees on one side or the other, by heavier mountain mass on one side, by a winding river course a little off center, every evasion of the exact symmetry balancing some other evasion—such is the fashion in which these great composers established a very active and thrilling equilibrium and opened up great calming spaces.

In later picture-making the needful balance is often achieved by opposing a large inert mass with a smaller mass of an energized character. A force or thrust has the value of a greater mass of dead weight. The painters of the High Renaissance, Michelangelo, Raphael in his later works, Correggio, Titian, Tintoretto, are great adepts at this sort of balance. So are all the good baroque and rococo painters. It is the organizing principle of Delacroix, Millet, Daumier, Renoir and Cézanne—to cite at random the first great names that come to mind from an historic yesterday. This active balance of thrust against mass was carried to the most audacious extremes by the great Japanese painters and designers of color prints. A flying swallow will balance an overhanging tree or a toppling crag. And the most powerful and ingenious of modern picture-makers, Edouard Degas, learned this art from the Japanese print makers, and fairly outdid them.

This principle of apt deviation is most clearly exemplified in music, but since I have but little competence in this art, I must limit myself to summary and perhaps too obvious considerations. The smaller rhythm is the metronomic beat. It must always pervade the music, be ideally present, but the music itself will play around the theoretical measure in the liveliest way, with infinite variations. Even in the grand old geometrical music of Bach and Haydn, in which a general emphasis of the metronomic beat is of high esthetic importance, you will find these apt deviations. In the most all-overish compositions of Debussy the measure is still perceptible to the trained ear. This principle of apt deviation could readily be carried through the phrasing and development of the melodic motives, through the

variation of the harmonization, through unexpected progressions and telling dissonances, but all these issues are
rather for a critic well trained in musical composition and
not for a naïve music lover like myself.

Recent investigation of the voices of several accomplished singers casts light on this whole issue of give and
take with the paradigm. Among those studied, no great
singer attacked the note quite on true pitch. All began
something less than a quarter of a note off and gained the
pitch. No great singer ever lost the pitch when once
gained. In short, the well modulated singing voice operates
precisely like Vedder's well composed picture, which is
a little off balance with an active and highly pleasure-
giving tendency to return thereto.

Aristotle has somewhere remarked that a chief virtue
of literary style is to give novelty and distinction to a
familiar subject matter by a slight unexpectedness in the
diction. It is a golden maxim for the writer of prose, and
incidentally this discreet baffling of a reader's expectancy
exemplifies once more the function of apt deviation. The
nobility of Greek sculpture, so natural in effect yet so apart
in appreciation, depends again on deviations from ordinary
proportions so slight that they evade analysis and measurement. Modern esthetic has sought to identify such deviation with that distortion which it regards as the guarantee
of artistic originality. This is an error both in observation
and in psychology. The effect of apt deviation lies precisely
in the fact that it is not perceived as such by any genial
art lover, while distortion is always perceived. The Greek
reader, unless he were an analytical critic like Aristotle,
never realized that what he relished in such a prose as

Xenophon's was a constant slight unexpectedness of form. This distinction is urged, not to contest the artist's freedom to distort—which is a separate issue—but in the general interest of clear thinking.

All fine poetry shows as richly as music these apt and highly expressive deviations. One might insist that the good poet follows any fixed metrical scheme only sufficiently to keep the scheme in the background of the reader's consciousness, or only when he, the poet, because of lagging inspiration and for lack of finding any telling variation, falls back on the bare paradigm. This statement needs qualification in view of the individual development of the artist. The young poet, or artist of any sort, properly keeps close to the traditional schemes or to such as he invents, gaining increasing liberty as he finds himself and matures. The first and the last manner of almost any great painter, Raphael, Titian, Rubens, Velasquez, Gainsborough, Constable, Turner, Manet, Winslow Homer, Whistler, Renoir—would demonstrate very eloquently the normal progress from relative dependence on the paradigm to relative independence thereof. Correspondingly, the mature work of art swings still further from its theoretical equilibrium.

Both the artist's move towards emancipation from schematic restrictions and our process of apt deviation find conspicuous illustration in the case of Shakespeare. We may recall that the country boy become an actor and soon an actor manager first revamped old plays and only in his thirties began to write plays of his own. His early dramatic blank verse was naturally in the manner of his greatest predecessor, Marlowe. The meter marched pretty steadily according to the scheme of a line of ten syllables and five not too unequal stresses, the even syllables being normally stressed. Such a form was reasonably called iambic pentameter.

When Shakespeare was writing perhaps the first of his really great plays, *Henry IV, Part* 1, in 1598, being about thirty-four years old, this rather even and heavy beat of Marlowe's blank verse was plainly his pattern. In elevated passages he tends to vary it, but, one may say, cautiously. Take Sir Richard Vernon's famous description of the young scapegrace Prince Hal become a resolute and militant king.

> "I saw young Harry, with his beaver on,
> His cuisses on his thighs, gallantly arm'd,
> Rise from the ground like feathered Mercury,
> And vaulted with such ease upon his seat,
> As if an angel dropped down from the clouds,
> To turn and wind a fiery Pegasus,
> And witch the world with noble horsemanship."
> —*Henry IV, Part* 1, Act IV.

Of the seven lines, five keep the strict pattern, they are separate and do not run over and merge into larger oratorical units. The only real deviation is one already common in Marlowe, the inversion of stress in the phrases, "Rise from the ground" and "gallantly arm'd." The verse is manly and stirring, but the flashing effect depends largely on such Aristotelian unexpectedness as the understatement "rise," saving "vaulted" for crescendo effect, upon "feathered" where winged was more likely, upon "seat" where saddle seemed indicated, upon the bizarre unexpectedness

of an angel taming a Pegasus, upon the felicitous verb
"witch" where charm seemed likely.

Throughout this justly famous passage there is a certain
lack of balance between a rather uniformly wrought versification and a highly varied and elaborated rhetoric. One
may say that the inexhaustibly resourceful rhetorician in
Shakespeare was the angel dropped down from heaven that
did not always successfully turn and wind his Pegasus. At
the moment of the verses which we have been studying, the
rhetorician not infrequently outweighed the poet; the form
somewhat dominated the meaning.

Some ten years later we shall find the poet and rhetorician in vital cooperation. Witness the oft quoted ejaculation
of Macbeth when he learns of his wife's death and tragically
faces the futility of whatever happens in time.

> "Tomorrow, and tomorrow and tomorrow,
> Creeps in this petty pace from day to day,
> To the last syllable of recorded time;
> And all our yesterdays have lighted fools
> The way to dusty death. Out, out, brief candle!
> Life's but a walking shadow; a poor player,
> That struts and frets his hour upon the stage,
> And then is heard no more; it is a tale
> Told by an idiot, full of sound and fury,
> Signifying nothing."
>
> —*Macbeth*, V, v.

Of the ten complete lines only half conform even remotely
to the ideal canon of iambic pentameter. There are lines
where only three accents are possible, lines with four
accents, six inversions of stress, one sharply run over line.
Statistically there is about six times as much apt deviation

as there was in the quotation from *Henry IV*. Very interestingly, the elaboration of the metrical form has worked a simplification of the rhetoric. Here everything is more straightforward and natural, the unexpectedness more delicately nuanced, while there is nothing of the earlier preciosity.

It remains only to note that profounder meanings rather than deliberate metrical research have worked this enriching deviation from the norm of the verse. And it should also be observed that the severe pattern of blank verse is really always ideally present in this passage. Rather few lines do conform to type, but all seem to do so. To keep in constant variation the sense of regularity may seem to be the ultimate refinement of the art of the poet, considered merely as a craftsman in metrics. More broadly considered, it is just one more instance of the solution of the problem of the one and the many through art.

Readers of contemporary poetry need not be reminded how audaciously and often successfully our newer poets practice the art of apt deviation. Humbert Wolfe would afford excellent examples, so would John Masefield and Elinor Wylie. There is something thrilling, though I fancy it is after all a specialist's joy, in finding in these apparently interminable runs of melodic syllables just the familiar pattern of good old common meter or of the five stressed decasyllable. The wide swing from the norm gives much of this new poetry a very special fascination. It also deals shrewdly and often very successfully in the old Aristotelian unexpectedness by substituting assonance for the anticipated rime. It would be pleasant to go deeper into this matter, but it lies a little apart from my main theme.

In leaving the subject of apt deviation, I do not wish to leave as well the impression of an unlimited license or a lawless liberty. The law is simply that the deviation must not be so extreme as to banish the ideal presence of the underlying metrical pattern. When the pattern is for any reason effaced we have simply confusion and ambiguity— the many has devoured the one. Particular cases—whether, for example, Walt Whitman in his worst moments ignored all patterns including his own—are to be settled not by precepts but by individual taste. And obviously when we envisage new works which seem to us merely to transgress the old forms, we shall be prudent to ask ourselves whether what troubles us as an unwarranted variation on an old form, may not instead be a new form which we have not yet understood.

An important characteristic of the good work of art has been especially emphasized by Professor DeWitt H. Parker. It is thematic variation. The process is most readily studied in musical composition which consists in repetition, variation, and enrichment of a limited number of themes—in their calculated and orderly interplay. No one who has understandingly followed a symphony needs any further hint. In literature the rôle of thematic variation is only less clear. We have already noted in Wordsworth's poem to Lucy the lovely variations on the theme of loneliness, the intimation that praise was due and would have been grateful, the sudden drop from the exaltation of the theme of loneliness to the bitter lower level of the poet's personal bereavement. Here we have all the repetition, elaboration and resolution of the themes of a musical melody, and again the melody is subtly counterpointed by emphasizing consonances. Of this sort is the structure of any and all great works of literature. Even the extraordinary divagations of *The Odyssey* are held together by the recurrent and ever variously modulated theme of Ulysses's home-seeking. Stendhal's *Rouge et Noir* may fitly be described as variations on the theme of ruthless ambition; Flaubert's *Madame Bovary,* as variations on the theme of that romantic self-deception which is sentimentalism. Naturally such schematic generalizations are over-simplifications. No thematic analysis of a symphony is a symphony or completely accounts for it. But so far as it goes, the analysis may be sound and enlightening.

On careful inspection all good pictures show such thematic variation. It consists in balances or repetition or contrast of lines, color areas, textures, masses, implicit stresses and motions. It has often been observed that the parts of well composed paintings are generally acceptable independent compositions, and that these parts are always in relation of varied repetition or contrast to certain dominant shapes of the picture. All this can be readily studied in Raphael's "School of Athens," in Titian's "Pesaro Madonna" or "Entombment," in Rembrandt's "Syndics," and Renoir's "Bathers," in Albert Ryder's "Siegfried and the Rhine Maidens," indeed in any well made picture. Probably the greatness of a work of art depends upon the extent and richness of such thematic variation. Thus, despite the aversion of most recent esthetic to all notions of hierarchy, we may reasonably hold any symphony of Beethoven to be a greater work of art than the best song of Schubert, a good Winslow Homer to be a greater work of art than the finest Oriental rug. Such notions were laughed away in the 1890's as bourgeois, by esthetes who confused great art with exquisite craftsmanship and disliked the pains of thought. Had I written the above forty years ago, I should have seemed a despicable *bourgeois* to my fellows, nay to myself. I trust I shall not seem it now.

In its merely formal aspect, any fine pictorial design may be described as a balance between pattern-making, mass-making and space-making. Every painting or work of graphic art is a pattern of lines and areas of tone or color—materially is just that and nothing more. The good artist always takes account of this ineluctable fact and consciously or unconsciously so contrives everything that implies mass, space, action, emotion that actively balanced organization shall result. Much, indeed most, bad painting lies in disregarding pattern for, say, projection, or highly detailed representation. Most French academic painting of the nineteenth century, most English genre painting of the same century, German painting of the same period almost without exception, agreed in disregard of the pattern, and the pattern has had its revenge, for these patternless paintings are dead beyond revival. The complete energizing of any pictorial organization depends on all features doing triple service as pattern-making, space-making, mass-making.

One must think of the features of the organization as in active cooperation or opposition. A line of a given direction or force calls for a line to enhance it by repetition or to balance it by contrast. Introduce a spot of red, and it calls for repeats through the surface. The gamut of straw yellow and azure so characteristic of Vermeer of Delft repeats itself by a sort of chromatic necessity. An area of the blue commands one of the yellow and vice versa. Watteau's triad of rose, azure and pale yellow comes and goes intermittently across his pictures with the inevitability of the exits and entrances of a song in the form of a canon.

Returning to thematic variation in pictures, the analyst sometimes meets the difficulty that several consistent analyses of a great pictorial composition may often be made, with nothing to choose between them. For example, that most complicated composition, Leonardo's unfinished "Adoration of the Kings," has been analyzed in terms of a dominant central circle with concentrics and radii, and also in terms of a dominant central triangle with its derivatives. Either analysis holds together, and there is no way of knowing which was in Leonardo's mind or whether either was in his mind. Nevertheless such multiple schematization tells much about the extraordinary richness and variety of the organization of any great work of pictorial art.

Naturally the esthetic value of thematic variation of the work of art lies simply in so modulating the meaning as to make it fully and richly expressive. But thematic variation may sometimes have a kind of value in itself. Trivial or even unworthy themes may thus receive a kind of magnification which is of an esthetic sort. The old motets in their calculated ingenuity have their own esthetic appeal. Even Bach now and then seems merely to play with his themes. Recently Ravel's "Bolero" has taught us how a vapid theme can be promoted to musical importance simply through orchestral elaboration and a mechanical sort of *crescendo*. But the effect necessarily hovers between the bizarre and the sinister. We have not in this most ingenious *tour de force* the richness of a great work of musical art.

Obviously the richest thematic variation is invited by the opera, which enlists, organizes, blends, the scene painter's and costumer's art, the ordered posture, gesture, and song of the actor-singer, with the constant diapason of the orchestra. That the greatest works of art, then, are the great operas might seem to follow, but does not necessarily. For after all, only a few great operas fully achieve the synthesis, and even these generally betray holes, soft spots, disproportions, *longueurs*.

Here I am conscious of treading on quaking and perilous ground when I suggest that there are in the world many more perfect light operas than grand operas, and that even Wagner at his height may be said to be squandering thriftlessly his magnificent orchestration and overplaying his spectacular effects. I think a sound argument could be made for "The Meistersinger" as Wagner's single perfect opera— light opera it will be observed—and for "The Flying Dutchman" as his next best from the point of view of complete coherence and fitness of form.

The form of poetry when metrical is easily felt. It consists of rhythms measured off into verses, skilfully varied, and often enriched by rimes or assonances at the end of the line. Further enrichments, which are, while common to prose and poetry, more affected by poetry, are alliteration, inner rime and consonances. The longer lines of verse are usually broken by a pause, a caesura, which occurring normally at one place, may actually occur at almost any place.

One might reasonably illustrate these formal and rhetorical characteristics of metrical poetry from such masters of elaborate orchestration as Poe and Swinburne. I choose instead a less egregious example, the opening lines of Coleridge's *Kubla Khan*. On analysis it is in all conscience elaborate enough.

> "In Xanadu did Kubla Khan
> 　　A stately pleasure-dome decree
> Where Alph, the sacred river ran
> Through caverns measureless to man
> 　　Down to a sunless sea."

Here are few metrical peculiarities, nothing but the effective reversal of stress in the last line—

> "Down to a sunless sea."

Euphonic enrichments abound. "Xanadu" and "Kubla Khan" have the same vowels in reversed cadence. Out of this mere coincidence grew much of the vocalic elaboration. Notable are the alliterations at the end of every line— "Kubla Khan," "dome decree," "river ran," "measureless to man," "sunless sea." It is probable that the initial alliteration in Kubla Khan induced the rest. Similarly the first stressed syllable of Xanadu induced the later rimes "ran," "man." Because of the stressed vowel in "Xanadu," the river had to be "Alph"—an assonance which the word cavern repeats. "Stately" similarly calls for "sacred." The reiteration of the dull vowel "a" is soothing and hypnotic. Finally "dome," "down" and "sunless" are approximate consonances. It should be clear that without such ornamentation the simple metrical form would yield little effect, and also clear that the ornament is meaningful.

Now the task of the poet is to make such verbal and euphonic enrichments serve the meaning, as they do in *Kubla Khan,* and not to make such embroidery for its own sake, as Poe and Swinburne, with the French symbolists as a group, not infrequently do. We have to do with that apparent conflict between the exactions of form and those of meaning which is the problem of every artist in whatever art. The good poet, the good artist of any sort, composes the quarrel to the advantage of both parties. Thus the good work of art is simply a balance between the pressure exerted respectively by meaning and by form.

When poetry is not metrical but freely composed and rimeless, such an analysis as we have made above becomes difficult. But this probably only signifies that while we know very well the norms of the traditional metrical forms, we have not yet learned those of free verse. It does not follow that such new norms will not reveal themselves on sufficient study.

Except for the specialty of forensic oratory, the considerate study of the forms of prose is, after more than two thousand years from Aristotle's *Rhetoric,* still in its infancy. Usually such study has been confined to diction which, important as it is, is in many great works of art really unimportant in comparison with the larger construction. It would be absurd to set Rabelais down as a poor writer because *Gargantua* and *Pantagruel* have not the lapidary diction of Lord Bacon's *New Atlantis* or Dean Swift's *Gulliver's Travels.* Rabelais has the style that is proper to his genially gigantic imagination—the diction that is right for his meaning. Alexander Dumas is not an inferior historical novelist because he did not polish the style of *The Three Guardsmen* as Thackeray polished *Henry Esmond,* or Walter Pater *Marius the Epicurean.*

One may say roughly that in the work of prose the diction is important in an inverse relation to the scale. An essay, a short story, a descriptive sketch, an oration, cannot be finished too highly. It is the obviousness and superficiality of such finish that has militated against the vigorous criticism of Macaulay, while that of DeQuincy, William Hazlitt, Charles Lamb, Emerson, Thoreau, and Macaulay's detractor, Matthew Arnold, has kept its value. And here we should not fail to note that the limitations of Macaulay's diction are those of his feeling and thinking—of his meaning.

But for the longer work in prose, it may actually be disadvantageous to have too rich a style. Stendhal, with his nonchalance of a Napoleonic campaigner, may very well outlast Flaubert to whom stylistic perfection was a torture. The torrential iridescence of Ruskin's prose style, which enchanted my young manhood now becomes cloying to me. I read best *Modern Painters* and *Stones of Venice* by chapters—as a series of short prose compositions, and Ruskin is most alive to me today in such brief masterpieces, as *Sesame and Lilies, Seven Lamps of Architecture,* and the political essays in *Unto This Last.* All of which goes to validate the familiar Horatian maxim that in no writing should the "manner surpass the matter."

Now except in the drama and in oratory, this larger construction of the extended work in prose has received insufficient study. If the characters seem real, if they do things which seem compatible with their character and are interesting, we let it go at that; the history, the biography, the novel are good. But this merit is actually achieved by a most elaborate proportioning of parts, by apt impetus and retardation of narrative, by continuity of mood never allowed to become monotonous, by apt reference to the mind chiefly concerned with the action and only in the last instance by artfully modulated diction. All this awaits a study which I am able only to suggest. The best discussion of these problems within my knowledge is Henry James's *The Art of the Novel*. For present purposes I wish only to remark that the unending battle between form and substance is less acute in prose literature, as it is also in music and perhaps in sculpture, than it is in poetry, the theater and painting. The conflict is radical only in the prose writer who cannot control his virtuosity—a Maurice Hewlett, a James Joyce, a Gertrude Stein.

The drama as literature has been carefully studied in its formal aspects ever since Aristotle. Probably his categories, the dominant motive, the entanglement, the climax, the retardation, the solution are sound not merely for the drama but also for most literary composition of a larger sort. Perhaps a vague sense that this is so has unhappily prevented the needed specific study of the epic, the narrative poem, the biography, the history, the novel.

When we come to the drama as acted, we reach the most complicated formal problem, save possibly that of the opera, which the arts present. Until quite recently it has been assumed that the business of the art of the theater was to make the Aristotelian categories—taken not in their letter but in their spirit—audibly and visually effective to an audience. As to that, Dumas *fils,* Scribe, Freytag, Henry Arthur Jones, Augustus Thomas and the critics William Archer and Francisque Sarcey would have agreed across their national boundaries. Latterly we have a single and simpler doctrine—namely, that the good play is any acted thing which for an entire representation successfully imposes its mood on hearer and beholder. Whether this be a notable reform, or a notable aberration, only time will tell.

Assuming for the sake of simplicity the Aristotelian position, the art of the theater is actually exercised by a manager interpreting a play. Into the representation enter the manager's taste, the script, the persons of the cast, the lighting, and naturally all the persons who make or handle the setting; and, as if this were not enough, the Russian managers have added the cinema. Last but not least enters the dire need of an immediate success with the public and of consequent ultimate profits. The task of the stage manager is nothing less than that of harmonizing all these interests.

Historically such reconciliation has rarely been effected. Perhaps the nearest approach thereto was in the Greek theater. The stage setting was conventional and relatively fixed, was unobtrusive and taken for granted. The dramatic poet and the actor, including the chorus, dominated the scene. The manager's part was a minor one and he was often the dramatist. The public was pleased in advance, for the play was given by the Archon to gain votes and to honor the god Dionysius. There was no issue of profit. Finally the play was built upon sacred themes, heroic or mythological, which tended to impose the dramatist's meaning upon the actors and the chorus, and, perhaps most simplifying condition of all—there were no women in the cast. I do not think one is merely a lauder of times past in feeling that the Greek theater attained an artistic unity which has rarely been achieved since.

With the development of comedy, the growing prominence of the actor unbalanced the theater. With the heroic out of the play, and mythology present only in burlesque, there was little in the themes to control the actor. On the contrary, everything encouraged him to exploit his own idiosyncrasy for comic effect. With the emergence of the new comedy and the disappearance of the chorus—champion of the poetical element in the play—the prominence of the actor further increased. One can think of the comedies of character and eccentricity of Plautus and Terence only in terms of the actors. These comedies do not ask to be read and contemplated as did the old tragedies.

The book becomes of less importance. The actor, if generally under critical reproof, develops the tendency to change the lines. The setting is still simple and conventional. The characters are few and typical. The task of the manager is comparatively easy. Under these conditions, the new comedy developed a real unity, but perhaps of a somewhat cheap and sparse nature. In both the tragedy and comedy of classical antiquity declamation was of first importance. Oratory was the art most highly considered and naturally influenced the theater. The conventionality of the characters and the use of the comic mask tended somewhat to check the growing usurpation of the theater by the actor.

Through the Middle Ages, the actor on the whole continued to gain prominence. The book was of such small literary worth that no actor need take the text too seriously. But the fact that the actor was no longer a professional but an amateur prevented anything like an anticipation of the evils of the modern star system. The stage setting, perhaps borrowing from the pageant, assumes an importance and splendor unexampled in classical antiquity. This, through the masque and the opera, will later become a somewhat dubious inheritance for the theater. A good mystery or miracle play must have been less a unity than a bewildering and perhaps alluring mixture of elaborate setting, extravagant acting of an amateurish sort, and casual declamation. Since the Middle Ages took allegory with all seriousness, the greatest unity of impression was attained by the few good morality plays, as the revival of *Everyman* has atttested.

In the European revival of the poetical drama during the Renaissance, the play assumes once more the importance it had had in Grecian times. In such playwright managers as Shakespeare and Molière we have once more the dramatist in charge of the representation of his own play. The diction is again of a beauty to impose itself upon the actor. The problem of the cast is only beginning to be complicated by the presence of the actress. Shakespeare did not have to deal with the problem. The stage is sparsely decorated, with little scene shifting, and the broad projecting apron serves really as a rostrum. Declamation is the chief concern of the manager and actor. It is controlled with difficulty as Hamlet's famous instructions to the players amply testify. The actor is getting out of hand, aspiring to become the leading feature of the art of the theater.

Probably the best renditions of the theater of Shakespeare, Molière, Davenant, and Sheridan came nearer the fine balance of the Greek theater than any of later times. Something of the richness afforded by the chorus and by the stateliness of the outdoor theater was doubtless lacking, but this lack was offset by a greater intimacy and variety of action and characterization. Among the high pleasures of the theater a representation of Racine or Molière, with the conventionalized diction, the disciplined action, the nondescript but fitting scenery and costuming of the Theatre Français, still counts first with many theater goers of experience and taste. Everything is balanced about the play and the manager embodying the tradition.

The instability of all the composite artistic forms is strikingly shown by the fact that the course of the theater was to be profoundly altered by a simple mechanical invention, that of bright footlights. When the stage was really in the theater, the necessary distance between the play and the audience was maintained by the artificiality of the diction and by the generalized character of the setting. One might say that because the stage was too near, the play, the setting and the actor had to keep a balancing remoteness.

Footlights and the proscenium arch cut the stage off from the audience, made a separate world of it, greatly increased the visibility of the actor and the setting, with consequent temptations to the actor and the scene painter. The individuals of an audience cannot be distinguished across the footlights, the whole audience is a blur. This meant that for the old, direct, quasi-oratorical appeal of the actor had to be substituted an appeal of another order. It was to be that of the actor's personality made more conspicuous through footlights, and later through the spotlight and the opera glass. Earlier the task of the actor, cruelly exposed on the apron stage and in the same light with his audience, had been to keep his distance; now his task was to diminish the distance created by the new lighting. The star began to ascend. He or she will soon have a dazzling resplendence at the expense of the play.

Meanwhile, quite illogically, the scene painter was encouraged to compete with the star. The enhanced visibility of the setting lured him into inventing new elaborations of a realistic order, new decorative splendors, new mechanical devices.

Before the converging aggressive of the actor and the scene painter the play had to yield. To exploit the actor's personality it was cut, transposed, interpolated. Competing characters and scenes were eliminated. All this amounted, if not to rewriting, at least to radical reconstruction. In the interest of the scene painter the old plays which were written for a different stage, were arbitrarily redivided into scenes. As the most continuously presented, this transmogrification affected the best plays—those of Shakespeare. In part this was a commonsense renovation of the old scripts, to meet contemporary conditions; more often it was sheer vandalism. New plays had to be written to meet the caprice of the actor and the pedantry of the scene painter.

The star system also reduced the already declining authority of the manager. The star moved in his or her own orbit, or declined to move. Thus the manager's effort turned to what was still left in his hands—to the stage setting. In short, the manager joined with the actor and the scene painter in a triple alliance against the playwright and the play. Naturally the play dwindled in importance for a full century.

Had the managers conducted their innovations in stage setting with anything like taste and intelligence, great benefit for the art of the theater might have resulted. There was a place for decorative splendor which should reinforce the lines in analogical or symbolical fashion, should introduce elements of illusion of a generalized sort—which should somewhat offset the always too personal and specific appearance of the actor, should in short make the actor accept that reasonable distance which he was desperately trying to abolish. But unhappily the new experiments in stage decoration were guided not by the traditional wisdom that the stage should have reality only to the imagination of a sympathetic auditor, but by the fallacy that the stage should seem as real as the forest to the forester; as the castle to the stone mason; as the furnished room to the cabinet maker. Thus the esthetic distance which the actor imperfectly maintained the stage setting sacrificed utterly. It was to end with the grandiose archaeology of Sardou, with Augustine Daly and his properties in period furniture.

The lowest depth of this drive for an inept realism is appropriately the bottom of a river made in Germany, the Rhine. In *Rheingold* in a famous scene unforgettable for any beholder endowed with a whit of the comic spirit, lightly draped buxom Nordics are reeled up and down by wires attached to a harness. A blue netting signifying water mercifully conceals them somewhat, but not sufficiently, as they swing massively on their shortening and slackening wires and sing the most heavenly music. Only the beauty of the music and the shortness of humor in Wagnerian audiences has prevented this scene from being laughed off the opera stage. I repeat it is the lowest depth of nineteenth century stage realism, for even under the preposterous conditions imposed by the book, the scene could be put on much better. Gracile Nordics even more lightly and appropriately draped could be reeled and unreeled and swing much more convincingly if unburdened by the responsibility of song. Meanwhile the melodious buxom Nordics would evidently function more pleasurably were they unseen. But to Wagner who, with all his genius, was obsessed by the realistic heresy, for a Rhine maiden to be sung for would have been an insincerity—as if the art of the theater did not consist in what in ordinary living seems insincere.

The advent of the well made play and the rise of Ibsen some sixty years ago caused a temporary balance between the play and the setting, but did nothing to abate the evils of the star system. Being of contemporary scope and realistic, with no tinge of poetry, the well made play rarely called for elaborate setting and accommodated itself reasonably with such realistic setting as was provided for it.

Reviewing this summary but perhaps too long survey, the difficulty of achieving any artistic synthesis in the theater is inherent in the fact that while the play itself and the setting are artificial constructions, the actor is a real person save in so far as he achieves a suitable artificiality. In the opera the difficulty is really less, since the performer does an artificial thing, sings—in an artificial medium, music. Thus, we meet the paradox that though the drama is one of the highest branches of literature, the drama as ordinarily played is ever among the lowest of the arts.

Certain purists, among them that extraordinary genius, Gordon Craig, have alternated between drastic counsels of reform and despair. The reform, as Mr. Craig, Mr. Appia, and Mr. Norman Bel Geddes conceived it, consisted in treating the setting, not as the actual location of the action, but as a visual and symbolic accompaniment for the lines. This seems in the right direction, as shifting the balance in the traditional direction, from the actor and the scene painter towards the *régisseur* and the play. Theoretically at least this was entirely sound, and, as I have already suggested, a return with much decorative enrichment to the better estate of the theater before the star and footlights. By insisting on very great distance in the setting, something of that distance overflowed to the always too near actor. Could we restore also the distance once established by a reasonably artificial diction—a distance still observed by the state theaters of France—the actor, even the star, might cease to frustrate that very delicate balance which any fine art of the theater requires.

As to the actor and the star, Mr. Craig indulged a moment of complete and perhaps too logical despair. He virtually framed this syllogism: Without an artist in full control there is no art. But no manager, and the manager is the artist in control of any theatrical production, has ever controlled the star actor by much, or the star actress at all. Ergo, so long as the theater admits the actor and actress, it cannot be an art.

The remedy was plain: eliminate the actor, and substitute what can be managed, the puppet, whose lines should be sympathetically declaimed by an invisible reader or readers. On these principles Mr. Craig conducted amazing and delightful performances on his tiny model stage at Florence, nearly thirty years ago. But Mr. Craig had to live, and, after putting himself stalwartly on record in *The Mask* and in his books, he continued under difficulties to set plays for the living actor, which for the art of the theater was a very great service. On the issue of principle involved in Mr. Craig's purism, I may merely recall my endeavor, in the first chapter of this book, to show that the complete control of the artist over the work of art is historically and factually non-existent. Hence the major premise of Mr. Craig's syllogism has at best partial truth. The situation of the theater, bad as it is, is perhaps not so desperate as it has seemed to him.

As an art involving the harmonizing of four more or less competing interests—that of the playwright, the manager, the actor, the stage setter—the art of the theater is surpassed in complexity only by that of the opera which adds two more competitive interests, that of the composer and the leader of the orchestra. But many of the arts are more cooperative than is usually imagined. All music involves the composer and interpreters, from the individual performer to the director of the orchestra with perhaps eighty musicians—not to mention the audience. All architecture involves an accord between the owner, the architect, the builder or contractor, the workmen. In short, only literature, painting and sculpture are, and then but relatively, under the artist's control, for there is often substantial pressure from public or private patronage.

This discussion of the art of the theater shows in an extreme case what the problem of achieving formal equilibrium is in any highly composite art. It should also permit me to treat more briefly the formal character of the other arts which, while apparently much simpler, is really complex enough.

The form of painting is conditioned by the frame or border, which may be considered as shutting the picture off from the ordinary world and into its own. Where there is not such a determinant boundary, as in the sketch which is not a composition or in the vignette, we have to make it with a mat or a frame. Precisely what distinguishes a landscape from the scene it appears to represent faithfully is in the first instance that the design of the painting is related to fixed bounds whereas that of the scene in nature has no such relations but fades off in every direction. The photographer acts like an artist when he chooses his scene with reference to the quadrangle of his sensitive plate. Any attentive observer of pictures composed within various frames—squares, uprights, oblongs, ovals, medallions, polygons—will not have failed to notice that the pictorial pattern is in active relations to the frame, relations generally of repetition or contrast. The absence of such relations makes an unsatisfactory composition. The minor Florentine primitives often simply set a composition conceived for a square into a circle. Competent painters, such as Lorenzo di Credi, Botticelli, not to mention such giants as Michelangelo and Raphael, always derived the leading curves of their figure compositions from the enclosing circle.

This principle of the bounds as determinant of the main lines and proportions of any well composed picture may most readily be studied in decorative design. Nowhere better than in the wedge-shaped spandrels in the Sistine Chapel, occupied by Michelangelo's prophets and sibyls, or in the odd half-lunettes where the families of the precursors of Christ are represented. The skilful filling of circular forms is admirably exemplified in the medallions which Titian and his Venetian contemporaries painted for the ceiling of the Library at Venice. In the ceiling of St. Roch's and that of the Ducal Palace Tintoretto displayed an inexhaustible ingenuity and tact in handling the most various and apparently refractory of areas. One need not go so far afield. Vedder's lunettes in the Library of Congress, Edward Simmon's decorations, Kenyon Cox's pendentives in mosaic, in the State House of Wisconsin, would equally well illustrate the matter. So would the admirable handling of the coffered ceiling in the Boston Public Library by John S. Sargent.

Beyond this necessary conformity to the fixed form of the painted field, the reader must consult one of the many books on pictorial composition. Here I need only recall that the fundamental patterns of linear composition are rather few. Central symmetry, diagonal, processional, and catenary are the usual patterns in old painting. Of central symmetry, Giovanni Bellini, Perugino, and Raphael are the greatest masters, ever enriching the simplicity of the underlying symmetry with the most exquisite variations.

The pattern that results from disposing the chief figure or motive diagonally across the rectangle has far more dynamic effect. Titian brought it to perfection, Rubens elaborated it magnificently, Delacroix revived it powerfully.

Processional patterns are self-explaining, from the mosaic nave of S. Apollinare in Classe at Ravenna to Hippolyte Flandrin at St. Vincent de Paul at Paris. Or Robert Blum's charming frieze, "Music," transferred from Mendelssohn Hall to the Brooklyn Institute.

Catenary compositions, apparently highly complicated, are in their elements quite simple. The unit is merely curves

Perugino. Deposition

Uffizi, Florence

Titian. Pesaro Madonna

Frari, Venice

in typical relations. A very usual unit is the geographical symbol for a mountain chain ⌒ . Considered merely as a linear pattern, Michelangelo's "Creation of Adam" is this sort of a composition. The curves may be variously related, say, reversed ⌣,)(, lateral or upright (). Tintoretto's admirable "Mercury and the Graces" is of the last sort. Raphael's "Sibyls" has this theme)(, and the curves of the figures are reversed catenary not only with regard to the figures themselves but also with regard to the two structural arches within which they are inclosed—an extraordinary elaboration of a quite simple motive. The pattern of Renoir's "Bathers" is again chiefly catenary. I may add that even the audacious and apparently lawless ceiling designs of the baroque painters will usually admit of a catenary analysis.

This summary treatment of the grammar of linear design is carried only far enough to remind the reader that there is such a grammar. I need not also remind him that linear design is only a small part of composing any picture, that it demands all sorts of reinforcements and contrasts from tone, color, texture; that in some pictures it is virtually absent, the design being built not merely over the surface but deep beyond it in space and volumes, as in El Greco's paintings. Of this sort are many of Rembrandt's finest compositions, but the very finest, such as the "Portrait of Jan Six and the Syndics," while subordinating the linear pattern do not renounce it. In the best Cézannes likewise, the linear pattern is only less palpable than the relations of the masses in depth.

Of course any well made picture suggests space and mass. Gradation of color and knowledge of its effect as advancing or retreating is the chief space-making service. But diminution in perspective and the inward direction of lines and planes may also be of space-making value. Every picture represents some space if only as an inference from the masses represented. In decorative, especially in mural, painting such space is usually kept shallow. In most of Giotto's frescoes, which are models of decorative spatiality, the space is just deep enough not to cramp the probable movements of the figures.

The masses in a picture may be made either by lines, by lines which swell and tend to become areas, or by planes, color areas, which actually suggest only the geometrical construction of the object represented, but are accepted by a cooperative beholder as a more or less complete account of the form. The relative tones and textures of such planes bring them forward or push them back. The whole arrangement is to be thought of as a dynamism behind the picture plane, the factors of which also make a relatively static pattern on the picture plane. It is this double or even triple function of every part of a well made picture that constitutes the difficulty of the painter's art.

Much modern painting in the effort to achieve a very active sense of mass neglects pattern. But much of Matisse in his more recent work gives little more than pattern delightfully elaborated. In the best painting the rhythmical movement across the picture plane is fully harmonized with those rhythmical movements in depth which give the sense of space and mass. Perhaps the fullest reconciliation of these really competitive functions is found in artists a little below the first rank, such as Paolo Veronese and Tiepolo. The greatest artists often push one function to the

Renoir. The Bathers

extreme. The best painting is seldom the greatest art, for apart from pattern-making, space-making and mass-making the picture has a primary emotional meaning which dictates both formal emphasis and formal sacrifices.

All these devices of the painter are again to be regarded as the terms of a grammar and not as qualities of things. Observation of things helps to make the grammar, but does not limit its use. Like any grammar the proper use of that of painting is to make new expressions which, however they may parallel appearances in the outside world, are actually novelties—additions to the former sum of appearances.

The form of free-standing sculpture is dictated by the need of making an infinity of aspects contribute to an effect of unity. Practically this means that a few typical contours must be emphasized. Here nature helps the artist, perhaps more generously than in any other art. For, dealing as he ordinarily does with the characteristic postures and actions of men and beasts, the sculptor finds that these many aspects are variants or reciprocals of one effect. He has merely to make the exaggerations and eliminations that will enhance the impression of organization. Because he really has less to do than the painter and because that little is so subtle, his task is really more difficult. As we have already noted, great sculptors are the rarest type of artists. To use to the full the favorable aspects of nature while conveying them in the terms of art seems to be the problem. Auguste Rodin, in his habit of letting the model move about the studio until the desired pose occurred, invited the fullest contribution from nature, but only to begin an intense activity of stylization. To his biographer, Mr. Anthony M.

Ludovici, he expressed as follows the main problem of the sculptor. I add for clearness a phrase in brackets:

"According to Rodin, therefore, the radical problem of all good sculpture consisted in discovering how an object moulded [or carved] from the outside could be made to look as if it had grown from an inner necessity."

In the voluminous writings drawn from his talks, Rodin elaborates a method of modelling, which could also be one of cutting, in planes. The essential surfaces are to be looked at not as so many areas but as the nearest extension of volumes thrusting towards the observer. The detection and rendering of these limits of protruding volumes will yield that variety of expressive contours upon the joint effect of which the unity of sculpture depends. This thought is very concretely elaborated in his book *Art* to which the reader is referred, with telling reference to famous Greek statues. This larger structural modelling also provides the facets which will reflect the light favorably.

Ultimately, as Karl Hildebrandt has observed, the statue which is made with the focused eye from a model again seen with the eye in focus, is going to be seen with the unfocused eye—as a distance picture, *Fernbild*—as a picture without the isolating advantage of a frame, hence more or less liable to confusion with adjacent objects. This needful isolation the good sculptor gets, along the lines described by Rodin, through greater forms of construction which, analogous to those of corresponding nature, are also transformations and simplifications. More arbitrarily, such isolation is attained by the sound habit of making the base of the same material as the statue and setting both on a pedestal of a different material—as it were, an insulator.

Hildebrandt assumed a plane at the point fixed by the projection nearest the spectator. All proportions were to be regarded as measured from such a plane. What is important in this view is that a sort of ideal solid geometry underlies all good sculpture.

Generally sculptors have insisted on an ideal geometrical content for the statue, a keeping of limits. Michelangelo expressed this when he wrote of the statue as contained in the block of marble and only needing to be liberated; and more sensationally, when he said that the good statue could be rolled down hill without damage. Many of his own famous statues would suffer under this test, and many quite inferior statues of our contemporary sculptors would endure it unscathed, which should make us sceptical of universal formulas, even of those of great artists. Still, the presence of such an implied containing form is important as a point of permanent reference for the spectator, who, as he observes one aspect, must build up a composite memory experience from other significant aspects. It is the difficulty of building up this memory picture which makes any full esthetic experience of sculpture very difficult. There are too many pleasant halfway houses tempting one to linger in partial appreciation.

Naturally the form of sculpture varies greatly according to the executive method—modelling up, cutting away, and according to the very various materials which the sculptor may choose. But something of this will be discussed when we consider the effect of material on form, while as regards sculpture in general, the reader may be referred to the elaborate analyses of Lipps and Volkelt.

Since sculpture in relief and sculpture in the round which offers a single aspect, as in a niche, is really a plastic form of pictorial design, its peculiar conditions need not detain us. Suffice it to say that the problem, as in the picture, is that of the single aspect and of the design isolated by clear boundaries. The difference between the two apparently similar varieties of sculpture, which really have nothing in common save varying degrees of projection, can be visualized by imposing bounds upon free-standing sculpture. George Barnard's much disputed "Lincoln" fairly cries for a niche. Within bounds, it would be as impressive as Donatello's "Zuccone," which suggests that as free-standing sculpture Mr. Barnard's admirable statue has patent defects. Contrariwise great statues in the round suffer surprisingly from imprisonment limiting the beholder to one aspect. Some years ago it occurred to certain wags in the Princeton Graduate College to install a reduced plaster cast of the "Venus de Milo" in a Gothic niche in the courtyard. The nobly balanced goddess thus displayed had the air of executing a decorous *danse du ventre*. I am ashamed of confessing that, most unfairly, I have never since seen the "Venus de Milo" with quite the old untroubled rapture.

The unique character of the architect's approach to form would deserve rather a book than a few paragraphs. He begins where the sculptor ends, with geometrical abstractions, plans, sections, elevations which no eye ever sees in the completed building. Alone of artists he may be thought of as beginning with an anterior form which appears only as derivatives in his finished work. The appearance he has to divine or forecast from its skeletal elements. As things go today, it is at a rather late stage in design that he makes some prophecy of the future effect in a generally flattering and quite specious rendering in perspective. In the Renaissance and earlier a more reasonable simulacrum of the finished building was promptly created in the form of a model to scale. This procedure, as we have already noted, had certain advantages in giving a reasonably free hand as interpreter of the design to the master builder.

Again, the architect is the only artist whose form is necessarily conditioned by practical considerations. His task of bringing a manifold into unity is extraordinarily difficult. As is the case in sculpture, the beholder must build up a composite memory image in order to appreciate any great building as a whole, and it may be doubted if this composite image is for any great monument of architecture, ever even relatively complete. Much of the best appreciation remains entirely fractional. One thinks of the transept with the five sisters in York Cathedral, of the Chapter House at Salisbury. Estheticians of a puristic sort suggest that the esthetic appreciation of any building consists of several typical and unrelated images. We should think of the interior of Chartres without any awareness of the exterior. In the first place it is entirely doubtful if this be possible, next if it be, we must abandon the formula of the work of art as a unified manifold. Except in small buildings, which may be regarded as a sort of architectural sculpture, the form of any great building as apprehended seems to be a smaller within a larger manifold rather than a unity. For this reason the purists in esthetic theory have prudently fought shy of architecture. I shall prudently do the same, admitting frankly, however, the difficulty of the situation.

Like music and the play the form of architecture exists only through the activity of an interpreter—the master builder. Its serial and generally incomplete appreciation, developed largely through memory, recalls that of music, the theater, the opera and literature. It is with much appropriateness that architecture has been called frozen music, though such it is only if considered in the abstract and apart from the experience of the beholder, the difference being chiefly that the music moves; in architecture, the beholder moves. Psychologically the two experiences are entirely analogous, and perhaps if we rarely attain a complete architectural appreciation, we also rarely reach a complete appreciation of music, of a play, or for that matter of any longer work in literature. What is important in these perhaps necessarily partial appreciations is their direction, that they should be tending towards the center, which is the creative experience of the artist.

Obviously the artist is highly subject to the law of his materials. In our own day we have seen the successful fight of a Louis Sullivan against falsifying the structural logic of the new material, steel, justly requiring that it be embodied in appropriate architectural design. Something of this must occupy us later when we consider the artist.

Certain isolating characteristics are proper to the work of art. It must be distinguished from the great mass of common objects, must have a distance that aids its appreciation. Such distance is often supplied by the art itself—the frame of the picture, the pedestal of the statue, the curtain, the proscenium and artificial lighting of the theater, the rhythm of poetry, the special diction of literary prose, the arbitrary scale and harmonies of music—these are intrinsic methods of producing distance. Often distance is brought about more or less adventitiously and extrinsically. The uniform dress of the orchestra, the formal rows of seats, the darkening of the auditorium—all this contributes towards the distance of orchestral music.

Since much of this has already been touched on in connection with the several arts, nothing but a reminder of the universality of isolation or distance seems now necessary. Obviously many, perhaps most, of the accepted conventions of the arts are means of establishing a right distance. Often there is a tendency to rebel against the law of isolation. The baroque painters who, following Correggio's lead, painted away the architecture, bringing clouds and figures down into the church, were making a world unsevered from that of the spectator—abolishing the distance which the Renaissance decorators had ever observed. But the architecture could not wholly be painted away; the sense of it persisted under its superficial disguise; thus in spite of itself, the best baroque decoration keeps its distance sufficiently.

When that able theater director Meyerhold does away with the curtain and brings actors on stage through the auditorium, he is reducing the distance traditional in the art of the theater. One feels that the expedient is more suitable for the patriotic melodrama in which he excels than for plays of a more serious esthetic import.

It may be added that the distance-making conventions become so much taken for granted that a more natural and unconventional disposition of the form of a work of art may actually effect a disconcerting distance. It was hard for a picture lover accustomed to the dark tradition of landscape painting to accept the iridescent and more resemblant landscapes of the Impressionists. The modern still-lives in Cézanne's fashion, with the bowls and apples apparently spilling off the table, give after all the true aspect of bowls and apples as one looks down on them. Chardin's still-lives, on the contrary, are conventionally staged, at the level of the eye. One never sees still-life this way except through squatting painfully. But through use and wont the Chardins seem more natural than the Cézannes. That is, distance and isolation are not absolute but entirely relative—psychological not physical. It may be added that the isolating principle of architecture is by no means clear. It may consist in the sheer rise of a building from the ground, but other things than buildings also rise sheerly. It more probably lies in some subtle intuition of the underlying abstract and geometrical activities of the architect.

A characteristic of the good work of art which is generally ignored in esthetic discussion is scale. For every composition and technique there is an appropriate scale which is ignored at some loss. With a just tact the best painters in the smooth and linear manner of Holbein chose the scale of a quarter life or smaller. The same technique on the scale of life tends to become empty. Contrariwise the rough and loaded painting of the very able pictures of Segonzac often seems to require a scale larger than his. That very accomplished modeller, Mr. Macmonnies, often makes a statue in three scales—that of life or nearly so, that of a statuette about eighteen inches high, and that of a figurine a few inches high. In almost every case the smallest version is the best—expressing more of the sculptor's verve and virtuosity. As a practical standard, when any design can be greatly enlarged or diminished to advantage there is something wrong with the design.

This is perhaps most fully understood in the graphic arts. Few copperplate etchers today would make the big plates that beguiled our fathers. It is well understood that the thin etched line is effective only on a rather small surface. To use it on a large surface is a sacrifice not merely of executive economy but of esthetic effect. On the other hand the coarser line of the etched zinc plate or of the wood block may effectively be used on a large surface. Similarly there is a right scale for marble statues. The very big ones tend to be bleak and repellant; even Michelangelo's "David," at best the mere exploit of a great genius, is an unpleasing object. Marble statuettes are generally weak and trivial in effect. With a just tact, the Greeks made their colossal statues in gold and ivory or in bronze, and their statuettes in bronze or terra cotta. With a similar right instinct, the Gothic sculptors made their small statuary in ivory or wood.

Any well designed work of art tends to look much larger than it is—to magnify itself in the beholder's eye. It will be a surprise to most of my readers to learn that virtually all of the famous portraits of Titian are hardly of half the scale of life. The scale of Giotto's frescoes is about the same. Portraits over the scale of life are almost invariably hideous. Perhaps the most variously beautiful changes of scale are those in Michelangelo's ceiling of the Sistine Chapel. The scale runs a gamut from Adam eighteen feet long, through the gigantic prophets and sibyls in the pendentives, to the so-called slaves who are about of life size, but something in the function of the figures, in the space they occupy, in their decorative relation to the whole, justifies differences of scale in themselves preposterous. Any serious changes in this gamut of scale would make of one of the most beautiful fresco decorations in the world a positive eyesore.

The Dutch genre painters found a rather small scale right for their familiar subjects. This virtual canon was transgressed at hazard. The big Jan Steens are not the good ones. Even the magician Vermeer of Delft is below himself in his few large compositions. The few big Chardins are his inferior works. I think Cézanne often missed his scale. The big painting of nude bathers seems to me less satisfactory than the lithograph which he made of the same subject. On the other hand, Gérôme, a pale and empty painter on his Salon scale, is occasionally quite charming in his small pictures, as was Meissonier in his book illustrations. In general a mediocre composition gains through reduction, while a fine composition, if rarely gaining from enlargement, at least bears it with relative impunity.

Such illustrations may sufficiently suggest the principle of scale, and we shall here and there return to the subject in a more concrete aspect as we in the chapter on the artist discuss the effect of material upon form.

Since, apart from any ulterior meaning it may possess, the work of art is merely so much formed material, the chosen material, wishing a form congruous with its own nature, properly influences and conditions the esthetic form. When the material must mean something other than itself, as the painter's pigments, the adjustment between form, meaning and material may be very difficult. In such cases the skilful artist in effecting his reconciliation will always take the claims of the material into account. In the decorative and applied arts, there is no acute problem, for the material means only itself and chiefly determines the character of the esthetic form. Yet the decorative arts often make the most perverse use of their materials, which only goes once more to show that the taste and intelligence of the mere craftsman are normally on a lower plane than that of the artist.

To achieve an expressive form without doing violence to the idiom of the material is perhaps the major technical problem of the arts. It is difficult or the contrary to the extent that the material does or does not impose its idiom. The more refractory the material, the less difficult the creation of the appropriate form. It is easier for the sculptor to go wrong in marble than in basalt or jade; in clay than in marble. The composer in the traditional sonata and symphony forms has an easier problem than he who is creating a less defined form. The poet who accepts a fixed metrical scheme has a guidance towards esthetic form which is denied to the writer of prose or free verse. It is simpler to design a fine building in brick, stone or wood than in the far more tractable materials of steel or reinforced concrete. But the good artist ever seeks and regards the laws, overt or occult, of whatever material he is shaping into form.

The case is best illustrated from sculpture which commands a great variety of materials each of which has its own idiom—an idiom that is frequently disregarded. The basalt and porphyry of the Egyptians encouraged sculptural design in rather simple geometrical solids, a general roundness, no rapid shifting of contours, little interior modelling or elaborated linear definition, static, firmly balanced arrangements tending to be symmetrical. One may reverse the situation and say that the hieratic and strictly formalized thinking and feeling of the Egyptians called for expression in such simplifying and magnifying materials as granite, basalt and porphyry.

The crystalline and somewhat translucent marbles of Greece encouraged a modulated surface, the flow of which should be unbroken by sharp changes of contour, by deep shadow-forming pits, by linear accentuation. Such marbles are the ideal materials for the youthful nude. When they are used, however ingeniously, for struggling muscular giants, as in the famous Pergamene frieze, there is abuse of the material. Such design is for modelling in clay and casting in bronze. Again the marble statue should be self-contained as regards center of gravity. Where you see a marble held upright by an urn, a dolphin, a tree trunk you may assume that the design is ill-judged or that the marble is a copy of some original designed for bronze. Naturally, amazing marble sculpture has been made in rank defiance of the law of the material—the "Laokoön," Bernini's "Rape of Proserpina," and "Apollo and Daphne." It remains true that such exploits are not exemplary.

Soft opaque stones, limestones and sandstones generally, admit of variety of contours, interior modelling, sharp linear accents. Such stone from Assyria and Egypt down has been generally and rightly used for sculpture in relief— semi-pictorial sculpture. Most medieval sculpture in the round is only technically so, being set in a niche or against a wall and calculated for a single aspect. Such sculpture appropriately borrowed linear and pictorial features from manuscript illumination.

The bronze statue, being supported by an iron armature, permits all audacities of posture, gesture, and balance. Here great variety of silhouette, emphatic linear contours and accents, a general liveliness and tension as compared with marble are in place. There may be more attention to texture and to details of modelling, subject always to the sharp and somewhat obscuring reflections from polished bronze which drive the eye to the contours. If there is to be much interior modelling and detail, the patination should be dull. Since the bronze is cast from a model, the model itself should have bronze character. It is for this reason that the lost-wax process of casting provides the best bronzes. The wax-covered model carefully worked out has more bronze quality of surface than any clay model. In an idiomatic bronze statue cast from a clay model, the accidents of the clay technique are chiselled or filed away with all care. The fact that so able a sculptor as Jacob Epstein simply models up a portrait in clay and casts it in bronze does not justify the practice. Impressive as Epstein's bronze portraits are, I feel sure they would be finer in terra cotta.

Since clay can be manipulated in almost any manner, the idiomatic character of modelling by building up lies in great freedom, in a varied and picturesque surface, affording a lively play of light and shade. Minute modelling is feasible; sharp linear accents can be made with a stylus. The good clay modeller will naturally tend to avail himself of all these resources of his material. A terra-cotta bust of a Roman patrician at Boston is an admirable example of clay modelling from antiquity. All the characteristic lines of an old face are indicated without smallness. Joys for the art lover are the clay sketches of Bernini, the French terra-cotta portrait busts of the eighteenth century, the frankly sensual figurines of Clodion. In general, clay is an informal material, fit for gay and familiar themes. Yet it will yield tragic effects that would strain the resources of marble or bronze, witness the colored terra-cotta depositions of the Lombard primitives Mazzoni and Begarelli. Clay can achieve dignity, but does not exact it.

Very often terra cotta is merely the core of a statue finished in painted plaster or in glaze. In such case, that of the Tanagra figurines, of the enamelled sculpture of the Robbias, in many reliefs or free-standing figures of the Middle Ages and Renaissance, the ultimate modelling is reinforced by painting. Of this sort are the charming porcelain figurines of Chelsea and Meissen. While a very accomplished sculptor like Luca della Robbia achieves admirable and impressive results with his enamelled figures, he does so by keeping the theme simple, the scale rather small, and the color scheme restricted. This seems to be the law for completely polychromed statuary. Luca's successors, who increased the scale, elaborated the color scheme, essayed complicated themes, by no means improved on his work. Terra cotta, like soft porous stone, seems to call for painting as giving a more agreeable surface than its own.

To treat polychromy in sculpture at large would lead us far afield. From what we know of Greek polychromy it was generally a mere tinting or a filling in of a background, with no representative character. It may very well have been a beauty in marble statuary exposed to the bleaching

Mediterranean sun. Despite interesting experiments of modern archaeologists, it remains a lost art.

Of course the fundamental difference between sculpture, accurately speaking, and modelling is that between cutting away and building up. The cutting-away method implies great respect for the material and some residual sense of the tool in the finished object. The building-up method may take its highly tractable material less seriously, and the tool, which is chiefly the thumb and fingers, may or may not assert its presence. It would be easy to illustrate these principles from wax modelling, wood carving, ivory carving, and carving in jade, but it is unnecessary. In general, the severer the style, the more intractable the material, and vice versa. The modernistic sculptors who are trying to revive in marble the geometrical massiveness of Egyptian sculpture, might more appropriately use basalt or porphyry. But here intrudes both a consideration of expense and a suspicion that these ingenious designs are not worthy of the nobler materials. It may be added that no sculpture makes a more subtle and accomplished use of the tooled surface than do the ebony fetishes of the Congo blacks, and this technical perfection of negro carving has led its extravagant admirers to claim for it further merits which it does not possess.

It is in the interest of literary style and metrics that war has been most frequently waged in the name of the law of the material. The commonest criticism of an unusual style has been that it is contrary to the genius of the language, and if the conception of the genius of the language could be clearly defined, there could be no more valid criticism. On this ground John Lyly, the Euphuist, was condemned.

He had introduced into English the alien mannerisms of a Spaniard—Guevara. For their excessive latinizing, various critics have upbraided John Milton and Dr. Johnson. Victor Hugo was attacked for shifting the pause of the Alexandrine, and for using in poetry such colloquial words as *mouchoir,* when the genius of the language required the more elegant *serviette.* For using simple language in poetry and renouncing most of the customary ornamentation, William Wordsworth was written down as an inferior poet. Walt Whitman offended through presenting as poetry his dangling and prolonged tirades in rhythmical prose. So it has been, and so it ever will be as often as a diction or metric unfamiliar to the critic or the proverbial gentle reader shows its unhallowed head.

Now there probably is a law or genius of every language to which an author is bound to conform, but in practice it is desperately difficult to define what we mean by good literary usage. Was our good literary usage of the 1890's that of W. D. Howells, Henry James, Stephen Crane, Walt Whitman, O. Henry, Mark Twain, W. C. Brownell, Theodore Roosevelt, Peter Finley Dunn?—it would be hard to say. Unless there be, as in France, an authoritative academy which awards prizes and makes dictionaries, good literary usage seems to be merely what each writer or reader thinks it is. His duty seems to be that of obedience to a standard which he himself has established. Obviously such a standard lacks all general authority.

From the Greeks down, an alternate and more tangible criterion has been suggested in the conversational usage of polite and cultured society. From this, good literary usage should not too much depart. Where there is a polite and cultured society recognized and respected as such, this is a concrete standard. It is one that French literature has on the whole accepted. The conspicuous merits and the equally conspicuous limitations of French literature are undoubtedly due to this fact. And such reference to conversational centers has probably been advantageous to French letters, has brought about its characteristic sobriety, poise, and reasonableness. Genius, as Delacroix admirably expressed it, was merely being reasonable in a very superior fashion—after the pattern of *honnêtes gens,* but on a higher plane.

Such a standard is comfortable, and where there is a cultivated minority, whose culture is generally admired, its good usage is a practical point of departure for the poet or prose writer. Such has been the case in Italy, and in Spain; in England, if now on a diminishing basis; in the old Austrian Empire; in many of the compact and coherent small nations—such as Denmark, Norway, Sweden, Holland. For a time it was the case with us. For fifty years before say about 1905, one could hold that the conversational usage of the Century Club, with its sisters, cousins, aunts and wives, was the norm for the American author. It is no longer the case in America, and it has never been the case in Upper Germany, where owing to minute national subdivisions and perhaps to the domination of an academic class more learned than cultured, there never has been a standard of polite good usage to which a hesitant writer could repair. No group could really be said to be in charge of the genius of the German language. The same situation holds in Russia today. Whatever slight traditional authority existed, and it was of a rather exotic sort, has gone down the wind of revolution. Without a political revolution, we are in about the same case in America.

Now while a society that is well nourished from good literature should develop a conversational usage which any sensible writer will more or less take into account, it is equally true that the idiom of good talk and that of great literature only exceptionally agree. A Plato, a Xenophon, surely had the best chat of Athens always in mind, but no Greek ever talked like Homer, like a chorus of Aeschylus, like an ode of Pindar. The material of such exalted poetry being entirely different from that of the choicest conversation, no law based on conversational usage can be imposed. When we have an *entente* between conversational and literary usage, as in the eighteenth century, we have a pause, a certain lowering of creative endeavor.

This gulf between the language of conversation and that of poetry has been ingeniously surveyed and charted by the great symbolist poet, Stephan Mallarmé. He would deny even a speaking acquaintance between the two styles, and his own literary language had little enough to do with the genius of French speech as it had previously been understood. But Mallarmé's exaggeration of theory and practice after all emphasized the profound truth that poetry, indeed imaginative writing of any kind, more or less remakes the language in which it is written, and is not bound by the conversational habits of the best conceivable literary society.

The upshot of this discussion of the law of the material in literary composition seems to be that there often is a law of polite and cultured usage in conversation which a certain sort of writer naturally and reasonably consults. The familiar essayists, the moralists, most historians and biographers, writers of comedy, novelists of manners, narrative and satirical poets—properly observe this law. Epic and lyric poets, writers of tragedy and romantic fiction normally disregard any such law. Is there, then, some other law of the material which applies to them?

Probably there is, but it evades anything like a formulation. It lies perhaps in the tradition of these more imaginative and impassioned forms of literary art—the tradition as individually sensed by the creative writer, and also as cherished and transmitted through formal criticism and vitally persisting in the experience of well read and sensitive contemporaries. Here if not a law is a background of judgment which a wise author, however conscious of his own taste and capacity, ignores at his peril. And here the case of Proust may be instructive. His novels consist in almost equal proportions in study of manners and in research of certain morbidities and curiosities of human psychology. For this latter aim his highly complicated and prolix style was well invented. For the residual novel of manners in every book of Proust, it was very ill adapted. The ultimate ambiguity and unsatisfactoriness of Proust's amazingly ingenious and perceptive works may well rest on such intermitted attention to the law of the material.

In this chapter I am conscious of having merely glimpsed a few aspects—I hope important ones—of a vast theme. I have tried to show the esthetic form and the material as contributing to, obstructing, in happier cases always furthering the ultimate form and content of the work of art. It is indeed rather in mediating these a priori pressures from form and material than in his relation to nature that the

task of the artist consists. It is here especially that he con-
fronts the facilities and obstacles bequeathed to him by the
history of his art. The finest artistic creation in the past
has always involved the delicate appraisal and prudent
reinvestment of this legacy. I doubt if the urgent present,
with its cult of the isolated individual, offers to the creative
artist any more promising procedure.

Finally the reminder may be as ever in order that as
we study the form of the work of art we should regard it
merely as the imprint of the artist's creative activity and as
the stimulus to the art lover's experience of appreciation.
Between these two psychical realities, the work of art with
its form is merely a linking symbol—an abstract middle
term. Independent, unrelated existence, it has none; it is
something that has been worked upon and works.

CHAPTER VI

THE ARTIST

SOMEWHERE in the abysm of prehistoric time we may imagine a potter looking with dissatisfaction at the vessel he had moulded. It was finished and ready for the fire, but it seemed to need something more. A sharp stick was lying near. Picking it up, he scratched as evenly as he could a zigzag around the shoulder of his pot. He was the first decorative artist.

Perhaps about the same time—we have no reason for thinking it either earlier or later—a neolithic hunter was scratching the outline of a stag on the bone handle of his flint knife. Perhaps he was merely doing so because he thought it would bring good luck in hunting. All the same, he was the first representative artist.

These two remote ancestors of the modern artist were starting competitive activities of the most interesting sort. Sometime a representative artist was to paint or inscribe the silhouette of a beast on a pot. From that moment what had been flat pattern was to have a tendency to assume plastic effect. Far later, when the representative artist had achieved plastic effect, he was to give himself much pains to retain in such effects the sense of flat pattern. And the decorative artist also was sooner or later to feel that his pattern must seem plastic, must become to the eye a relief.

Out of these attempts to combine endeavors essentially alien was to arise in both branches the most unexpected problems, compromises, failures, triumphs. The whole course of the graphic arts was, had there been a prehistoric critic, already predictable. It was to be, like the first decorative pattern, a zigzag, for the adjustment of the claims of a decoration on a flat surface to seem flat with those of the representation of a solid object to seem plastic—this adjustment admitted only of infinite experimentation and not of any ultimate reconciliation. In potentiality, Bonnat and Puvis were already present when first the dilemma was felt.

And it was ultimately to apply to all the arts though bearing more heavily on some than on others. Musician, poet, architect, sculptor were to think of their respective arts as requiring merely an agreeable handling of some sort of a surface or as suggesting something in the space behind a surface which should produce an illusion of plastic existence. Most artists would try to do both, with very varying success. The decorative artist would normally compose out of his own head, using nature only incidentally, so far as she served him; the representative artist would continually consult nature, would be in a broad sense an imitator, seeking to make of his work a sort of transformed nature perceivable more or less on the terms of nature itself. The problem seems to have emerged consciously in Hellas, possibly in the twilight of the Mycenæan era, possibly two or three centuries later, in Homeric times. It has ever since been, if intermittently, the main problem of the European artist. To this fundamental distinction of the artist as decorative or representative I shall not recur. The reader is begged to carry it in his mind as we consider other aspects of the artist.

Those rhythms which pervade the animate and inanimate universe evade most of us, but are vividly sensed by the artist, for they correspond to the rhythms of his own inner experience. We are all parts of the organized energies of the world, but generally unmindful of our participation. In these ordered energies the artist finds analogies with his own, finds in them a fund to which he may contribute, a source from which his own activities may be nourished and refreshed. In some artists this sense of correspondence with the whole rhythmical ongoing of things is entirely conscious. It was so with the great landscape painters of China; it was so with the great artist St. Francis, who found his kin everywhere in nature. Nine hundred years before St. Francis the Chinese poet Lu Yün wrote—the translation is Arthur Waley's—

"My spirit is tuned to the spring season:
At the fall of the year there is autumn in my heart,
Thus imitating cosmic changes
My cottage becomes a universe."

In some such sense, and generally through unconscious activities, does the artist live in the whole of things, with the result that his work is a microcosm. Naturally the great artist is here in mind, and the whole in which he lives is not to be thought of mystically, but in terms of those energies of the universal rhythm which actually knock at his gates.

It is this sensitiveness of rapport with surrounding activities that constitutes the superiority of the artist—his glory, his capacity as a seer which was lauded as early as Aristotle. And this impressionability of the artist may be also his burden of loneliness and maladjustment to the ordinary concerns of living. Some three hundred years before Boccaccio had announced to the dawning modern world that

the poet was a seer, the Chinese poet, Su Tung-p'o, petu-
lantly resented the distinction. Mr. Waley translates him
thus:

> "Families when a child is born
> Want it to be intelligent.
> I, through intelligence,
> Having wrecked my whole life,
> Only hope the baby will prove
> Ignorant and stupid.
> Then he will crown a tranquil life
> By becoming a Cabinet Minister."

It is this paradox that the artist, who is admittedly the most
representative of men, the fullest expression of our human
intelligence and dignity, is often of men the most isolated
and unhappy—it is this paradox which must occupy us.

It should be clear that the artist is naturally happy in
that world of certitude and order which is his work. Surely
a Théodore Rousseau, who longed for a picture so taxing
that with its completion his heart should cease to beat,
enjoyed the stern rapture of the struggle. Where the artist
suffers is in the frustration of his work through outer circumstances beyond his control. A few great artists have
managed happily to build their world that should be
within the world that is—a Giotto, a Raphael, a Goethe;
more have not. Aeschylus, Dante, Milton, Shakespeare,
Molière, Pascal, Michelangelo, Rembrandt, Beethoven,—
one does not think of these as happy men. Every mode of
life has its price, and the price of aspiring to live in the
whole is discontent with that fractional living which is the
lot of a bread-winning world. For the many artists who

are chiefly craftsmen, the conflict is often not acute; for the great artist it frequently is.

For well over two thousand years we know how men regarded the artist. During most of this time he merely had the standing of an exceptionally skilful and resourceful craftsman. In the widely scattered great periods of art, there was a tendency to think of the artist as quite different from the craftsman—as a super-man, a seer, a magician. Greece and China will agree in assigning a kind of supernatural capacity to their great poets and painters. Boccaccio, in the apology for poetry in the preface to his *Genealogies of the Gods,* revived this conception, and it fairly stood fast to our own times, which have advanced the counter-theory that the artist is merely a conspicuous example of nervous maladjustment, technically a victim of hyperaesthesia which expresses itself, as all neuroses do, in various abnormalities and eccentricities.

Artist biography can be abundantly cited for either of these polar characterizations. Great artists have been exemplary citizens, model husbands and fathers, good business men; and great artists have also been, much more rarely to be sure, wastrels, drunkards, drug addicts, libertines. There is no record of any great artist, unless Charles Méryon and Vincent van Gogh be regarded as such, who was actually insane, but there are plenty of instances of good artists who were either habitually deranged or lived on the border line of insanity. With artists I have had a considerable acquaintance. I have known those who had qualities of the seer—La Farge, Vedder and George Barnard. Highly intellectual and merely clever artists have come my way, and also very stupid artists. Among artists

I have found aggressive conceit and appealing modesty; sobriety and chronic alcoholism; extraordinary practicality and general slipshodness. All this makes me slow to accept any single formulation of the character of the artist.

As a starting point, we may assume that the view of the artist as a seer, having held its own for centuries, cannot be wholly devoid of truth, while we shall feel that the view of the artist as a neurotic, being of yesterday, has still its way to make in the critical world. Here it is instructive to note that Vasari, who told quite ruthlessly all the truth he knew about over a hundred contemporary artists, makes no bones of their foibles, frailties and vices. He thinks of these as interesting bits, and as really having nothing to do with anybody's art. If Vasari, being no psychologist, understressed the relations between the artist's character and his work, modern psychology perhaps stresses these relations unduly. The truth seems to be that the artist, like all trained professionals, functions *qua* artist in a sort of better self with which an ordinary personal self may have rather little to do. Thus Charles Baudelaire was pitifully maladjusted and prone to devastating vices. Something of this passed into his poetry; nothing of it, into his prose criticism, which is a model of delicate good sense and of unclouded moral vision. We do not after all require our banker to be chaste. It is enough if he be able and honest. Vincent van Gogh painted as well when he was in the asylum as he did before his overt mental breakdown.

So even if it be true, and I believe it far from proved, that statistically there are more mad artists than mad hatters, the fact would seem to me of small importance, for the artist necessarily creates not with his weakness but with his strength—at his highest point of sanity and efficiency. All that is true of the artist as neurotic seems to me to be that his nervous balance is unusually sensitive. But such oversensitiveness is the indispensable condition of his successful activity. It summons the compensations and stabilizations which make him in his own work perhaps the best balanced of men. He may not be able to keep a checkbook, but he can carry through to completion processes the delicate organization and complexity of which would stagger any expert bookkeeper.

By long-standing common consent, the distinguishing capacity of the artist is a vivid imagination directed towards the understanding of a certain sort of meanings and the embodiment thereof in a certain type of forms. In treating the imagination one is tempted to fall back on Coleridge's classic and eloquent definition. But I think the matter calls for a more modern, more psychological formulation which with many misgivings I shall now undertake.

For me the imagination is merely the capacity which sees and multiplies relations in their aspect of interest and value. For most of us the area of relatedness is very small—that of our practical concerns; for the artist the area of relatedness is very large. Everything he experiences tends to organize itself by analogy and correspondence into groups, and these groups generally develop unexpected interrelations. He lives in constant expectation of the extensions of such correlations—in a world that, being always open and flexible, is progressively becoming of a wider and richer orderliness. This capacity to organize experience rather than that of image making is the essential gift of the imagination, though the artist is also more prone to see in images than is the layman. It is this breadth of apposite reference which allies the artist with the creative scientist, the inventor, the great organizer of any sort, just as on the purely executive side he has kinship with all men of high physical and mental dexterity—the surgeon, the tennis champion, the successful yachting skipper. I need hardly add that while this correlating activity may and often does work on the conscious level, it is essentially a gift of or from the unconscious. The poet is mostly born, and to a very limited degree made.

On the other hand, no great work of art makes itself entirely in the unconscious. The first and apparently chaotic assembling of possible raw materials is consciously made. The artist prudently treasures up what he knows he may sometime need. The process has been tellingly illustrated by Professor Lowes in his elaborate study of those notebooks of Coleridge which underlie *The Ancient Mariner* and *Kubla Khan*. Here we may follow the most esoteric workings of the poet's mind; and in the final shaping of the work of art conscious choice and rejection enter actively. Without them no notable work of art seems possible. We may follow this ultimate working of consciousness in Coleridge's revisions of *The Ancient Mariner*.

We have recently had under national investigation a number of great captains of industry and finance. What must have struck any attentive follower of these inquests is the narrowness of the highly specialized imagination of our leaders in the practical activities. Outside their customary adjustments, many of them betrayed an astonishing degree of infantilism. With the most usual and urgent ethical and social issues they simply had no means of coping

—could not frame a suitable evasion or a seemly lie. Now such people are merely very common people promoted by luck or highly specialized endeavor, generally by both, to a rather casual prominence. Like the common man, they live in a very small world which is tightly organized mostly by use and wont. Outside of this little world of small heart's and big head's desire, lies in a blur the rest of the world and the cosmos. The blur cannot be negotiated, indeed it is seldom even glimpsed; it is wished away.

In the case of the artist, the organized world is much larger in area; it tends to invade and diminish the surrounding blur, which is not wished away but confronted and through progressive organization drawn into the ordered area. To extend his bounds is a problem accepted by the good artist of every rank; to maintain his narrow bounds is too often the customary endeavor of the captain of industry and finance, as it is of his little brother, the forgotten man.

It follows, then, that the wider the interests of the artist without dispersion or loss of intensity, the richer will be his art. It is well that so far as his specialized activities permit he should share the feelings of his public. Here the adjustment is highly individual. It was advantageous to Delacroix that he thrilled to the revolution of 1830. To Corot it was equally advantageous that he faced the revolution of 1848 with a bewildered indifference. The law is that the artist should turn these extrinsic interests to his own creative ends and not overindulge them for their own sake. With fine sententiousness André Gide has expressed the real import of this issue:

"The artist should put his work in order, and not the world which surrounds him." ("C'est *son œuvre* que l'artiste doit ordonner, et non le monde qui l'entoure.")

What we divine through the work of art is rarely its creator's character in its totality; it is rather that aspect of his character which he regards as most worthy, which he enlists in his choicest activity. One may say that, as he creates, he banishes his smaller and merely idiosyncratic self and puts on some more central and generally valid self, as Buffon put on formal raiment before taking his pen in hand. The works of Poe tell us almost nothing about the ill-fated dipsomaniac; those of Oscar Wilde, very little about the homosexual in him. We get the artist about as he wished us to get him, and we get him only through sensitive inference from his work. Hence the artist's way of working is the only aspect of his total experience and activity that really concerns deeply the student of esthetics.

What I am to write about the artist's way of working will amplify and to a certain extent repeat what I have already sketched in the chapters on The Esthetic Transaction and The Work of Art. The artist has an innate will to create which in part causes, in part may be caused by a constant uprush of images or schemes of things that may be made. I think this swarm of themes seeking a form is invariable, hence that the artist is naturally prolific, and in the few cases in which he is not, we have to do with exceptional personal hesitations or with badly competing activities—a Laurence Housman or Leonardo da Vinci occur as instances under these two heads.

These mental images or schemes seldom have to be sought out; they readily emerge from the well stored subconsciousness. As they appear, they are accepted gladly or with cautious reservations or are rejected. Here the preliminary sifting or censorship may be instinctive or conscious, or a choice made at one level may be confirmed or vetoed at another. My judgment may insist that the exclusion made instinctively is unsound, or my instinct may rebel against an acceptance made by my judgment. In such differences it is instinct that is the safest guide and usually prevails. In a far higher degree than the layman, the artist has a sense of what is makable, and in this matter is less dependent on actual trial and error. He better foresees the whole process of making.

Now these possible themes may be merely felt and thought of in disembodied fashion, or they may from their inception begin to assume a provisional form in the ultimate material. We should then have at the outset a partially materialized theme, a sort of embryo, seeking elaboration and definition. This I think is usually the case. It is an adumbration of a painted picture that haunts the painter; of a statue in a chosen material, the sculptor; of a musical composition with phrases and motives at loose ends, the composer; fragmentary acts, scenes, dialogues, the playwright—an incipiently organized whole needing further organization. The original vision I believe is rarely a mere scheme at any stage. From the beginning it normally has a certain concreteness and a tendency towards the ultimate structure.

At this stage creative practice differs sharply. With certain artists, embodiment of the theme in the rightly formed material seems to me almost effortless; with other artists there must be an intervening period of travail. The whole scheme must be tested in provisional form or material; details must be worked out, studied, accepted, rejected, adjusted, readjusted, corrected, while even the apparently completed work must still be subjected to delicate retouching by the Horatian file. The great compositions of Mozart grew into their complex, lovely form without committing anything to paper, without trying anything on a musical instrument, without false steps or even hesitations. The great musical compositions of Beethoven involved the most painful trial and error, revisions, eliminations. Corot in his maturity painted as the bird sang; his friend, Théodore Rousseau, agonized over his slightest picture. Goethe wrote:

"I let objects act passively in me; I observe their action; and I try to render it truthfully; that is the whole secret of what men have agreed to call genius."

But Leopardi put his poems through the most drastic revision. Byron threw off the great poem *Don Juan* in the intervals of four years which saw no less than eight other long poems or dramas. Dante was at least ten years concerned with the *Divine Comedy* producing on an average a canto every thirty days—an amount of writing which would have been the task of fewer hours for Byron.

Were poetic justice in charge of the work of art, the labored work ought to be the more valuable. Here we lack a measuring stick. One feels, or the contrary, that the music of Beethoven is more valuable than that of Mozart; the poetry of Dante, than that of Byron, but it would be difficult to prove the validity of the preference. Again, disconcertingly, much-labored works often are as easy in style as works wrought with ease. Nothing in Mozart is more gracious and accessible than Beethoven's Seventh Symphony. All that can be safely asserted is that the work that has been elaborated through travail will usually have a denser richness of every sort than that which attains its form without effort. Whether such greater density of richness implies higher artistic merit—personally I believe it does—can hardly be demonstrated and is best left to individual taste.

In books on esthetics it is customary to treat creative activities—certain polar differences of which we have been considering—as first times. As such activities occur, they are almost never first times, being rather a part of a series of such activities. Thus each new activity is profoundly conditioned not only by the previous creative activities of the artist but also by such activities of earlier artists as have commanded his admiration and approval, hence have suggested imitation or emulation. Into what is becoming a new work of art passes much of the artist's own past and much of an older past of other artists. No work of art is uninfluenced by the going taste or tastes, whether by conformity or by revulsion. Hence, despite many estheticians to the contrary, taste as a social and collective experience, is a relevant and necessary part of any complete study of esthetics.

Nothing more clearly marks off the great artist from the throng of his merely passable fellows than his intelligent reverence of tradition. In choosing traditions there is as much skill as in picking friends. If you take up readily with such casual and exotic acquaintances as Persian miniatures, Indian textiles, Byzantine mosaics, Japanese prints—if you do this and have talent, you may become a Henri

Matisse. A Delacroix, a Mary Cassatt, a Renoir will wish to
assimilate a richer and more coherent tradition—that of
the Renaissance. A Rembrandt will make something rich
and personal out of the apparently unlikely precedent of a
Caravaggio's tenebrism, and from the same traditional
source a Velasquez will draw very rich and personal novelties. A Dante is inexplicable without a Virgil and St.
Thomas Aquinas; a Shakespeare, without a Kyd and Marlowe; a Thackeray, without a Fielding; a Wagner, without
a Beethoven. All the greater expressions of art imply such
an apostolic succession, and the best art when out of such
succession is generally qualified by eccentricity, hence is
well below the first order. On this lower level survive after
all notable artists—the Brownings, Walt Whitmans, the
Courbets and Monets; the Debussys and Scriabins; the
Henry Jameses and the Prousts of this happily much varied
world.

Concerning the traditional attitude, the late Kenyon Cox
eloquently wrote:

"It would have each new work connect itself in the mind
of him who sees it with all the noble and lovely works of
the past, bringing them to his memory and making their
beauty and charm a part of the beauty and charm of the
work before him. It does not deny originality and indi-
viduality—they are as welcome as inevitable. It does not
consider tradition as immutable or set rigid bounds to invention. But it desires that each new presentation of truth
and beauty shall show us the old truth and the old beauty,
seen only from a different angle and colored by a different
medium. It wishes to add link by link to the chain of
tradition, but it does not wish to break the chain."

The writer of these weighty words illustrated in his own person the difficulties of the modern traditionalist. Kenyon Cox never fully made the transition from bad executive habits acquired at the Ecole des Beaux Arts to the traditions of the great Venetians whom he deeply admired and understood. And the growth of the museums and the wide extension of the history of art dangle before the artist in every field the most perplexing variety of traditions. How find his own? How avoid a shifting eclecticism? The task is far from simple, yet it remains the essential task of the good artist to exercise such a critique of tradition. For an innovator like Masaccio, Giotto represented the only thinkable worthy tradition; for Raphael, passing beyond his master Perugino, to betake himself to such guides as Masaccio, Leonardo and the antique was inevitable. Even he nearly shipwrecked under emulation of Michelangelo's alien genius.

But the modern painter, sculptor, author, musical composer with the whole backward-reaching panorama of their respective arts before them—how shall they find their own in the past? How hold their course among exotic traditions—oriental painting, far-eastern and Negro sculpture, oriental literature and music? Until the new way of judging is found, as I am sure it will be, it behooves us to be tolerant of much eclecticism and trial and error, which may after all prepare the way for a future richer synthesis.

To the traditionalist, the rebel artist is the natural contrast. In quantity he is quite a recent phenomenon, a product generally, as I have elsewhere tried to show, of inevitable maladjustment to a rapidly changing social order, of isolation and undeserved hardship. The self-righteous Hebrew marvelled that the heathen raged. They possibly raged largely because of the Hebrew habit of smiting them hip and thigh in Jehovah's name, and the modern artist can be forgiven a certain resentment against a world which smites him no less damagingly, if negatively, through misunderstanding and neglect.

There is, however, a good and a bad rebel attitude. The good attitude generally consists in repudiating a nearby bad tradition for an older and better one—in short the salutary rebellion is usually a Renaissance, and a Renaissance is just a restudy of nature in the light of a suitable tradition. In quitting Delaroche's atelier Millet was a sort of rebel, but he quit in order to interpret nature with the aid of Correggio and Michelangelo. In rejecting the dryness of the eighteenth century tradition, a Chateaubriand fortifies himself from the fuller eloquence of a Bossuet and from consultation of the richer Latin tradition generally.

The rebels who have successfully gone on their own without consulting earlier tradition are singularly few. In painting I can think only of Caravaggio, and he drew much from such apparently alien exemplars as Giorgione and, probably, Leonardo da Vinci. He represented also a needed reaction against the far-fetched and limited elegance of the Eclectics. From time to time such rebels are needed, but they play their useful part at a pathfinder's sacrifice. What justifies Caravaggio is less his own painting, impressive as much of it is, than that made under his influence—Rembrandt's, Velasquez's, that of the best baroque masters of Naples and Venice. In short, for one rebellion of this heroic and successful sort, there are thousands which are cheap and nasty gestures of so many maladjusted individuals.

Oddly a heroic rebel like Courbet, who after all drew chiefly from the old tradition of Spanish realism, may as a person act like a small and negligible rebel, which again illustrates the fact that the artist creates from a sort of higher self.

I return from this digression on artist psychology to the more concrete theme of the artist's way of working. The luxuriant growth and weeding out of associations as the work of art progresses we have already studied in the chapter on The Esthetic Transaction. We may then proceed to the consideration of the artist who works with much conscious revision and through manifold trial and error. Such a procedure postpones the merging of the theme with the ultimate material, and as well involves trying out the scheme as a whole and its essential features in materials of a provisional sort—studies and composition sketches of whatever kind which clarify the form before it is committed to the material. Classical examples of this sort would be the mass of experimental notes underlying any great composition of Beethoven, the great body of notes and trial drafts for any novel of Flaubert's, or, even better, the scores of figure and composition studies for Leonardo's unfinished "Epiphany," which have been skilfully arranged and elucidated in the excellent book of Jens Thys. Before the work was thought of in paint, there was an incredible amount of thinking with the quill pen. In the final executive activity we may think of the compositional form as dominating the material. It was perhaps the difficulty of such domination rather than Leonardo's habitual procrastination which forced him to leave the work unfinished. In the underpainting he had achieved a density and richness that in the finished painting might have been restless and confusing. Leonardo perhaps did well in letting well enough alone.

Where the form, with little preliminary study, is worked out directly in the material, the material tends to dominate. Such is the case with all the painter-like painters, the great Venetians, Velasquez, Rubens, Frans Hals, Delacroix, Renoir, or rather the material contributes more positively to the total effect. This is true of all artists in whom the craftsman is strong. From the first they think about the material. One can imagine the polished couplets of an Alexander Pope waiting for an antithesis to fill them.

Whether the creative activity begins with a theme which invites a form, or with a form which invites a theme has been variously argued. It seems to me it may begin either way, but that it begins most reasonably and profitably with a theme. There were plenty of undergraduates in my day who had up their sleeve a sonnet waiting for a content, and there are probably today certain undergraduates who carry in their poet's scrip some scheme of free verse similarly hoping for a meaning, but such sonnets and such free verse are rarely memorable. In general, where an empty form is the beginning of the creative process, its end is some sort of mannerism. The substance is drawn into the form in an arbitrary way, is not wholly assimilated. The scheme imposes itself unduly as a scheme. Obvious examples are the prose of John Lyly the Euphuist, the lapidary closed couplets of Pope at his worst, the studied simplicity of Wordsworth consciously employing folk speech, the average sentimental song, the trip-hammer prose style of Macaulay, most of the prettier writing of

Mr. Cabell, all of the painting of Bronzino, save his portraiture, much of the painting of Whistler and Arthur B. Davies. It will be seen that I am not herding together all mannerists for wholesale condemnation. Among the chronic or occasional mannerists, who are great artists, I recall only El Greco and William Blake. No one would deny that substance has come richly to the rescue of their manner.

Among the legacies from the past that the artist has to appraise for acceptance or for renunciation, none is more serious than the going conventions of his craft. For example a landscape view is ordinarily tipped towards us so that we may see much that is in actual vision foreshortened away and may receive a satisfactory impression of height. Even in our days of making all things new, few landscape painters eschew this convention, and they do so at their peril. Such conventions are generally means of attaining esthetic distance, of establishing a difference between the thing represented and the thing as seen. These conventions rest upon an entirely unconscious sense of the fitting, upon the need of transforming an appearance or an occurrence into conformity with the nature of a material, upon the general principle that the work of art for its best effect wants a certain isolation. Until the contrary is proved, such conventions are to be regarded as respectable. It is better that the base of a statue should be of the same material as the statue itself. A picture looks better in a frame, and despite recent experiments, in a frame that is not an extension of the picture. When a rare piece of porcelain is promoted from the china closet to the collector's vitrine, we properly celebrate its promotion as a work of art by putting it on a base.

Any change of the convention involves a serious change of esthetic effect. For example the modern still-life with the apples and bowls spilling off the table towards you—it is after all just the way you see apples and bowls as you sit at the table. The effect is exciting and perhaps disturbing since it involves so little convention of arrangement. Think how the Dutch masters of still-life and the incomparable Chardin staged their little worlds. For your convenience the table is raised to a level at which, unless you squat painfully, it never actually is—at the level of your eye. The effect is of security, stability; it is highly tranquillizing. If you want your still-life on terms of domestic serenity, that is the way to paint it. If you want it on terms of excitement and the unexpected, then paint it with a minimum of convention as nearly as possible as you see it. That will abolish the old distance, bring it nearer to you. It is a question of what you like.

Of course this problem of the conventions and of distance which I have treated coolly in descriptive terms, is a most urgent and vital issue for the artist. If he conform too supinely to the body of conventions, he may not achieve originality; if he throw over any or all of the going conventions, he will pretty certainly make a fool of himself. Remains the glittering off chance, usually a will-o'-the-wisp or fool's fire, that he may start a needed revolution.

What should be the attitude of the artist towards nature has for over two thousand years been the chief theme of esthetic criticism. From Aristotle down to yesterday, there has been a general agreement that the artist should be a

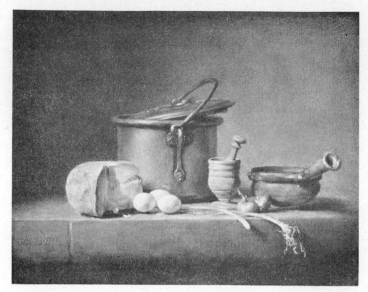

Chardin. Still Life

J. v. Ruysdael. Winter

Cézanne. Still Life

Cézanne. Provençal Landscape

Moscow

selective imitator of nature. Of course such a dogma applied chiefly to literature, painting, and sculpture. It was and still would be hard to show that the architect imitates natural appearances, or for that matter the musician. The application of the doctrine of imitation was really limited to the popular equation "poetry is like painting"—*ut pictura poesis*. For literature, painting and sculpture the doctrine of imitation, if genially interpreted, still seems valid. Surely the repertory of the man of letters and that of the painter and sculptor is largely drawn from his observation of man and nature—from something lived in relations with something outside himself.

Of course the catch in the maxim *ars est imitatio naturae* lies in the word nature. Does it mean natural appearances? Does it rather mean the principles of nature? If it means, as all defenders of the doctrine from Aristotle down insisted, that only the more orderly, normal, and seemly aspects of nature—*belle nature*—may be imitated, then we are begging the whole question. Who knows what these aspects are? Is there a code, or may the artist choose for himself? If so, when we speak of selective imitation, we have said nothing that will guide the artist or art lover. Such considerations have completely discredited the old doctrine of imitation with modern critics. All the same, the fact that till today virtually without exception all artists have regarded themselves as imitators of nature, have regarded the truthfulness of their imitation as their chief merit—this general acceptance of the law suggests that, with its obvious dialectical shortcomings, it does after all correspond to something deep in the artist's soul.

Winslow Homer, who habitually painted in the open air, was once asked if he ever changed anything he observed. Shocked at the mere possibility, he denied emphatically that he ever changed anything. As a matter of fact, Winslow Homer made freely and ably those transpositions and simplifications which are proper to the good landscape painter. A little comparison of his sketches with his finished pictures would prove the point abundantly. He also painted from memory much that could not be done from nature. What is important in the case is that Winslow Homer was entirely unconscious of the transformations he instinctively made—thought himself a faithful transcriber of nature.

Such an attitude is usual with good painters, and if you show them a feature they have painted but could not possibly have seen, they will generally answer that they saw it that way. This admiring humility towards nature, this unawareness of the value or even of the existence of his own transforming processes is probably the best attitude for any painter. For one of a certain sophistication, and of course many painters, as artists generally, are introverts, the attitude is impossible, and their consciousness of their own creative distortions in design brings very serious dangers of mannerism. Returning to the painter who is lucky enough not to imitate nature while thinking he does so, it is of the slightest importance whether he paint from nature or from memory. To be a merely competent painter—or for that matter to be a competent artist in any field—the memory must be highly developed, and no painter who has not worked much and faithfully from nature, possesses the elements of his craft. The power and fertility of the

Renaissance painters as a class lies in the fact that they were so highly trained that they could represent almost anything from memory. On this basis the good painters readily achieved style; the poor painters, at least an able mannerism. Evidently the painter who has difficulty in interpreting actual appearances in terms of design will do well to work from memory. Here we may recall Cézanne's pathetic ambition to make Poussins after nature—an impossible emprise, since in the presence of nature the quantity and quality of Poussin's reflection is out of the question. It wants four walls. Unhappily Cézanne had inherited the theory and practice of the French schools,—that one can only paint with something before him. The art of the museums which he studied devoutly and from which he learned much, failed to teach him its chief lesson.

Now I by no means decry the admirable paintings that have been made in the face of nature. The ink drawings of Claude are preferred by many fine critics to his paintings. The drawings were made swiftly, outdoors; the paintings carefully and slowly, in the studio. The really important matter is merely that the painter needs continually to consult nature; whether or not he consult her brush in hand, is of no importance. Of highest importance is his general attitude towards nature—as something conveniently furthering his talent; as something reverenced as far greater than any capacity of his own.

Such humility is the master trait of the great artist. Proud or humble as a man, when he deals with man or nature, he feels he is dealing with something greater than himself. Here arrogant geniuses, the Dantes, Miltons, Lord Byrons, join in respect for their theme. They seek to express its greatness, never regarding it as an occasion for expressing a greatness of their own. It is no mere conventionality when Dante implores the aid of higher powers as he begins each of the three poems of the *Divine Comedy*. It is this profound sense of nature as inspiration and goal which distinguishes the true artist from the mere decorator, for whom nature is something from which one may pick cleverly, an opportunity for exploiting one's own ingenuity. The reciprocal attitude of nature towards the painter was admirably suggested by perhaps the most intellectual and self-sufficing painter who ever lived, Leonardo da Vinci, when he wrote that the artist is the child of nature—owing her the veneration due a parent, receiving from her not commands, but solace and unfailing encouragement.

I recall once reading in a guest book after a great number of entries to the effect that the guest had enjoyed himself immensely the entry of a guest who had enjoyed his host and hostess immensely. Here the dilemma of the artist is suggested: shall he be most interested in his themes, or most interested in himself? Shall he look up to nature, or look down at her as a serviceable auxiliary, and up at himself? The character and grade of the artist are pretty well determined by his answer to these questions. If he puts nature first, he will look at his own position as ambassadorial; he has the proud function of representing and extolling her. If he puts himself first, his duty is solely that of self-expression with such aid or hindrance as inferior nature may provide. In the former case, while he thinks he is imitating nature, he will instinctively so transform the appearance that he will find a style that is his own; in

the latter case, he will consciously exploit his own idiosyncrasy, and the result will be not style but mannerism.

In short, style is normally a by-product of a deep concern
with something else—a natural appearance to be faithfully
represented; the thinking and acting of persons to be understood and to be made tellingly clear; the building to be
made fit for its use and worthy of its purpose; the play
to express the full meaning of the action; the symphony to
give utmost definition and richness to its themes and to en-
gage the full power and variety of the orchestra; the statuary group to commemorate the sage or hero worthily—
it is in such fashion that have come into the world the
great Ruysdaels, the novels of a Tolstoy, the cathedrals,
the music of a MacDowell, the rare triumphs of a Saint
Gaudens, as in the Shaw Memorial.

Similarly the other procedure—to think of your theme
chiefly in terms of your own skill, to aim consciously at
style, will generally produce only mannerism. A style is
reached from the inside out; a manner is applied cosmet-
ically. Naturally the manner may have its own charm and
distinction. One thinks of the slighter exquisiteness of a
Whistler, of the more joyously audacious Sargents, of the
festal architecture of a Stanford White, of the sensitive wit
of an Oscar Wilde, of the languid poignancy of an Anatole
France.

Such commonplace observations after all need to be
made, for an entire generation of painters is being brought
up in the deliberate research for style. As a reaction against
a period in which narrow ideals of vision and technique
had produced a painting completely without style, the
modernistic endeavor to recreate style by taking thought

may seem justified, and it may be hoped that ultimately some good may come from the onesided effort. Meanwhile the waste of good talent along individualistic bypaths is lamentable. The truth remains that the artist's highroad to style is through a deeper concern with the appearances of nature and the activities of his fellow men.

Here it should be frankly admitted that the good artist's outward orientation towards nature is, psychologically considered, in the nature of a beneficent illusion. What is all important for art is the disposition of the soul of the artist; nature is merely the warehouse from which he draws the materials for a construction wholly his own. But here we only meet once more the Saviour's paradox, that he who loseth his life shall save it. An initial and complete abnegation is the condition of all great creation as it is of all great appreciation. In whatever art, it is essential that its maker should work worshipfully.

In every great artist, John La Farge once wrote, "there is a humble craftsman who knows his trade and likes it." In general this is true. The artist normally likes to handle his tools and shape his material. Yet there have been great artists in whom the love of the craft was merely sufficient. Only for a moment, in the painting of the Camera della Segnatura, and in a handful of portraits, can Raphael be thought of as a great craftsman. His craft always does its work, but his meaning is such as calls for an utterance rather lucid than rich. Leonardo plainly loved the quill pen and the silver point, conceived and drew with unceasing zest. But his great unfinished pictures, his scanty production, his unduly prolonged execution—all suggest that actual painting was irksome to him. Elihu Vedder rightly

maintained that while Leonardo was unquestionably a
very great artist, it was absurd to think of him as a great
painter, as Titian or Rubens was. The late Abbott Thayer
affords an even clearer instance of maladjustment between
the artist and the craftsman. Mastering early, under
Gérôme, the official style of Paris, he practised it brilliantly
for a few years, then finding it unfit for the sort of monu-
mental ideality he sought to express, he renounced the
French style utterly. The formation of a new style gave
him infinite trouble and drove him to the most unhandy
expedients. He would paint a picture into a botch, then
have the botch copied and corrected by an assistant under
his instructions, and finally paint the finished picture over
the assistant's work. Possibly Thayer's incessant study of
protective coloration in nature was a serious and competing
activity. If so, his case would more or less parallel that of
Leonardo da Vinci. One of our greatest American painters,
Albert Ryder, undoubtedly loved to load his little panels
with varnish stains until the moon shone and the waves
danced, but this year-long labor was as far removed as can
be imagined from anything like dextrous craftsmanship.

Since at all stages the experience of beauty, whether
creative or receptive implies a very delicate balancing of
opposites, it is easy for the artist to miss the equilibrium
between his imaginative and executive self. It is possible
to have too much craftsmanship or too little. I know a
painter who worked admirably in the Beaux-arts style and
exhibited successfully in the Salon at seventeen. He never
found a meaning for his technique, wisely refused to keep
on painting and devoted himself to other artistic activities.
On the other hand, Jacques Louis David could paint much

more richly than he ordinarily did. A little sketch in oils of Marat has by good judges been taken for a Goya. But David found a somewhat bleak and thin handling really suited his great official pictures and his almost cruelly defined portraiture. His style was of the essence and his pictures would have been not better but worse if executed with the colorful and fluent brilliancy of his best pupil, Baron Gros.

Indeed the greatest artists are only exceptionally the finest craftsmen. They usually keep handling in a secondary place. The perfect balance which we find in a Titian or Rubens or Rembrandt is quite rare. And the finest craftsmen are rarely the greatest painters. It is impossible to paint better than Hals, Velasquez, Veronese, Tiepolo, or, for that matter, more brilliantly than Fortuny and Boldini —great painters some of these artists are, but none, the greatest.

Perhaps the most delicate professional problem of the artist is to form fit executive habits without immobilizing his expression. What he has already done properly conditions what he does, but this necessary conditioning of his habits should be a support and not a fetter. On the face of it, the artist's problem is in no wise different from that of any good craftsman, but the difference is really profound. Within a few years a good cabinet maker may acquire habits of thinking and doing, which, unless style and material radically change—as wood giving way to steel for furniture— should last him a lifetime. Not so the artist.

Progress and change are the very law of his successful being. In no instance can I recall a great painter who in his maturity worked in the manner of his youth. Ingres is the nearest example, but he is perhaps not quite a great artist. Now this change and refreshing of the artist's technique is best effected by indirection, by extending the scope of his meanings until they present new technical problems. The few academic painters who as a result of reasoned conviction have abandoned the representative for the expressionistic style, have hardly made pictures justifying their tardy conversion. As the artist copes with new meanings, he will insensibly seek new and fit technical methods.

Examples abound. When Henry James is dealing chiefly with the outer life, as in such early masterpieces as *Roderick Hudson* and *The Portrait of a Lady*, his prose style will be that simple and straightforward form of expression which is proper to the novel of manners—he will have Balzac in mind and the apostolic succession of the great British novelists from Fielding to George Eliot. When he deals with the involutions of esoteric experience, as in *What Maisie Knew* and *The Golden Bowl*, his prose style, following the new meaning, will develop kindred involutions. While it is possible that a style may be so central that its application is universal—such seems to be the case with a Hawthorne and a Thackeray—generally speaking, for a novelist to end stylistically where he began evinces mental limitations and hints of mannerism. Here Anatole France and George Meredith will occur as striking examples. Where the quest for a new style is too conscious, as in the case of Flaubert, the results are at best equivocal. *The Temptation of St. Anthony* and *Salambo* are no advance on *Madame Bovary*.

In painting the situation is even more palpable. Frans Hals began with a fairly odious display of virtuosity. In the great pictures of his maturity there is a fine balance between his technique and his meaning. His attitude is still superficial—his theme chiefly the he man of Haarlem in all his glory—but the great corporation groups subordinate *bravura* to expression. The balance is perfect—the method of exhibition completely right for the meaning exhibited. As he grew old, he developed a more interpretative attitude towards the *differentia* of personality. The style changed. The broad slashes of paint were more temperately applied. They expressed no longer the sitter in his spectacular and social value, but in his unique capacity as a feeling and thinking individual. The old garden-plot gayety of color, expressing chiefly wealth and health, gave way to a sober and thoughtful representation in enriched monochrome.

Rembrandt affords an even more striking example in the shift from coruscating sensationalism in his prime, to the tender and profound interpretations of his fellow men and the persons of the Bible in his premature old age. But we need not go so far in time and place. Our own great landscape painter, George Inness, in his fifties was painting the most solid and luminous landscapes America had seen. A careful sketch from nature underlay each masterpiece. For the materiality of the scene there was the most scrupulous regard. Then, as a result of the growing mysticism which he drew from Swedenborg, the materiality of nature no longer interested him. He now saw chiefly luminous organization as pattern or self-sufficing rhythm. The actual stuff of nature is merely glimpsed as reminiscence from another once-known world. There are no studies, no reference to specific appearances; everything is improvised at white heat in the studio. The old rich areas of paint give way to sweeps of translucent varnish stains, after the fashion of washes in water colors. Now it has no importance that I think the best Innesses are the luminously solid landscapes of his maturity and not the phantasmagoric visions of his old age. What is important is that the new vision and meaning evoked a new and appropriate set of executive habits. The change was made in the grand style, as a creative artist, and not in the spirit of an ingenious and worried craftsman.

Mood the artist gets from nature, and it often constitutes a very precious feature of his work. Mood is not precisely general psychical disposition—one's humor in the sense of the medieval psychologists; it is rather the weather in which one works. No one commands it, but one may profit from it when present. It is akin to the overtones of a musical note. Middle C natural has a very different quality and effect when sung by a soprano, contralto, tenor or bass—when sounded on a violin, a guitar, a flute or a horn. Such overtones may transpire in any act of creation and pass into the work of art, bringing a peculiar exquisiteness to its appreciation. Mood seems to be rather an emotional than an intellectual orientation, hence far more constant than the mental connotation of works of art which may be most various. It may be regarded as something superadded to an expression which without it would be formally complete. It may lend enchantment to an esthetic form in itself rather neutral or even negligible.

For this reason mood is an asset for the minor artist, or for the great artist in lyrical moments. The sonnets and the romantic comedies of Shakespeare reek with mood; there is little or none in *Macbeth, King Lear, Julius Caesar.*

We may hardly speak of a mood of Homer or Aeschylus, while no one can fail to sense the tenderness of a Euripides or the pensiveness of a Virgil. In the greatest works of art there are moods rather than mood, and the tinge of the moods is relatively slight and unimportant. The work is far greater than any weather which may have attended its creation. There is a mood of Mozart, a delightful mood, but not a mood of Beethoven.

The greatest music commands moods rather than conveys mood. Any symphony requires the modulation of its themes through a more or less set series of moods which afford to the hearer varieties of tension and relaxation, thus giving fit emphasis to the supreme musical moments. Of this general nature is the comic relief in Shakespeare's tragedies. Greek tragedy got less drastically the same effective change of weather from the music and dancing of the chorus.

Mood, to repeat, is at times almost the sole asset of the minor artist, and often a very precious one. The diffused benignity and mellowness of a Sir Thomas Browne are more important than anything he has to say. We value the lyrics of a Poe or a Verlaine chiefly for their mood. Eliminate it, and little is left. There is nothing save mood in the painting of that fantastic painter Monticelli; but it is enough to make of his pictures so many lovely day dreams. There is no mood of Rubens; his prevailing athleticism is active and conscious. Mood is passive and unconscious.

Again such music as that of Tschaikowsky and Debussy is mostly mood. So is the writing of Maeterlinck and that of Anatole France. Mood again dominates the plays of Sir James Barrie and is as nearly as possible absent in those of Ibsen—I am speaking of his so-called realistic plays; his early romantic plays almost superabound in mood.

Mood while a pure gift may be used or abused. The novels of Thomas Hardy are greatly enhanced by a circumambience of a tender and understanding pessimism; those of Joseph Conrad, by a pervasive compassionate acceptance of life. On the other hand, in the novels of George Meredith there is some abuse of his crackling ironic superiority; in those of Mr. Cabell, of his sardonic playfulness.

In his moments of high seriousness the great artist transcends mood. He indulges it in his minor creation, being mindful of the Horatian wisdom of now and then taking things easy. No lyrics more abound in mood than those of Goethe, and even the austere Milton is full of mood in *Comus*. So is Dante in some of his lovelier sonnets, or Beethoven in the Seventh Symphony, for its richness of mood generally called by his fellow countrymen, *Die schoene Siebente*.

Finally mood actively wishes to be shared. Hence the contagion of mood is the quickest and most effectual means of communication between an artist and a hearer or beholder. The greatest works of art have little or no penumbra of mood, and do not seem to need it. They do not reach out for our sympathy; they proudly await an understanding to which they seem relatively indifferent.

Throughout the arts the principle holds that virtuosity may be the artist's friend or foe. Mood may enhance high endeavor, while too much dependence on mood may make high endeavor impossible. It is for the artist to fix the relation, and usually no conscious solution is possible. It is an innate tact that must settle such issues.

We have seen that the creative activities of the artist normally begin well below the level of consciousness, in that strangely half-organized welter of half-made images, half-thought thoughts, inconclusive volitions which have come down virtually unchanged from our animal origins. The artist's control, indeed anybody's control of this obscure world lies simply in what he feeds it from the consciousness. He may feed it well or ill, but it assimilates even such selected nourishment very much on its own terms. Thus is stocked an inconscient stream carrying along potential forms and meanings, precious flotsam, which constantly emerges at the level of consciousness and gives the artist so many occasions for creation.

Until lately the artist has simply accepted the beneficent fact of a contributing and cooperative subconsciousness, has rarely attempted to explore it or to make it the subject matter of his art. Now and then an artist has plied his subconsciousness with alcohol or other narcotics, in general without noteworthy esthetic result. Of the inconscient and inconsequent undercurrent of our conscious and purposive activities art for some centuries has been aware. Literature has neither neglected, nor much emphasized, the matter. Romeo's soliloquy before he buys the poison is as much stream of consciousness as anything by Joyce. Until recently it was assumed that the milling about of the unconscious personality had little interest or value and that art owed it only a kind of minor recognition, sometimes to suggest the precariousness of our conscious activities, sometimes to emphasize their value through contrast.

Then came the new psychology, and the stream of consciousness, more correctly unconsciousness, was to become

a veritable River of Doubt challenging the audacity of the
artist to discovery and exploration. The task of the artist
was no longer to feed the unconsciousness well, and hope-
fully await results; now he wished to uncover the stream
and bring to view its confused yet powerful ebullition. In
pretty much all the innovating art of this century, the
conscious investigation of the unconscious has been a major
concern.

The endeavor has given us in James Joyce's *Ulysses* admirable episodes, but hardly a great novel; Eugene
O'Neill's *Strange Interlude*; the works of Virginia Woolf,
John dos Passos and Gertrude Stein; the painting of Kan-
dinsky, Chagall and Chirico. These are not negligible
accomplishments, but their ultimate value is still in the
balance. We may be dealing rather with a fashion which
will pass as quickly as it came than with a sound revolutionary movement. I may easily be wrong, but the stream-
of-consciousness group look to me like Kerenskys and not
like Lenins.

In the long run, only the kind of experiment that is
actually being made will prove or disprove the value of the
unconscious as subject matter of art. So far these experiments give me no great hope of any considerable enrichment of art from this source, and for these reasons:

1) It is a commonplace of psychiatry that any deliberate
tampering with the unconscious involves heavy risk of
nervous disorders. It is, to be sure, a risk any good artist
might cheerfully incur for the offchance of a masterpiece.
2) But it is at least theoretically doubtful if so highly
organized a product as any masterpiece of art can be made
through the contemplation of the disorderly or half organ-

ized. 3) While the goings-on of the subconsciousness are a fruitful field for psychological research, the actual human or esthetic values of the subconsciousness as such seem really to be very small. It is perhaps only in an auxiliary or ancillary relation to the consciousness that the unconscious activities first assume value. 4) If the more or less random and aimless movements of the subconsciousness are indeed to be the main theme of the arts, then the arts must forego the old sanction of relative values, for where everything is equally valuable, there will be no value whatever. 5) The most promising new movements in painting, and I think also in literature, are already moving away from the stream of consciousness to the more solid ground of an objectivity guided by judgment.

Such are reasons for thinking the artist on the whole does well to let his subconsciousness and that of his fellow men alone. The subconsciousness has hardly gained attractiveness from the inordinate amount of publicity it has recently enjoyed. And incidentally much that passes for audacious exploration of the subliminal depths is nothing of the sort, but rather a deliberate twisting into unrecognizability of quite familiar conscious patterns, is rather a trick than a discovery. Like many a good cat's cradler, the stream-of-consciousness artist generally knows what he is about. The fact that he is at the height of the fashion, and so promptly, is suggestive. The great seminal and revolutionary movements in the arts have not made their way so rapidly; the fashions have. The whole issue must ultimately be settled by results submitted to judgment.

An American artist in letters who had both achieved and failed greatly, Herman Melville, has given to the artist's problem of adjustment the most poignant expression, in the poem,

ART

"In placid hours well pleased we dream
Of many a brave unbodied scheme.
But form to lend, pulsed life create,
What unlike things must meet and mate:
A flame to melt—a wind to freeze;
Sad patience—joyous energies;
Humility—yet pride and scorn;
Instinct and study; love and hate;
Audacity—reverence. These must mate,
And fuse with Jacob's mystic heart,
To wrestle with the angel—Art."

CHAPTER VII

THE ART LOVER

THE central figure in esthetics is really the art lover. In the realm of beauty everything proceeds from him and ultimately returns to him. For the artist is only the art lover become creative, while the work of art finds its chief reason for being in the art lover's experience of beauty. Anything like continuity of appreciation, taste as a social and historical factor, depends on the unfailing succession of generation after generation of sensitive and discriminating lovers of art.

Indulge for a moment the fancy of a world exclusively peopled by artists. There would be no continuity of taste; most of the art of the past would be promptly immobilized, for with his own work, once finished, the artist is usually only mildly concerned, while with the art of his contemporaries his sympathy is usually very limited, and of the art of the past he normally loves chiefly that which furthers his own. Which is only to say that the creative attitude is naturally more concentrated and narrow than that of appreciation. One is obviously freer in what he enjoys than in what he makes. In a world of artists, the work of art would be stillborn.

Any characterization of the art lover must be of a sort too general to be very instructive; for of art lovers there are infinite varieties by nature's ordinance, and these natal varieties are confusingly multiplied by an education and discipline which are different in every individual. We must beware, then, of setting up a typical esthetic man in that air-tight cabinet where the once venerated economic man is slowly falling into dust.

Without attempting any complete analysis, some leading traits of the art lover may profitably be suggested. The crowning virtue of the good art lover is a pretty rare, hence probably distinguishing, virtue—that of humility. He is content to find himself in a world abounding in greater persons than himself. Any greatness which he may attain is for him not inherent—his own brought to light—but vicarious, the greatness of nature or that of finer fellow men, by experiencing and sharing which he himself may build up a modest and derivative greatness of his own. In short, any full experience of beauty involves a checking or suspension of that *amour propre* which psychology from La Rochefoucauld down has rightly regarded as the mainspring of human action. The art lover readily and gladly becomes as a little child, and to this extent his attitude is akin to that of the religious person.

Such humility tends to bring with it a flexible openmindedness, an absence of vanity of opinion, a ready and unabashed enthusiasm, a willingness to deal on friendly terms with the unexpected. Many art lovers for one cause or another fall short of this humility with its corollaries, but to this gentle law the true art lover gladly submits. It was to such *anime gentili* that the Tuscan poets who introduced in the "sweet new style" a new subtlety of feeling embodied in an unprecedented diction and versification—it was to such that young Dante and his fellow poets confidently appealed, and appealed not in vain.

Beyond this habitual humility we may perhaps predicate of the art lover an exceptional physiological sensitiveness.

Some day laboratory experiments may throw light on this question. It would be very interesting to see if there are measurable differences of nervous response between Mr. Royal Cortissoz, an exquisite connoisseur within his self-limited field, and, say, Mr. Alfred Barr with his broader responsiveness. The question has been already answered dogmatically by psychologists like Max Nordau and Lombroso who equate the artistic temperament with nervous instability and degeneration. Indeed such a view was dimly foreshadowed by Plato who regarded poetic inspiration as a divine madness, and by Horace when he described the race of poets as irritable. But for these views of genius, whether creative or receptive, as simply neurotic no sufficient evidence has ever been adduced. The argument is drawn from extreme and notorious examples, and it entirely ignores the fact that the genius who is in his general living highly indisciplined, is often highly disciplined in his art. Statistically I much doubt if a group of a hundred poets or painters or musical composers would show a higher ratio of erratic living than would a century of stock brokers or commercial travellers or housepainters. It would surprise me if laboratory experiments should show in the art lover any specific supersensitiveness of a physiological order. I should merely expect a specific supersensitiveness in esthetic orientation, a special sort of memory and perceptivity.

We are safe enough in thinking that no stolid or stubborn person can be a good art lover—safe also perhaps in asserting for the art lover a capacity for hyperaesthesia along esthetic lines. But when we use the big and rather ugly word hyperaesthesia of the art lover, we must divest it of its general and neurological connotations. The person who at all times feels too intensely will rarely be a good art lover. Moreover, the hyperaesthesia of the art lover is not a universal disposition, but a disposition in the limited field of beauty, a disposition that has become a habit and has been, as all profitable habits inevitably are, canalized and disciplined.

For an art lover of this sort, the constant experience of beauty is necessary, a prime need of the soul which cannot be foregone. He seeks it incessantly as other men seek money or sport or power. When teaching at Williams College, I had the habit of climbing the nearby hills towards sundown to see the glory fall and die on the great rimming mountains. On such solitary strolls, I often met a charming German colleague. He always beamed and with the solemnity and regularity of a ritual would say, "We must do this, else we die." It was a profound saying, for to be starved of beauty means to its lover to lose a chief value of his living.

The art lover's sense of beauty has a transporting function. It takes him out of a world where nothing is secure and much is confusing and troublesome and makes him free of a world where rules a secure, orderly and serene activity. This world is mostly of his own making, but of this he is generally unaware, and he gives thanks humbly to those works of art and revelations of nature through which he has found a dynamic peace.

So far I have treated the art lover as a naïve person without intellectual curiosity as to his own esthetic processes. He grows and opens towards beauty as the flower grows towards the sun. He loves deeply such works of art as speak to him, buys them as he can afford them, enjoys them regardless of what others may think of them or of him. All this becomes a very intimate part of his living. As a sociable being, he talks over his enthusiasms with like-minded people, generally avoiding those who are not like-minded. He is the *anima naturaliter aesthetica,* and in the mass he constitutes the indispensable infantry of the esthetic army. No region is really conquered for the beautiful until he is in occupation.

People, I think, are born that way. Small children often have the most uncanny insight into beauty of the higher and more complicated sort. As a lad my mother was equally likely to take me to Barnum's circus, to the old National Academy, or to the new Metropolitan Museum. I thought of them all indiscriminately as exciting and pleasurable experiences, with a tendency to prefer the galleries to the sawdust ring.

But if the predisposition towards beauty be natal, as I think it is, it may be greatly developed and enriched through experience. And here I mean experience of the unreflective sort. In the field of beauty works auspiciously a sort of inverse Gresham's law; in repeated esthetic experience the finer tends to drive out the cheaper. At worst, a naïve taste for the beautiful remains static; it rarely goes down; it tends to go up. The art lover naturally goes where he gets the richer nourishment. He finds it without being told.

But under modern conditions the completely naïve art lover is very rare. He is beset with informational and critical writing of all sorts; even the radio endeavors to refine his taste. He is interested in his favorite artists and reads about them, travels with handbooks. All this allures him to rationalize his experiences of beauty. It is, I feel, a temptation he should avoid, unless he be willing to see it through. His better part may easily be to rest on his natural enthusiasms. But the art lover endowed with intellectual curiosity will inevitably become increasingly conscious of his esthetic processes and will ultimately begin to analyze them, if only to show a reason for the faith that is in him.

At this stage, our art lover is incipiently a mute inglorious critic, and a critic he will certainly become if he achieve articulateness. With art lovers of this sub-critical sort largely rests the direction and destiny of collective and historic taste. In this unconscious social construction, the sub-critical art lover is substantially guided but not dominated by the professional critic, who shall be my next theme.

Now for critic or layman the coming of self-consciousness into appreciation involves certain esthetic hazards. Humility is no characteristic of the analytical mind, and the constant practice of analysis may impair the art lover's essential humility. The old wonder at the greatness of the work of art may be perverted into wonder at the cleverness of one's own analytical processes. And here we meet the inevitable paradox that though the art lover's state of mind is the all-important factor in esthetic experience, the art lover concerns himself with his own state of mind at considerable peril.

At this point, to avoid a kind of esthetic bankruptcy, an entire clarity is indispensable. Between primary experience of beauty and reflection thereon there must be no confusion. Analysis ministers to intellectual curiosity, which is not an esthetic motive, and not to esthetic experience itself. If this distinction be not firmly held, the art lover turned analyst may easily end in a kind of priggishness very disabling to all activity of appreciation and even calculated to make such activity odious.

If, however, the art lover succeed in keeping the above distinction clear, his analytical effort, though not undertaken for any such end, may incidentally enrich his receptive experience. Whatever intensifies and clarifies his thinking may ultimately intensify and clarify that eminently composite psychic state which is the experience of beauty. If he can win through an analytical phase, without lurching into the pitfall of vanity, his subsequent appreciation should be richer than that of the naïve art lover who has refused the analytical detour. And the analytical art lover who can pass through analysis unscathed, is simply a potential critic. If he talks or writes of his experiences, he is in actuality a critic.

In order to keep the professional critic in his place, he is frequently reminded of the fact that in the great creative periods formal criticism is significantly lacking. It pullulates, on the contrary, in periods of declining creative activity. If written criticism be meant and the long stretch from Caravaggio to Picasso be arbitrarily regarded as a period of decline, this statement is historically true. On the other hand, it seems impossible that in the great creative periods there was not much oral criticism of an influential sort.

Are we to suppose that the Greeks of the eighth century B.C., who adored the new marvel of the *Iliad* and had in memory its sonorous hexameters, never talked about their enthusiasms? In nearly three thousand years of recorded

Greek history, not talking has never been a characteristic of that volatile race. Are we again to suppose that the artists who designed, the artisans who carved, the officials who ordered and paid for the marbles of Olympia and those of the Acropolis held no opinions about these masterpieces, or holding opinions, never expressed them?.

Again, shall we think because Florence towards the end of the fifteenth century had produced only the casual written criticism of a Ghiberti, a Leonbattista Alberti and a Leonardo, that the two generations of conscious experimenters who worked out all the main procedures of a humanistic art never met and talked things over? In such periods there must have been equivalents for the meetings of the Impressionists with Manet at the Café Guerbois, for the afternoons of the Symbolists with Mallarmé, for the solidarity of the pupils of Thomas Anschutz—who bore Eakins's mantle—and of Robert Henri in America. That is, the absence of written criticism by no means implies the absence of criticism orally transmitted.

Then the extraordinarily early appearance of written criticism in India and China reminds us that written criticism implies a favorable background of written psychology and philosophy. Where this background is lacking or tardily formed, written criticism must also emerge tardily. There may be, probably must be, an antecedent, oral criticism doubtless unsystematic but nevertheless effective, just as we must suppose a long stage of oral discussion and transmission before the Indian and Chinese wisdom was committed to writing.

Moreover there is always much more critical writing on esthetic matters than is imagined, but it is often writing incidental to other themes, hence overlooked. Offhand, a few years ago, the average medievalist would have said that there was no criticism worth mentioning between Quintilian and Petrarch. This would be to assume that the fine artists who made the manuscript miniatures, the superb glass windows, those intricate marvels, the Gothic cathedrals, were completely silent as to their dearest concerns. And even supposing written criticism were meant, the admirable book of Jacques Maritain shows in all the great medieval schoolmen an intense and intelligent interest in the main problems of esthetics. Less careful scholars have missed the fact, because such esthetic criticism is not under distinguishing titles, but indulged as an extension of studies primarily devoted to morals and psychology. In short, there has ever been more criticism than that which is written down, and more written criticism than is ordinarily recognized by the histories of literature.

For requiring of the professional critic a due humility, there are better reasons than the alleged and much exaggerated lack of criticism in the great creative periods. What is true of this saying is that in the aftermath of great creation formal criticism superabounds. And nothing much is to be made of this for or against criticism itself. The best criticism is rarely if ever of the contemporary scene. It is of objects scrutinized at a certain remove and in historical perspective. Criticism, like any other art, works best when its subject matter is richest and most abundant, and this moment is precisely that which follows by a generation or so any period of great and copious creation.

In discussing criticism, my own art, I shall confine myself to its proper ends, which are quite simple and understandable, and I shall ignore means, which are infinitely various and confusing. Teleologically, then, all criticism is primarily directed to the definition and clarification of the esthetic experience of the critic himself. Secondarily, like all the arts, criticism seeks communication, the sharing of esthetic experience with others. Good criticism merely facilitates and heightens appreciation in the critic and in the reader.

Concerning this issue Mr. Wilenski, whose unabashed dogmatism is always provocative of thought, has written:

"The only critic who can tell us anything about a work of art is the man who has discovered the attitude, motives and procedure of the artist; and that discovery I hold to be the function of artistic criticism."

Of this it may be said that such a critic's discovery of the attitude, motives and procedure of the artist is merely so many inferences from the work of art, while that critic is indeed presumptuous who supposes any such inferences to be infallible or even authoritative. What truth there is in the dogma is that the critic does his best to ascertain the artist's attitude. That best is only an analogy or approximation, but it is better than the inferences of a less experienced person.

While the minor procedures of criticism are infinitely various, there is a general wholesome pattern to which all sound criticism tends to conform. Right criticism is always of the total meaning of the work of art. The roads to such total meaning are many. Where the critic begins to go in is a matter of convenience; eventually he must tread all the main routes to the center. He must write in the order of his own growing understanding. If, like that most talented critic, the late Roger Fry, he is especially sensitive to the form of the work of art, there he will probably begin, but his critical task is incomplete until he wins through form to meaning. Mr. Fry usually did, but somewhat grudgingly.

As to what the critic actually does there is a good deal of misunderstanding. If he thinks he is fully interpreting any work of art, he sorely deceives himself, for every work of art is self-interpreting. What the critic can do, and it is really all that he can do, is to create in his own medium a new work of art analogous in spirit and effect to the work of art he criticizes. Through grasping the meaning of the analogy, the reader comes nearer the original experience from which the analogy was drawn. Good criticism merely puts the reader in a mood favorable to understanding, and the triumph of good criticism is when the reader forgets it, burns his bridges and moves on confidently into the world of the work of art itself. To experience a Mont Blanc a wise lover of nature does not climb it; he climbs a small mountain across the vale of Chamounix, the Brevent. Of the Brevent he thinks little, but from its modest summit the splendor of the great mountain reveals itself. So the modest task of the critic is mostly the skilful making of Brevents from which the grander mountains may be directly and conveniently viewed.

There is as well a judicial, even condemnatory type of criticism which usually treats rather tendencies than individuals. Ultimately, if of any force and eloquence, it affects the artist and art lover quite practically. Such criticism often well serves its times, but it is generally more ephemeral than the better type of appreciative criticism. A Sainte-Beuve and a Roger Fry may well outlast a Brunetière and a Saintsbury.

The proper objective of the art critic, then, is chiefly his less experienced fellow art lover. If he is wise, he does not directly address the artist. No critic can possibly know the procedures of the artist's task as well as the artist himself; no critic dissatisfied with a work of art can know whether the sacrifices and emphases that trouble him were or were not inevitable in the logic of the work of art itself. He does well always to give the artist the benefit of the doubt. From the critic, as from any sensible and experienced fellow mortal, the artist may of course learn something to his purpose, but such a gain is usually of so minor and incidental a sort that the critic does not take it into his reckoning at all. His concern is not with the work of art in the making but with the appreciation of the work of art when made. He serves the artist best simply by furthering and extending appreciation of the artist's work. In this endeavor the true triumphs of criticism have been won.

Here we meet the paradox that while the best and most permanently valuable criticism is retrospective, the most efficacious criticism is that of contemporaries. One loves to recall Baudelaire's and Zola's generous championship of such suspected innovators as Courbet and Manet; the gallant and successful guerrilla warfare of the Pennells in favor of Whistler; Charles de Kay's early advocacy of the derided great painters of Barbizon and of our great ignored dreamer, Albert Ryder; James Huneker's genial and breathless fight for Arthur B. Davies and Ernest Lawson, and George Luks and George Bellows; Roger Fry's persuasive yet ever cool-headed analysis of the merits of the detested Cézanne and his followers—of recent criticism these are the heroic sagas.

Here of course there is a diversity of gifts, and each critic contributes what he can. It took me years fully to perceive the merits of such highly idiosyncratic painters as Albert Ryder, John Marin, and Cézanne, but in an unforgettable hour the ineffable glory of Chinese landscape painting dawned upon me. I promptly expressed the experience to my small American public, was, I believe, the first American critic so to do. Thus the historically minded critic, while admittedly off the firing line, may yet serve in some unheroic fashion of his own.

Indeed the recovery from the past of what has been lost or ignored, the reformulation of old opinion without unnecessary deformation so that it merges with that new opinion which has to be re-expressed for every generation —this is the specific task of the art critic as biographer and historian. It is a task requiring, with less audacity, perhaps a higher degree of tact and subtlety than the discovery of new genius. Personally my rediscoveries have cost me more in reflection than my discoveries, and I believe such is usually the case.

As a specialist, and presumably a heartless one, all estheticians of puristic stamp exclude the connoisseur from esthetic consideration. So drastic an exclusion seems to me unwarranted in view of the fact that as a museum official in charge of the purchase and display of works of art the connoisseur plays a large and ever growing part in the formation of social taste. Museum management is or at least should be mainly the orientation of connoisseurship towards public education in art. As such, its function is obvious and needs no elaborate treatment.

While the connoisseur is merely a specialized sort of critic, his difference from the critic is also considerable. Like the critic, he is primarily concerned with grasping the total meaning of works of art, but these meanings he interprets in terms of period, authenticity and authorship—more or less extraneous considerations which the critic is usually privileged to take for granted, since the work of art, authentic or the contrary, is what it is and has its own kind of meaning, which again, esthetically, is what it is. It is with these irreducible values that the critic, somewhat under difficulties, deals; the connoisseur must reduce them to terms of time, place and author. Concretely, he is the man who can tell you or thinks he can tell you whether there are only eight or upwards of seventy Giorgiones. In such problems the connoisseur is the invaluable ally of the critic. For if any criticism of Giorgione is to be valid, it must rest upon what he painted and not upon the work of his numerous imitators. Unless indeed the critic be wise enough to waive the central problem for its difficulty and write about the Giorgionesque ambience. This Walter Pater did, and his essay after fifty years still remains paradoxically the most illuminative criticism of Giorgione himself.

In more solvable problems than that of Giorgione's *œuvre* the connoisseur serves the critic in warning him off from marginal and doubtful works. To be sure, the critic's taste and common sense should set up the danger signal, but often in unfamiliar fields it fails to do so. So the wary critic must exercise a critique of connoisseurs, studying their propensities and vagaries, learning whom to consult for what. But I am suspicious of any critic who is not something of a connoisseur; of any connoisseur who is not something of a critic.

As for the methods of the connoisseur, they are really more like those of the critic than the literature of connoisseurship would indicate. The connoisseur must have a vast empirical experience and a retentive memory thereof. He knows the feel of a Leonardo da Vinci. If he has the same or closely the same feel before a disputed Leonardesque picture, it is for him a Leonardo. If the feel is different, it is not. The reality of all connoisseurship is as simple as that. The connoisseur knows his art as the tea taster knows his tea, or the wine taster his qualities and vintages. A wide experience accurately remembered is the whole thing. If Mr. Berenson is a far greater connoisseur than his rivals it is chiefly because he has a far greater repertory of remembered feelings about pictures, can for purposes of comparison visualize ten pictures where they can visualize one.

It would be highly impolitic for the connoisseur, who must have the air of a greater authority than can ever be his, to betray the instinctive character of his judgments. Since he cannot say frankly "This is the way it feels to me," for purposes of exposition and demonstration, he alleges all sorts of *materialia,* which, while confirming, have not really influenced his judgment. Thus we write about morphological ear marks, costume, patina, linear characteristics, color schemes, and cite the evidence of the X-ray and eke that of the ray of ultra-violet hue; of chemical analysis or microscopic observation.

Now of such apparently objective evidence it should be clear that it is of use only when connoisseurship has failed, and then not of much use. Where these tests serve is merely in checking a necessarily subjective judgment. They cannot increase in any way the weight of a sound instinctive judgment, but they may very usefully confute a judgment that is premature and unbased. Accordingly the wise connoisseur, knowing the fallibility of his own instincts remembered or immediate, uses and cites tests which he knows to be generally superfluous. He does this, not to mislead his public, but to avoid misleading himself.

Since the critic and connoisseur necessarily work by comparison and contrast of experience, a word on this process is desirable. By purists of the type of Lipps and Parker it has been emphatically condemned as anti-esthetic. They hold that the experience of every work of art, being unique, should be completely isolated. But under the ordinary law of association of ideas this is to demand the impossible. Can we suppose that Rodin when through months he modelled, say, "The Thinker" was entirely unaware of the statues he had made earlier and of those he meant to make? And if the required isolation be in creation impossible, how can it be possible in appreciation? The kernel of truth which is present in this as in most hard dogmas, is simply that contrast and comparison may be abused. All knowledge of any sort rests largely on contrast and comparison. For esthetic knowledge there is no exemption from the general psychological law. But practically we must beware of so misusing contrast and comparison as to define experience, not positively but by elimination and negatively. The question is always what is the experience? and not what is not the experience? Comparison and contrast may very usefully by elimination clear the way for an ultimate affirmation. Indeed there is seldom any other method available.

Since the opinion of the connoisseur has commercial value, he is under temptation to sell it. Sell it he may legitimately, as any other expert opinion is rightly sold. But the selling usually involves dangers to connoisseurship itself, and only too often ends in an odious charlatanry. Suppose the picture to be in the hands of a friend or financial benefactor. Without the expert's certificate, it is worth $1,000, with his certificate it is worth $100,000, and he is honestly in doubt as to the picture. It may or may not be a Rembrandt. Insidiously the picture gets the benefit of the doubt, and with each such surrender of scepticism the next surrender is easier. Such is the too frequent descent of the connoisseur turned expert. The critic who at best makes a bare living by his criticism may well rejoice that he is not beset by the deceitfulness of riches.

On the whole, the touch of the connoisseur with esthetic experience is incidental and rather remote. He may be conceived of as trimming up the always rough edges of the taste of his times. His happiest occupation is probably that of expert curator in a museum; his next happiest that of collector. In either capacity he may aid in the formation of social taste.

As for the collector, again all estheticians of puristic type absolutely exclude him from consideration. But since the conservation of the art of the past and the patronage of that of the present largely depends upon the collector, he must evidently be included in any esthetic which takes taste into account. In his best estate, the collector is merely the art lover who has the desire and the ability to own works of art. Where the esthetician regards him at all, it is usually to deprecate his desire for actual possession as impairing that ideal possession which is appreciation. Such an esthetician, I fancy, has never collected himself nor even studied the collector with any insight. For nearly forty years I have been a collector in many fields. If anyone tells me that because I have wanted to own and do own my pictures, prints and drawings I appreciate them less than I do similar works of art in the museums, he tells me simple nonsense. I love and enjoy them more, not because they are mine, nor yet because of sacrifices they have cost, or adroitness in acquiring them, but because I can experience their beauty frequently, conveniently and without competing distractions. The critic who finds possession anti-esthetic by the same token should not buy books, but should extol and practise the superior virtue of doing all his reading in public libraries.

There is of course much collecting that has little to do with love of art—collecting for personal prestige, as an expression of what Thorstein Veblen called conspicuous waste. But even here there are often ultimate esthetic benefits. The unloved treasures of art may pass to a museum and acquire lovers. Whatever the motive for collecting, some esthetic good seems to accrue. To the mere looting of Roman conquerors, we owe most of our finest examples of Hellenistic sculpture.

Besides it is a simple snobbishness to assume that because a collector is rich, has little time for studying his collections and is rather inarticulate about their beauty, that therefore he does not enjoy them. Here and in Europe I have known in their collections some twenty very wealthy collectors. Of these five might reasonably be called connoisseurs; ten more showed a discriminating pleasure in their pictures, while only three seemed to me entirely insensible to the beauty of art.

Of the ways and foibles of the collector I have elsewhere written. Here I shall only consider the possible harm or good of his dear pursuit to his own esthetic life and to the formation of taste generally. Far more than the non-possessive art lover is the collector subject to the esthetically disabling fault of vanity. His possessions tend to loom large in his eyes because of the difficulty of acquiring them or simply because they are his. Thus may come about a general distortion of values. Many a collection looks important when the ardor of the collector expands it, which after his death, in a museum, seems ordinary enough. This is true of famous collections which discreetly I will not name. Such magnifying zeal is a perversion of right esthetic experience. The true collector looks as austerely at his treasures as the true artist looks at his own works.

A second pitfall for the collector lies in commercializing his activities. His finds are salable at a big profit, and he is tempted to cash them in. Next he is tempted to buy in order to sell. At this point he becomes an art dealer under cover, or at best a long-range investor in the beautiful. In either case the quality of his collection will suffer, for he now buys not out of love and for himself, but for another and for gain. I have rarely seen a *marchand amateur* who died with a fine collection, for the collection ultimately consists of what he never really wanted and could not sell. It is not the selling that works the deterioration. At times every collector sells—the things he has outgrown, a poorer thing to get a better. But the moment he has selling in mind when he buys, he is no longer a collector but a dealer, and under the head we shall later consider him.

For the rest, his collecting is esthetically helpful in every way. With leisure and intelligence he will insensibly add to the grace of his love of beauty the dignity of criticism and connoisseurship. The great critic and connoisseur, Giovanni Morelli, when told of a promising young critic always said, "show me what he has collected." It is the high privilege of the true collector to domesticate beauty, to crown the ardor of pursuit with the serener rapture of possession. In the realm of esthetics he is the ideally married man.

The heroic type of collecting is that of collecting one's contemporaries. Of such, Maecenas is the patron saint. Than discovering and fostering living talent I can hardly imagine a nobler and more rewarding activity. If generation by generation we have had the beauty of art ever renewed, it is because of the continuity of such sensitive and magnanimous patronage. Such amateurs not merely keep the artist alive, but also feed his soul. Happily they have never failed the world. In our country such men as Luman Reed and Robert Gilmore made possible the career of a Thomas Cole. In our own days a Mrs. Harry Payne Whitney, a Duncan Phillips, an Alfred Stieglitz—for we cannot consider a man who all his life has lost money selling the pictures he loves as anything but an amateur—have made the artist's career possible for a hundred good talents. They are merely the figures nearest to us in a long apostolic succession.

The museum that deals with contemporary art must act in the spirit of the collector—indulging audacious enthusiasms and joyously taking risks. The museums that do this successfully such as the Whitney Museum, the Phillips Foundation, the Museum of Modern Art, and others less notable, generally are founded and managed by collectors. The museums of contemporary art which try to follow the precedent proper to the historical museums of avoiding risk, on the whole buy very badly, safety for them lying, where in any long run it never is, in following current fashion. Let the walls and lumber rooms of the Luxembourg and Metropolitan Museum speak! They will tell eloquently that while there may be a fine amateurism in contemporary art, there is no sure connoisseurship. To attempt it is a folly.

As the salvager of much beauty that has gone astray and is in peril of destruction, as assuring to the artist a livelihood and moral support, the collector is the natural breeder of enthusiasm for the art of his day as he is eventually the feeder of the museum. As such he contributes substantially to the formation of taste. All collecting serves this useful purpose whatever its motive or whatever the insight of the collector or lack thereof. A Charles IX who piously looted Catholic Germany for conscience's sake did as good a turn to the museums of Sweden as if he had been actuated by a more creditable purpose. Hence if social taste has any place in esthetics, and for me it has a very prominent place, the esthetician must take the collector very seriously into account.

Collecting older art is a relatively safe and unheroic activity for the collector who commands adequate connoisseurship or avails himself of competent expert advice. Sheer poverty has limited me to this unenterprising branch of collecting. The living artist has to live and some sort of living wage must be paid for his work. The deceased artist does not have to live, and if his work drift into back channels, it may be bought by a discerning eye for a ludicrous figure. Hence connoisseurship is the whole thing in this sort of collecting, while criticism in a broad sense is the whole thing in collecting contemporary art. For the above reasons, while I have been free to write as a critic, I have been forced to collect as a thrifty connoisseur. The result is that while envying the audacity of the heroic collectors, I have rarely been able to emulate it. Poverty has held me down to my modest collection of drawings and paintings by old masters.

On the face of it, if only for his relatively disinterestedness, the excavating archaeologist might seem to be the high type of collector of older art. He wants to discover and publish, not to possess. But from his scientific disposition the archaeologist is rather a purveyor than a contributor in the esthetic field. Prone to be equally interested in drains and Dianas, he rarely gives his finds a critical interpretation. At least he constantly provides for criticism new material, and incidentally extends and enriches the tradition of taste.

When I include the art dealer in an esthetic survey, I expect a clamor of protest. Yet the social facts are what they are, and for more than a hundred years past, if there had been no art dealers, there would have been practically no painting, and that little the product of gifted amateurs blessed with independent incomes. Concretely, we might have had something of Corot, Puvis, Manet and Cézanne, but Courbet, Monet, Degas, Renoir, Van Gogh and Gauguin would have been driven to other pursuits. In the main, only the illustrators would in the nineteenth century have continued the tradition of picture making.

I have elsewhere studied the shift of patronage from the private buyer to the middleman and have tried to show its dubious results. Here I need only note the fact that the average painter of talent today simply could not live by his art unless some art dealer who believed in him took him in hand. This was not always so, and perhaps should not so be, but so it is. The situation began even in the Renaissance. The seventeenth century was already a heyday of dealers, and the tendency since the French Revolution, and the ending of the old aristocracy and personal patronage, has merely been greatly accentuated. Hence the dealer today at one remove does precisely the concrete service to art that the collector renders, with the really negligible difference that the collector sells rarely but the dealer as often as he can. As to the objection that the art dealer is a mercenary, living by the sale of other men's pictures, it may be answered that so is the artist a mercenary, living by the sale of his own works.

On the effect of such middlemanship on the status of the artist and upon social taste there would be a long chapter to write. Here is not the place for it. Broadly speaking, within my experience the more intelligent dealers have done about as well as the more intelligent collectors, have done remarkably well considering that they must make money. In the Durand-Ruel's long-range investment in the Impressionists there is much of the audacity of the amateur. They won, but they might easily have lost. Without the faith of the Durand-Ruels, Monet, Sisley, Pissarro, Signac, Renoir could hardly have painted. Examples of this sort of far-sighted commercial patronage abound. Our own Albert Ryder could hardly have attained his slender livelihood but for the confidence of Daniel Cottier and other dealers in his work.

Where many inexperienced and rich collectors are making galleries, recourse is naturally had to the dealer, and generally he serves his client surprisingly well. Such dealers as the Knoedlers and S. P. Avery to be sure passed on to our American collectors many mediocre pictures that happened to be in fashion, but they also persuaded hesitating clients to buy the Rousseaus, Corots, Millets and Baryes which were not at all in fashion, with the result that far the greater and finer production of the Barbizon School is in the United States, much of it in public museums. Such dealers in old masters as the Duveens, Agnews, Kleinbergers and Knoedlers, with many of equal merit but lesser note, effected a similar transmigration of masterpieces to America, to the eventual enrichment of our museums. The better class of dealer is merely a connoisseur who sells his connoisseurship, and under that category he might most reasonably be treated.

It might readily be argued that our collectors would have done better and might still do better to interpose an artist or critic between the dealer and themselves, as three hundred years ago the Earl and Countess of Arundel consulted Rubens rather than the art dealers of Antwerp, or only yesterday Mrs. John L. Gardner depended on Mr. Berenson's advice, or the late John Quinn and Dr. Albert C.

Barnes on that of Mr. Glackens. Certainly such examples commend the procedure. But it is also natural that a collector who is a man of great affairs and means to spend much money should prefer to deal with a great merchant who has backed his opinion with much money. Besides, if the dealer is obviously an interested party, it is by no means easy to find a completely disinterested expert. On the whole, I think it would be better if the wealthy and inexperienced collector depended more on the artist and critic and less on the dealer for advice. Yet I feel too that since it is simple good business to treat a good client well, and since many dealers are good lovers of art, the dominance of the dealer in *de luxe* collecting is not too deeply to be deplored.

On the broader issue of the function and influence of the art dealer I think it might more justly be argued that the dealer stepped in to save a desperate situation for art than that the dealer is a usurper or exploiter. I should welcome the return of a more direct and human relation between the artist and patron. Until it comes, the dealer will be an essential contributor to the formation of collective taste.

Any complete elucidation of the theme merely broached above would involve a study of the *entrepreneur* in all the arts—the publisher of books or music, the librarian, the book club, the theatrical or musical manager, the foundation, the museum, including the docent, all teachers of the history and appreciation of art, the exhibiting societies and academies, the art schools, etc. But I have chosen to follow the broad outlines of the problem in the art most familiar

to me, and any alert reader will readily find the relevant
analogies for himself.

And this survey of the marginal esthetic activities is
made for a larger purpose. If I have followed the art lover
in all of his varieties, it has been to suggest the wide social
ramifications and reverberations of the experience of
beauty. In one aspect the most individual experience
conceivable; in another, it is the most social. And if much
writing on esthetics has been merely so much psychological
moonshine, it has been because too much attention has
been given to the soul in wholly isolated rapture before a
masterpiece, forgetting that the soul is after all one of many
souls similarly yet variously occupied, and that far short
of the masterpieces are found the great majority of esthetic
satisfactions.

Of course I am aware of the shortcomings of my roughly
descriptive treatment of the art lover. I have merely
sketched a set of preferences and habits with esthetic implications in the social field. The real problem of the art lover
is of course psychological and would require wide collation
of evidence and searching analysis. Obviously the quality
of all esthetic experience is deeply colored by the temperament of the hearer or beholder. Goethe, so far as I know,
was the first critic to try to bring such *differentia* of esthetic
experience under a classification. Earlier we may assume
that everybody took it for granted that the "four temperaments" would have their say in esthetic as in all experience.
And really, despite the ingenious researches of Vernon Lee
and Anstruther-Thomson, we are hardly in a position to
assume more today than that the prevailing character of
the individual necessarily modifies his experiences of

beauty. Within this very general statement, the moment we make subdivisions we have a confusing variety that defies either separate interpretation or useful classification. In reading Professor Chandler's careful summary of many laboratory experiments, I find no consistent results. What seems likely is that the unity and integrity of the work of art dominate in a very similar fashion persons of quite various temperaments. Goethe's tabular distinctions will at least serve my purpose of making the reader see the problem.

Goethe's method of approach was singularly concrete. He made the large and very miscellaneous collection which he had partly inherited and partly acquired himself serve as a touchstone for the numerous visitors who betrayed their idiosyncrasies by their talk. The material is presented charmingly, in the literary tradition of the *Spectator* in a series of letters called "The Collector and His Possessions," *"Der Sammler und die Seinigen."* The results as tabulated give three main types of amateurs and artists. Since there are difficulties in translating Goethe's fantastic but also suggestive nomenclature, I give the table first in German.

ERNST ALLEIN	ERNST UND SPIEL VERBUNDEN	SPIEL ALLEIN
Individuelle Neigung	Ausbildung ins Allgemeine	Individuelle Neigung
Manier	Stil	Manier
Nachahmer	Kunstwahrheit	Phantomisten
Charakteristiker	Schönheit	Undulisten
Kleinkünstler	Vollendung	Skizzisten

SERIOUSNESS ONLY	SERIOUSNESS AND PLAYFULNESS IN LEAGUE	PLAYFULNESS ONLY
Idiosyncrasy	Development to- wards uni- versality	Idiosyncrasy
Mannerism	Style	Mannerism
Imitators	Truth of art	Visionaries
Characterizers	Beauty	Grace seekers
Little masters of analytical sort	Perfection	Sketch lovers

While the categories are not quite consistently worked out, the table is at least made on sound psychological lines, and its implications are highly suggestive.

Either too much or too little seriousness will result in mannerism. To cite examples—if Frans Floris is a manner- ist, so is Gerard Dou. The high point of art is attained through no sort of absolutism but through some delicate synthesis involving a reconciliation of the apparent oppo- sites, playfulness and seriousness. Style is the fine flower of such reconciliation, as mannerism is of all unilateral en- deavor. This is the application to esthetics of Goethe's two memorable maxims *"Man muss entsagen"* and *"Im Gan- zen, Guten, Schönen resolut zu leben."* So while the table might suffer under close psychological criticism, for a humanist it holds the essential truth of the matter. Like everything concerning Goethe, it has the grace of ancientry without in any way seeming merely dated. Since I cannot

myself more clearly express what the psychological problem of the art lover really is, in borrowing Goethe's ingenious tabulation, I combine an act of utility with one of
homage.

CHAPTER VIII

ON TASTE AND THE VARIETIES OF BEAUTY

IN THIS last chapter I may gather together certain left-overs, aspects of beauty which for one reason or another have not seemed to find their place earlier in these pages. This apparently unsystematic procedure I am ready to defend. Any very complicated theme may perhaps be best set forth by successive illumination from many angles. It may be better for the reader to combine such aspects as he may than for the writer to impose a premature and perhaps partial systematization.

The truth of the work of art is truth of illusion, truth within a restricted field of reference established by the artist, consistency within the work of art itself. Such truth may or may not be that of the good human life. On this ground Professor Lowes has valiantly defended the truthfulness of *The Rime of the Ancient Mariner* which a literalistic criticism, from Wordsworth down, has sharply contested. For shooting an albatross, two hundred of the Mariner's shipmates must die and he himself be condemned to an eternity of homeless wandering. The sympathetic observation of parti-colored water snakes lifts the burden but not the penalty of his guilt. All this in the world of ordinary living is morally absurd, nay, monstrous. Not so in the world of pure glamourie which Coleridge has created. There the moral disproportions are not felt.

For a whole class of works of fantasy, the plea is perfectly sound. No sensible reader brings the gustatory or amatory feats of Pantagruel before the bar of common sense or considers the unlikelihood of finding an Ariel, a Puck, a Falstaff, a Bottom the Weaver around the corner. We do not cavil at Titian for assembling about the Madonna saints who lived centuries apart from her, in a Venetian picnic speciously called a "Sacred Conversation." But the title justifies the anachronism. Spiritually all the saints are contemporaries—that is, in Titian's frame of reference, their coexistence is truthful.

Yes, the truth of art is truth of illusion, but in the greatest works of art this truthfulness is singularly close to that of life and rarely contradicts it. One can live according to Homer, Sophocles, Dante, Chaucer, Montaigne, Shakespeare, Voltaire, Fielding, Thackeray, Tolstoy, and many another writer; one can hardly live according to Ariosto, Coleridge, Dumas *père,* Poe, and Ibsen. What is true of the Pheidian marbles is equally true of heroic living generally, but the truth of Bernini is valid only for his own elegantly fantastic realm.

Perhaps the truth of illusion is really proper to what my friend the late Irving Babbitt, possibly too condescendingly, used to call recreational art. Such art as commands high seriousness does not seem to require this dispensation from the common human standards. When we speak of the truthfulness of Rembrandt, Ruysdael, Addison, Flaubert, Browning we are speaking not merely of esthetic truthfulness, but also of that of our own living. Truth of illusion there is, but we do not necessarily perceive it as such, nor need to do so. The work of art was probably not intended to be applicable to our individual need of living the good life; by a peculiar grace, it is applicable.

On all this matter Mr. Santayana has written with eloquent and robust good sense in *The Life of Reason in Art*. He sees in the history of art a growing tendency towards approximation of the two orders of truth, and he looks forward to an ultimate disappearance of the immemorial distinction. His hope I moderately share, for, as he does not fail to point out, it involves an ultimate perfection of the art of living which may make the other arts superfluous. This will not come about in his time nor in mine, and as an art lover I can face the distant prospect with equanimity.

Where Mr. Santayana's esthetic moralism is valuable is in restoring to art in a reasonable way the old sanction of imitation. It is a principle which in the prevailing anarchy of artistic theory and practice has been generally and wrongly discredited, and modern esthetics has unhappily authorized if not encouraged the most unpromising and unprofitable excesses of barbarous individualism. So Mr. Santayana does well to remind us that the measuring stick for the greatest art is merely the usual moral measuring stick, perhaps turned over, like a measure that is cut both in feet and meters.

In music unassociated with words I find no truthfulness save that of illusion—inner coherence and consistency. Other truthfulness music may vaguely intimate, but cannot express. That is why music is generally and properly regarded as the purest, not necessarily the greatest, of the arts. It seems to be able to live wholly on its own resources, while the other arts must draw at least their raw materials from outside themselves.

The higher truth of all really great literature is only such higher truth as there is in life. The truthfulness of architecture is that of expressing the functions and structure in the form, but architecture also rightly employs truth of illusion in the use of ornament and in reasonable evasions of the logic of structure in the interest of delectation. Painting and sculpture may emphasize either sort of truth, but again seem to be at their greatest when their truthfulness is at peace with that of the good life generally.

Of course neither Mr. Santayana nor I would define the good life by hard moralistic formulas. We are thinking of the man who is at once liberated and self-disciplined. It is he who is really the judge of the truthfulness of great art, and under his own going standards. This does not mean that there shall be no "cakes and ale" in the way of a recreational art which in a sort of moral irresponsibility has its own eminently pleasure-giving but also inferior sort of truthfulness.

To treat the subject of the comic after the researches of Coleridge, George Meredith, Henri Bergson and J. C. Gregory requires a certain hardihood. I shall accordingly handle the matter very briefly and only in its most general relation to esthetics.

A very simple instance of the comic may be instructive. A pompous young fop superbly attired in top hat, black cutaway, tan waistcoat, pearl gray trousers, and spats, and carrying a gold-headed cane and wearing a monocle, slips and falls into a puddle on which his top hat floats away. The occurrence is comic, and we laugh. Why? Clearly not out of *Einfühlung* or Esthetic Sympathy. If we put ourselves in his place, we should not laugh at him, but be sorry for him. If he has hurt himself and is clearly suffering, his mishap is no longer comic. Since *Einfühlung,* which would make us laugh with but never at another person, is plainly not involved in the usual experiences of the humorous, the witty, the satiric, etc., such advocates of *Einfühlung* as Theodor Lipps have been inclined to exclude from esthetics all experiences that grow out of the comic, or at least to regard these experiences as sub-esthetic.

Against such exclusion common sense protests. No lover of the archly humorous operettas of Gilbert and Sullivan will admit that their enjoyment is entirely alien to that of music with no comic connotation. When we pass from Hamlet to the sardonic humor of the gravediggers, we do not feel we have moved out of a great play into another and foreign territory. In a picture gallery when we exchange the exquisiteness of a Vermeer for the homely and drastic humor of an Old Bruegel we feel no solution of continuity. It would go hard to admit that our relish of Falstaff, Bottom the Weaver, Don Quixote, Mrs. Malaprop, Colonel Mulberry Sellers, Tartarin, is outside of our esthetic experience.

To return to our young dandy recovering his top hat and gold-headed cane from the puddle—why do we laugh at him? In the first instance precisely because we do not put ourselves in his place, but regard his ill-hap as something entirely exterior to us, in short because we see his plight without any exercise of sympathetic imagination. To this extent the esthetic, which implies a complete activity of the sympathetic imagination, may well seem the antithesis of the comic. We laugh at the really pitifully bedraggled exquisite simply because of the unexpectedness of his plight. Everything that normally should not happen to him has happened. The pattern under which we perceived him has suddenly been ripped away and replaced by a new and entirely incongruous pattern. He doesn't belong in the puddle, and the outrageousness of his not belonging amazes and delights us. And paradoxically we seem to get out of a sudden vision of incongruity and disorder an esthetic pleasure very similar to that which we draw from the vision of congruity and order.

With this paradox, the theory of *Einfühlung* simply cannot cope. Possibly the theory of a universal analogy of rhythm is in better shape to meet the difficulty. May not the shock produced by a sudden lapse of normal experience into disorder, be a kind of negative tribute to a prevailing orderliness? Without such reference to a general orderliness, would its sharp suspension produce any effect on us whatever? In the background of that nervous surprise upon which the comic rests is, it seems to me, a sense of what would be fit in the circumstances. With this goes often a feeling of discrepancy between means and end. The mountain that labors to produce a small mouse is ridiculous, and not really the small mouse.

Such elementary comic effects can hardly be said to be esthetic experiences. Much that seems ridiculous is so only to jumpy nerves and dull imaginations. Too much of it falls under La Rochefoucauld's cynical maxim, "We all have courage enough to bear the misfortunes of others." I feel that the merely ridiculous rises to the comic and begins to have esthetic quality only where there is some sense of the entire situation involved in the unexpected event. For example, one's laugh at the dandy in the puddle is in part a vote against dandyism and for modesty. Had a shabby newsboy fallen into the puddle, the mishap would probably seem comic to his mates, as young barbarians, but not to any grown-up. In short, the merely laughable may have to esthetic humor and wit about the relation that the simpler pleasures have to esthetic delight.

Esthetics has, then, rather little to do with the obviously comic until an artist or a work of art is involved. A man who not merely relishes but makes ludicrous situations may be a considerable artist. Many clowns have richly deserved the title. One who can tinge sheer clowning with shrewd worldly wisdom, like Will Rogers; or with pathos and a general sense of illusion, like Charlie Chaplin, may be in his fashion a very great comic artist. In such cases there is always reference to a general order outside the ludicrous.

Beyond trying to suggest the broad relations of the comic to esthetics, there is no need of pursuing at length a familiar and already admirably studied theme. Nor shall I remind the reader more than briefly that as the sudden perception of incongruity passes beyond sensation and perception, becoming more fully intellectual or conceptual, humor is merging into wit. Here the distinction is clear only in the extreme instances. Indeed, the most delicious cases are those which may be regarded either as humorous or witty, and have in truth both graces.

"What is more enchanting than the voices of young people, when you can't hear what they say?" So writes Logan Pearsall Smith. Here is the sudden crack of humor, the discernment of wit, with a precious tinge of quiet pathos, hinting—*Si jeunesse savait*. This is akin to the wistful forest wit of the Melancholy Jacques, and it is as far from Horace's airless vision of the vainglorious poet, crane-like, *stans pede in uno,* as it is from the metallic scintillation of Alexander Pope's wittily backhanded tribute to coquettes:

"With varying Vanities, from ev'ry Part,
They shift the moving Toyshop of their Heart;
Where Wigs with Wigs, with Sword-knots Sword-
     knots strive,
Beaux banish Beaux, and Coaches Coaches drive."

Before leaving an enticing subject, just a word on certain esthetic uses of wit and humor. What counts here is the general attitude of the humorous or witty artist towards the world. One may clearly perceive the incongruities of life, the breaking of its orderly and noble rhythms, and accept the situation with equanimity and without protest. Humor in the grand manner is always of this sort. Such is the humor of the Wife of Bath, of Gargantua, of Falstaff, of Sancho Panza; of a Mark Twain or Gilbert Chesterton at their best.

Again, you may accept the fact that our fairest dolls will, if you wound them, bleed only sawdust—accept it, but resentfully, wishing it were not so, yet with no intention or hope of changing it. Here humor is moving towards wit and irony. This it seems to me is the irony of Old Bruegel in his marvellous painted parable of "The Blind Leading the Blind." Much of the humor of Molière is of this sort. It is the prevailing note in Anatole France, reaching a paradoxical blend of elation and despair in the allegory of *Les Pingouins*. Of wit of this life-accepting but hopeless temper Norman Douglas is probably the greatest living master. An aftertaste of bitterness is proper to this brand of the comic.

Or you may regard the indecent unexpectednesses of life with disapproval and do your best to prevent them. Here wit and humor are conspiring to form satire, and we are passing away from the comic. There are few laughs in *Tartuffe*. Much of Molière, nearly all of his greatest comedies, are dramatized satires. Aristophanes shifts brilliantly from satire to humor in the grand style. George Meredith in *The Egotist* moves readily from a subsatirical basis to one of naïve relish of the goings on of his Sir Willoughby Patterne. Indeed, the richness of humorous literature rests largely on its mobility in finding in the comic, differences of level; in swift change from the comic to the serious. Thus the comic really illustrates better the general esthetic principle of organization, through tensions and releases, than does literature of the nobly serious sort.

I wish there were space to reargue the old plea for humor as a highroad towards general understanding. A latency of humor is one of the greatest prophylactics for art of however grave a kind. The raw material of wit and humor is suddenly broken rhythms, witness the um-pa of the bass horn in a solemn march, and obviously one may learn much about intact things by studying them when they happen to break.

I had hoped to dispense with a treatment of ugliness, but a tardy reading of Professor Stace's excellent book, *The Meaning of Beauty*, convinces me that the theme is not to be evaded. I agree with Professor Stace that the opposite of beauty is not the ugly, but what he aptly calls the "unbeautiful"—the ununified, unharmonized or merely neutral. And

I accept his paradox that the ugly so far as concerns esthetics, is often merely an exceptional type of beauty which for its unfamiliarity has been artificially set apart.

Generally speaking, ugliness seems to me not an esthetic but a moral category. Ugliness is not in things but in our associations, in states of mind, in motives, in acts. Whatever we associate with moral baseness, physical corruption, we call ugly—'tis thinking makes it so. But the morally ugly is not necessarily unavailable as subject matter for art, and when art takes it up, it often transforms it into a kind of beauty.

There is no formal or objective standard by which we may measure ugliness. Every conceivable phase of it could at least theoretically be envisaged in terms of beauty. The hunchback is often relatively as well formed as the athlete, everything about him has become harmonized with his curvature. Mr. Punch is as well formed as the Apollo Belvedere, I think, better formed, for his forms have more character. In esthetics the ugly may be regarded broadly as the extremely unusual and the ill understood, hence intolerable. When it is understood, its unusualness and ugliness will generally pass. Here philology comes to our aid. The Latin *novus* meant not merely new, but also unlikely and repellant. Whatever finds in us no pattern for its apprehension disquiets and perplexes us and is with difficulty brought into our organized (including esthetic) experience.

This is the realm of the ugly in esthetics. It means simply that something is being presented to us as beautiful which we think could not or ought not to be so presented. We feel the artist has gone out of bounds, and vehemently disapprove his adventure. But generally the artist knows the bounds that are good for him, and in the long run we usually have to accept his judgment. Experience seldom fails to prove us wrong. Velasquez's "El Gobbo," a deformed dwarf, is far more beautiful than his "Venus"— more beautiful in the sympathy the painter brought to understanding, more beautiful as exquisite workmanship, more beautiful even formally.

There probably are bounds, suggested in Aristotle's categories of the possible and probable, but nobody has ever been able definitely to draw the line where beauty ends and ugliness begins. And nobody ever will, for that would be to know to just what material the experience of beauty may extend. To imagine one knows this, is to demand the end of esthetic experiment. On the positive side, the ugly is what seems monstrous or intolerable to anyone. There is little uniformity in such judgments, and progress in esthetic experience normally consists in reclaiming for beauty much that one has earlier excluded therefrom. The ugly then is merely what sticks painfully in our esthetic crop. We may cough it up or get it down. If we get it down, it will surprisingly often turn out to have as good nutritive quality as any better accredited beauty. The category of ugliness would be an excellent basis for an unintelligence test in esthetics. In the length and character of a list of things and subjects written down as inherently ugly, one would have a singularly accurate measure of the writer's Philistinism.

In writing of taste I am not thinking of those intimate individual preferences concerning which Horace sensibly wrote we should not dispute. I am thinking rather of those broad agreements in taste, class by class and generation by generation, which profoundly influence both the creation and the appreciation of the work of art. For the purist, the social fact of taste is no part of esthetics. Every act of creation or reception is supposed to be absolutely personal, occurring in an isolated world containing only the artist, the art lover and the work of art. But such an attitude ignores the elementary processes of psychology. All the artist's previous activities of taste are more or less effective in each new work. All the art lover's earlier experience of beauty modifies and limits each new appreciation. In short, the esthetic transaction is never completely isolated. Moreover, the form of every work of art is necessarily much affected by the taste of a patronage either actual or prospective. And the going taste is equally a factor in creation, whether the artist's attitude be one of acceptance, indifference or revulsion. Indeed, the purists when they study the experience of beauty through art deal with a beauty based merely on a mass of weighty opinion.

Now the formation of these solid and widespread strata of esthetic opinion remains somewhat mysterious. Why did all the artists and patrons of the High Renaissance like the human form counterpoised—head, trunk, and limbs in various and actively balancing planes—in Michelangelo's very technical word, "serpentinated?" Why was this convention of pose in high favor for a full generation, only to give way to the lolling and sprawling and ill-contained poses of the mannerists? The answer may only be surmised. But the historic fact seems to rest upon the enthusiastically favorable response of a few persons of esthetic authority to the innovations in pose invented by

Leonardo da Vinci and Fra Bartolommeo and continued by such great painters as Raphael, Michelangelo and Titian. All these innovators were really drawing heavily on such antique sculpture as they knew. From these few arbiters, I take it, the new taste spread widely by a sort of swift contagion to all persons who were wide-awake esthetically. It seems a case under the general law of the power of all convinced and coherent minorities. It should be recalled that at the moment under consideration there was virtually no critical writing to reinforce by argument the general preference for the "serpentinated" figure. A little later such professional criticism was to become highly influential, as it is today, in the formation of social taste.

This theory of contagion from a few highly considered individuals seems to account for the starting of a taste. It is confirmed by humble analogies within everyone's experience. Why did I as a fifth-form schoolboy absurdly encase my legs in skin-fitting trousers, my feet in painfully pointed shoes, and disfigure my broad face by a derby hat all brim and practically crownless? Was it not because Mr. Berry Wall possessed fifty pairs of trousers of the skin-fitting type, while the Prince of Wales had appeared at the Newmarket Races with pointed shoes and a bowler all brim? In short, the pressure of a few arbiters was promptly brought to bear on the remote, suburban schoolboy.

But if the theory of contagion seems to account for the starting of taste or fashion, it does not account for the singular permanency of taste as compared with fashions. Fashions come and go. Taste changes, to be sure, but gradually and in keeping with itself. Michelangelo's "serpentinated" figure has never lacked champions for over four hundred years, whereas the sprawling and ill-contained figures of Giorgio Vasari and his fellow mannerists were in high favor for about a generation and ever since have been abhorred or ignored. For four hundred years there has been no serious challenge of Raphael's position as a great painter. Meanwhile we have had the Protestant Reformation, the abandonment of the duel, the end of absolute royalty, the prevalence of representative institutions, their threatened overthrow by the one-party system, the introduction of easy divorce, the Newtonian physics, and the new relativity. This list will show that, considered simply as a solid social fact, the approving taste for Raphael has been more permanent than any of the main attitudes in morals, religion, science and politics. As a going concern, esthetic taste seems to be at least as sure and as important as any of those cardinal principles by which we are governed, or profess to be governed, in our practical living. And this is true even if we admit, as we must, that taste enlists much mere lip service, for so do our most cherished maxims in morals, religion and politics.

Now the cause of the relative permanence of the greater formulations of taste eludes us. We may fall back on evolutionary phrases, mere words, that since in the psychical as in the physical field there is a tendency for the fittest to survive, what actually does survive is *ipso facto* the fittest. "Whatever is excellent, as God lives is permanent." But here we are logically in a vicious circle. We may perhaps insist merely that the fact that a spiritual preference has maintained its prestige through the centuries at least suggests that such a preference corresponds to our spiritual needs, that a sensible person will always take it into consideration, no more flouting casually the going taste than he would the going morality.

It should further be noted that social taste is not static but evolutionary, and, withal, that it involves a group element and a time element.

Professor Vladimir Simkhovitch has ingeniously traced the variability of the taste for Greek sculpture. It started about 1500 with an exaggerated admiration for such late Hellenistic sculptures as were about that time discovered— the Cleopatra, the torso of Hercules, the Laokoön, the Venus de' Medici, the Apollo Belvedere. All this was ultimately codified by Wincklemann some hundred and seventy years ago. Here it should be said that these admirers of what now seems Greek sculpture of an inferior order, rather deserve credit for divining the residual greatness of the Hellenistic decadence than discredit for ignoring the greater excellence of sculpture which they never saw.

With the coming of the Parthenon Marbles to London, fell the twilight upon the Vatican gods. The supreme excellence of Greek sculpture now meant the excellence of the school of Pheidias.

That taste held for half a century or so until the excavation of the more primitive marbles of Olympia. These promptly became the glory that was Greece.

Then the maidens of the Acropolis were dug up, and even earlier archaic statuary was recovered from the soil. Partly as a taste, but principally, I feel, as an archaeological fashion, archaic sculpture became the greatest Greek sculpture. You could trace its dominating influence up and down in the sculpture of the late nineteenth century.

Came then the great darkness or the great enlighten-
ment, as it may turn out to be, and all Greek sculpture
of whatever sort was rocked on its pedestals by the ebony
fetishes of the Congo blacks. Signs point to this being not
a revolution in taste, but merely a sharp shift in fashion.

Professor Simkhovitch shows without difficulty that the
formula of the supremacy of Greek sculpture has meant
historically the successive supremacy of at least four kinds
of Greek sculpture of very different quality, and there
with a philosophic and charmingly sceptical smile he
leaves his neatly developed theme. What he fails either to
note or to explain is the singular permanency of the formula
itself.

It is not for nothing that during four centuries of the most
intense development of Western culture, the Greeks have
seemed the greatest artists. Has not the varying content of
the formula been due to archaeological chance and historic
accident? Can we doubt that Raphael would have preferred the Venus of Cyrene to the Venus de' Medici, or
Rubens the Pheidian marbles to those garden sculptures
he assembled for the Earl of Arundel? Then the occasional
intrusion of mere archaeological fashion has now and
then temporarily perturbed the going taste for Greek sculpture. We shall not always accept as masterpieces the
old quantity manufacture of big archaic statues, though
high authority bids us so to do. With all shifts of reference,
the formula that somewhere in Greek sculpture we shall
find sculpture of the highest quality, still seems perfectly
sound.

The group element in social taste is too obvious to need
extensive illustration. At all times the best taste, or, more

accurately, the several varieties of better tastes, have been the possession of relatively few individuals forming loose but fairly coherent groups. The Tuscan poets who in Dante's lifetime and with his aid introduced the "sweet new style" with almost tedious repetition address their poetry to a small audience of "gentle souls." This public in the year 1300 may have been limited to a few score people of patrician or clerkly class, among whom the lyrics of Guido Guinicelli, of Guido Cavalcanti, of Cino da Pistoia and Dante Alighieri passed by oral tradition aided by rare manuscript copies. This group doubtless included many of those who admired the rising star of Giotto in painting, of Giovanni and Andrea Pisano in sculpture, of Arnolfo in architecture. One may reasonably imagine an overlap between a larger and a smaller group. The directness and heartiness of a Giotto and a Giovanni Pisano would have attracted a public to which the esoteric subtleties of the "sweet new style" was inaccessible. If there were only a few score to read Guido Guinicelli understandingly, there may easily have been a few thousand, the larger group including the smaller, to whom Giotto's robust and forthright art deeply appealed. We may reasonably infer this from the obituary notice of Giotto, telling of his great fame, by that eminently sober historian of Florence, Giovanni Villani.

As the Renaissance came with ever accelerated impetus, the number of "gentle souls" grew. Here much credit is due Petrarch, the legitimate heir of the "sweet new style." His influence swept throughout Italy and overflowed into Western Europe. We can now speak of an Italian taste in poetry, where fifty years earlier we could detect only a Tuscan taste. In another century the group grows still

larger. It has passed from scores far into the thousands.
Still another century and the works of Petrarch sell edition
by edition, alongside the new idyllic poetry of a Poliziano,
a Bembo, a Naugerius, a Sannazaro, and the old poets of
the "sweet new style" are successfully reprinted. The Italian
group representing the best taste in poetry probably coin-
cides pretty closely with the group that adored the sculpture of Donatello, Desiderio, and Michelangelo and the
painting of Leonardo, Raphael, Michelangelo, Andrea del
Sarto, Titian.

And the group of gentle spirits that love high poetry is
now extended internationally. In France Joachim du Bellay
and Pierre Ronsard are members; in remote England, the
Earl of Surrey and Sir Thomas Wyatt, with Edmund
Spenser and Sir Philip Sidney soon to follow. It was a
golden age of patronage for all the arts in Italy and for
poetry everywhere in Western Europe. It need hardly be
added that the Italian group readily draws the new opera
into the field of its enthusiasm; the English group, the
regenerated drama. At all stages we are dealing with the
concurrent enthusiasms of at most a few thousand highly
cultured individuals, of a group still unorganized, but
beginning to receive a degree of organization through the
new criticism of a Castelveltro, Du Bellay and Sidney in
poetry, of a Varchi, Vasari, and Aretino in the fine arts,
of a Baldassare Castiglione on the good aristocratic life in
general.

We must imagine this group of elect spirits living amid
what they would have unhesitatingly called the base people—the run of the human herd which as ever found its
esthetic joys in such sub-artistic forms as the anecdotal

wisecrack, the humorously smutty story, the simpler types of sentimental song, the loose-jointed romance, the dawning melodrama. But here it is important to note that the base people after all admired, if perhaps at times grudgingly and never quite understandingly, the elect spirits and so contributed substantially to their great if informal authority. One can imagine a shrewd Italian tradesman to whom by report or slight reading some information of Castiglione's "The Courtier" had come, at once thinking it the nonsense proper only to gentlefolk while somewhat envying those who were free to devote themselves to a nonsense so gentle. If only by a sort of silent assent, what the gentle spirits approved was pretty generally regarded as admirable even if personally one lacked the wit or the inclination to admire it.

In our day it is the democratic unwillingness of the traditionally base people to admit their baseness, and the consequent inferiority of their esthetic enjoyments, that deprives the various small groups which may be said to represent the good taste of our moment of anything like general authority. Any dominating new taste must have a broad basis.

Before the sun of the Renaissance had set, the coherence of international good taste began to give way to diverging tastes and fashions. While the preference for the grand style inaugurated by Leonardo and Michelangelo was continued by conservative professional criticism quite to our own day, the laity and radical criticism formed new groups at the expense of the old.

Before Raphael died, Parmigianino rejected the principle of dynamic equilibrium and decorum in favor of far-fetched unbalanced poses and elongations in the interest of a new gracefulness. He won his followers, and mannerism ruled Italian painting through the Pontormos, Bronzinos, and Vasaris till the Carracci sounded the eclectic recall to order. Similarly, literary taste ceases to present a solid front. We have the metaphysical school in England, the clever affectations of a Marini and Fierenzuola, the mock heroics of Butler and Scarron, the sprawling copiousness of a Le Sage. And these new tastes, or as it may be, new fashions, evoke critical championship. Besides, the Renaissance taste is gradually undermined by perfunctory adherence. Through the eighteenth century almost without exception all intelligent persons nominally approved the grand style, but they bought the pictures of Watteau, Hogarth, Boucher and Chardin, and the books of Defoe, Diderot, Smollett, Richardson, Sterne and Restif de la Bretonne.

To trace the disintegrating process further is unnecessary. The facts are accessible to all persons of any reading. Progressively professional criticism has played a greater part in consolidating group opinion and keeping it separate. So that today if one wished to ascertain the conservative taste of the day in the fine arts he would only have to read my accomplished friend Mr. Royal Cortissoz. Should he wish to locate the taste of the right center, he might do well to consult my books; for the left center, the late Roger Fry would admirably serve his purpose; for the extreme left, Mr. Wilenski or Monsieur Ozenfant.

Now these analyses of the variety of tastes are by no means simply academic; upon artistic creation they have the most practical bearing. If on the whole the modern era has in the fine arts hardly equalled Greece at her best, the great period of cathedral building, the Italian Renaissance, it is precisely because there has been no such coherent body of taste to support the artist and guide patronage. If on the contrary we have surpassed the Romans, the medieval age, and the Renaissance, while fairly vying with the Greeks in literature, it is because there has been a substantial body of directing literary taste, because the literary battles have been fought on clear and reasonable issues, and because on the whole there has been less confusion than in the fine arts between considerations of mere fashion and those of authentic style.

And if in music we have excelled the entire past, it has been precisely because modern music from Bach down has enlisted a singularly coherent and intelligent taste whether in lay patronage or in professional criticism. All this has given to the great composers and interpreters of music a security and an esthetic support which the practitioners of the fine arts have too often lacked. For this reason, of the traditional arts music is the most alive today, while, except for architecture, the fine arts struggle on apparently as pale and diminishing survivals.

We have noticed the tendency of the like-minded esthetic group to expand and at a certain point to subdivide, with sacrifice of efficacious influence. The further question arises, what are the limits of such a group? For the whole of recorded history the answer is plain—the normal and narrower limit is that of a political unit—a city or state; the wider limit, that of a particular civilization. Thus the historical range of late Hellenistic taste is well expressed in the familiar adage "Conquered Greece conquered Rome."

So we may say that French taste dominated the Middle Ages in the West; Italian taste, the European Renaissance.

May such an esthetic group be formed across civilizations? There are recent signs that this is not impossible. What prevents is of course the hard edges and exclusions with which any coherent civilization naturally safeguards its integrity. May a wider tolerance and sympathy annul these exclusions? The question can hardly be dogmatically answered. I once had the high privilege of the acquaintance of the great Japanese critic Okakura Kakuzo, profound and discriminating student both of the art of the Far East and of that of Europe. The limitations of his sympathy were most instructive and most intelligently based. For lack of spiritual quality, he depreciated the exquisite art of Japan and China from the seventeenth century on. For the same lack of spiritual values, he used to say that great Western European art did not, as our critics maintain, begin with Cimabue but rather ended with him. Our Renaissance was a progressive derogation of spiritual ideals in favor of an unwarranted Humanism. Within our great period of painting, he saw nothing really significant save the drawings of Rembrandt and, with some reservations the etchings of the same master.

Now, though as a fledgling art critic with his pinfeathers unpleasantly visible, I was properly in a relation of pupilage to a great sage like Okakura, I used to feel that his formulas were too hard, that something was to be said for the nervous fastidiousness of a Korin, for the great Ming painters, even for the delightfully ingenious artistry of the Japanese masters of the color print. As an incipient humanist, I felt that Okakura gravely overestimated the spirituality of our medieval artists, who as a class were chiefly supreme decorators, while also failing to perceive the spiritual implications of the humanist attitude. I recall this experience merely to show how difficult it is for an art lover fully committed to the highest ideals of his own civilization to appreciate those of a civilization alien to him.

Nevertheless there are abundant signs that such bounds may successfully be broken and with advantage to him who breaks them. The early European enthusiasts for the so-called popular Japanese art, La Farge, Whistler, Degas, Van Gogh, Gonse, Burty, Fenollosa gave themselves generously to the alien civilization and in so doing enriched the art and the taste of their own. To the best trained of our fathers, a Chinese painting or statue of the great period would have seemed merely odd. Today many of us find in this art a tranquil exaltation which our own art very rarely offers us. As a devotee of Blake, a Sir Laurence Binyon finds himself at home with the poetical dialect of the great painters of China and Japan. Latterly the desire to break our Western bounds has been fairly hectic. To reinvigorate an anemic painting the miniaturists of Persia are called on for first aid, and the Negro carvers of the ebony fetishes of the Congo. How much of this is mere caprice and fashion, how much a real extension of esthetic sympathy, only the future can tell. For what they may be worth such facts at least point to the possibility of a real cosmopolitanism in taste, paralleling a similar new cosmopolitanism in recent political ideals.

This inconclusive discussion may close on a hopeful note with a quotation from Charles Baudelaire's reflections concerning the universal exposition of 1855.

"What would a modern Wincklemann (we are full of them, the nation bursts with them, the lazy minded go crazy over them), what would he say before a Chinese object, an object strange, bizarre, elaborately contoured, intense in color, and often refined to a vanishing point? Nevertheless it is an example of the universal beauty; but in order that it be understood, the critic, the spectator must effect in himself a mystical transformation—must by an act of will acting upon the imagination teach himself to share in the surroundings which have given birth to so unusual a flowering. Few men have in any full sense that divine grace of cosmopolitanism, but all may in various degrees acquire it."

That Baudelaire realized the full difficulties of esthetic understanding across national and racial boundaries is shown in a sentence on the opposite page from our long quotation:

"When judging other peoples, every people is academic; every people is barbarous when judged."

It is despite such hard historical facts that we must entertain the hope of an ultimate "divine grace of cosmopolitanism."

Books have their fates, writes Horace, and so have all other works of art. This absence or presence of the understanding and appreciative group means for the work of art, as we have earlier noted, its veritable death or resurrection or some pale limbo existence which is neither. Take the case of Giotto. For two centuries after his death there was a general admiration of his greatness, and the reason given was his gracious naturalness. This is stressed by two generations of that notable family of historians, the

Villani ; it transpires in the intelligent imitation of a Masaccio, in the eulogies of Lorenzo Ghiberti and Leonardo da Vinci. Then comes a change. Giotto exchanges the rôle of great artist for that of venerated ancestor. According to his lights he did well, was the finest expression of the childhood of our art, to be gratefully remembered despite his defects, because he after all started us on the right way. Such is the condescending note from Vasari, about 1550, for about two hundred and fifty years, during which Giotto survived only in a pale archaeological existence. The Italians neglected all his frescoes and actually marred and whitewashed his ripest works, at Florence.

Towards the end of the eighteenth century the highly intelligent Abate Lanzi, the first art historian to divide Italian painting into schools, praised Giotto as a very great painter absolutely and in his own right. But the new word fell on deaf ears. Only a few years later Goethe travelled through Italy without caring enough about the Giottos to note them. A little later the really sensitive Stendhal at least had the merit of freely plagiarizing Lanzi, while he added independently a tribute to Giotto's fine sense of color and a sensible warning that the modern painters had no reason to pity Giotto.

With the German Nazarenes, the English Pre-Raphaelites, and the Neo-Catholic movement, Giotto received a one-sided rehabilitation for his simple piety, which, though essential to his art, was perhaps its least individual feature. Some sixty years ago John Ruskin emphasized this point of view with great eloquence, adding little else. It remained for Mr. Berenson some forty years ago to convince us all of what only Masaccio, Leonardo, Raphael and Michelangelo knew earlier, that Giotto is great because of his artifice, because of his masterly way of conceiving and expressing and organizing forms into compositions. It took about five hundred years of partial understanding or neglect to put the fame of Giotto beyond the hazards that equally threaten books and all other works of art.

Again, this time element in social taste and patronage is not merely historical and academic, but has a most tragically practical bearing. Unhappy is that artist who is wholly out of tune with the taste of his times. A great but frustrated American author chose to plumb the sinister depths of personality, at the moment when the serene optimism of Emerson was in vogue, with the superficial urbanity of Irving and the gentle narrative charm of Longfellow. In his untimely endeavor, Herman Melville broke his heart and nearly burnt out his brain. Lacking the steadying support of a sympathetic public taste or even of an understanding criticism, Melville's most ambitious books, with the possible exception of *Moby Dick,* remained unclarified; he survives chiefly by such minor productions as *Typee.* He passed his last twenty years, which should be a writer's best, almost unproductive, on the pittance of an appraiser of customs. Had he followed instead of in a degree anticipating George Meredith and the great Russian novelists, his accomplishment and fame would have been far different. With a somewhat similar disposition, Melville's friend, Hawthorne, reasonably won through, partly because his themes were solidly based in the sacred and popular soil of New England, while his rather low energy and consequent restraint were current good literary form.

The right relation of the artist to going taste may briefly

be suggested. It is first of all a sense for such going tastes, for now there are always many, as correspond to his own. Generally the artist—and it is equally true of the man who seeks a good life—does well to accept a tradition wholeheartedly yet also critically. Such a chosen tradition should be not a trammel but a support. His attitude should be that of carrying a tradition forward, of fulfilling it through development and enrichment. In this way he has the support not merely of like-minded contemporaries, but also of like-minded predecessors. Here he finds the surest basis for self-criticism and self-development.

All this is easy to write and hard to do. Apprenticeship and discipleship, the normal way of entering into a tradition through the relation of pupil to master—all this has given way to the generally impersonal instruction of the art schools. Even the old sound traditions of good craftsmanship have yielded to confusion. Then, with the spread of archeological discovery and research and popularization of the history of art, available traditions are perplexingly various. This is perhaps especially true of the painter, sculptor and architect, but is true also for the artist in whatever field. The danger is that of eclecticism, of shuffling a specious new hand out of incompatible old cards. One sees it everywhere. All the same, the personal problem of the artist remains what it was, to find his public, present or past—to recognize his spiritual ancestors. The growing difficulty of the problem should be only a challenge to the judgment of the creative artist.

My silence as to laboratory experimentation in esthetics has been based on the fact that much desultory reading in this field has left the strong conviction that the results were in the main insignificant or at best are such as would have been more readily furnished by simple common sense. The opportune appearance of an extensive summary of these experiments in Professor Albert R. Chandler's *Beauty and Human Nature,* New York, 1934, gives me a chance to reconsider my old conviction, but changes it in no essentials. The problem of esthetic experience seems far too complicated to be covered or much illuminated by such quite elementary experiments as are possible in the laboratory.

Most of these experiments have sought to establish the inherent pleasantness or unpleasantness of single colors, or simple color combinations; of simple shapes or their combinations; of various proportions; of musical notes; of various musical instruments; of vowel sounds, and of single words.

In general, carefully conducted tests along these lines yielded entirely inconsistent results. Preferences were either capricious or probably based on associations extraneous to the tests. Even had the preferences been consistently explicable, their bearing on esthetic experience of the usual complication seems to be remote. For example, the person who reports he dislikes a disk of yellow will not necessarily dislike yellow in a picture; the man who likes red as a color may not like an excess of it in a picture; the person who prefers a particular vowel sound, may or may not find it agreeable in a given passage of verse or prose; he who loves a particular word may not find it appropriate in a given literary context; he who prefers a rectangle of a certain ratio of sides, might not like a façade of such a ratio; a musical note or a musical instrument may seem unpleasing to one who would like both in an orchestra. For such reasons I feel no more is to be expected from such experiments in the future than we have had in the past.

A curious and interesting experiment on the effect of the mere sound of poetry was conducted by Professor R. C. Givler. Taking passages from Wordsworth, Milton and Shelley, he recombined the sounds of these passages into blank verse lines which made no sense but kept approximately the rhythm and measure of the original lines. When these nonsense lines were read they produced pretty much the general mood of the passage thus travestied. What seemed to be proved was that the mere sound of poetry apart from any sense involved may have about the same evocative effect, as regards mood, as musical sounds. But was this really proved? Professor Givler's reshuffling of the sounds in a passage of poetry is no real equivalent for the sound of the original passage. Moreover the declamation of his nonsense verses rather than their inherent vocalic character may have induced the rough parallelism of mood. Finally, simple common sense might suggest that if a melody of musical notes will produce some vague effect which can be distinguished and described, so might well a similar melody of speech sounds. This kind of power of the human voice has long been recognized. Still, the experiment is one of the more interesting described in Professor Chandler's book. The reader may profitably consult in this matter his Chapter 14.

Beyond this, I glean not much except that music lovers who habitually have visual associations when enjoying music are not those best trained and competent. This nicely confirms my own mere surmise, page 14.

In general, the careful reading of Professor Chandler's very orderly and interesting book much strengthens my old doubt that the psychological laboratory can contribute anything really important towards the solution of esthetic problems as we actually meet them in human experience.

The beginning of the experience of beauty is, for me, simply an active sharing of the universal analogy of rhythm. At this point beauty is a one. But this sharing draws so immediately, richly and variously upon kindred experiences, which with every person are different, that beauty becomes a many. The only possible standard or fixed beauty conceivable is the total psychical activity of the artist in creating some particular work of art. Other point of measurement or reference there is really none. If we could recover this creative experience, then and only then should we have an absolute beauty. Since we never can recover this creative experience, not even the artist himself, beauty is necessarily relative and existent only in modalities. Of the collective experiences of beauty, the group taste we have already considered, relativity is the very law.

Hence for any real purpose of definition we need at least a rough classification of the chief varieties of beauty as actually experienced. Here the traditional nomenclature, though I agree with Mr. C. K. Ogden that it admits of no precise psychological analysis, remains practically very useful. The seventeenth and eighteenth centuries worked out a whole vocabulary of such qualifiers—the sublime, the beautiful, the charming, the attractive, the tragic, the comic, the idyllic and so on, words without end. Perhaps we may get along with a greater economy of adjectives.

Volkelt who of all estheticians has considered the matter most elaborately suggests contrasting pairs, namely: elementary, intellectualized; naïve, sentimental; objective, subjective; magnifying, matter-of-fact; typifying, individualizing. Now the test of such a classification is that the various kinds of admitted natural and artistic beauty should fit into the categories without too much overlapping, and it seems to me that Volkelt's classifications are so general that any work of art might have to appear under nearly every head. For example the first part of *Faust* is elemental, generally naïve, but occasionally sentimental, subjective, magnifying, and individualizing. This suggests, what is the fact, that Volkelt's classifications really repeat each other, and while they are soundly psychological, are to be regarded as qualifiers of larger and simpler categories. Other classifications are likely to be based on the usual divisions of the arts, with the disadvantage that such divisions are not psychological.

The classification which I have tentatively adopted and now offer with some misgivings seems, when checked against well understood beauties of art and nature, to hold everything without too much overlapping. The scheme is best presented in a table, which the reader will find at the end of this book. Here then I need give only briefly the reasons for the classification. Four very broad yet fairly distinct categories with their respective subdivisions have been checked for more than a hundred concrete instances and seem to work. They are the Sublime, the Delectable, the Characterful and the Comic. It should be noted that the sublime and delectable depend upon perceptions of harmony, and the comic upon perceptions of incongruity or discord, while the characterful may rest either upon the sense of harmony or that of discord.

We find the experience of beauty at its height in the sublime. It early engaged the attention of critics, Aristotle, Lucretius, and Plotinus, for example, and was the first esthetic category to receive separate elaboration, in the famous treatise ascribed traditionally to Longinus. Most investigators of the sublime find that it is evoked by impressions of magnitude of scale or power—effects in art or nature which produce an initial awe. Most critics regard the overcoming of such awe, its transformation into a tense serenity of acceptance, as the distinguishing mark of the sublime. Undoubtedly many experiences of the sublime follow this course, but not all. There is a sublimity about the massed and moving clouds in the heaven, even when they contain no menace of storm. It was this sense of a necessarily hostile or repelling element in the sublime, which has led many estheticians from Burke up and down to regard the sublime as transcending beauty and not to be classified therewith. This is to rob beauty of its supreme manifestation.

Psychologically, in comparison with other esthetic states, the sublime is experienced at very high tension and with little change of level. An analogy might be the short waves which carry a radio message for thousands of miles. It is the capacity to assimilate and enjoy this tension, to live unperturbed on this lofty level, which constitutes the pleasure-giving character of the sublime. On this the Pseudo-Longinus, not usually a suggestive author, writes admirably:

"For the true sublime, by some virtue of its nature, elevates us; uplifted with a sense of proud possession, we are filled with joyful pride, as if we ourselves had produced the very thing we heard."

Santayana has very subtly analyzed the process, merely sketched above, by which through exclusions and a consequent greater detachment we build up a magnified and more stable self.

"When we come upon a great evil or an irreconcilable power, we are driven to seek our happiness by the shorter and heroic road; then we recognize the hopeless foreignness of what lies before us, and stiffen ourselves against it. Thus for the first time we reach the sense of our possible separation from our world, and of our abstract stability; and with this comes the sublime."

This excellently describes the "Stoic sublime," to use Mr. Santayana's happy phrase. There is as well an "Epicurean sublime" which merely rests on greatly magnified and intensified experiences of order and harmony.

Accurately speaking, the sublime is experienced as a quality of an action, or of nature either acting or, through *Einfühlung,* conceived of as acting. In the arts, literature and music are the terrain of the sublime; in the visual arts generally, it seems to be a secondary or associational quality. In architecture, however, the sublime is at home. The sublimity of the interior of Santa Sophia is idiomatic and intrinsic, depending on no religious association.

In literature the great tragedies and the loftier flights of the great epics furnish the best as well as the most familiar examples of the sublime. It rests upon the hopeless conflicts heroically undertaken, upon clashes with some ineluctable fate only dimly perceived or not at all. The Œdipuses, Antigones, Hectors, King Lears, Othellos in their shipwreck illustrate the greatness of the human spirit, a greatness which we may share.

Since the sublime has always been regarded as the supreme esthetic experience, there has been a great endeavor on the part of the artists of the ages to attain it, and criticism has too generously credited with sublimity works of art that really fall under lower categories. For example, the interior of Santa Sophia seems to me sublime; that of Durham Cathedral heroic; that of Saint Peter's merely grandiose. These subdivisions are I believe practically useful. Shakespeare in *Macbeth* is sublime, in *Julius Caesar* heroic. It is a distinction that holds broadly for his tragedies and histories. Corneille is rarely sublime, almost always heroic, and at his worst merely grandiose. Swinburne's *Atalanta in Calydon* has its heroic moments, but is in the main of a highly melodic grandiosity. Victor Hugo's poetry and the tense episodes of his novels are in the main of a grandiosity deceptively raised towards the heroic and even the sublime through the color and intensity of the rhetoric.

Very little painting and almost no lyrical poetry seems to me to be rightly called sublime. Michelangelo is sublime in the Sistine ceiling with a tendency to lapse now and then into the grandiose—the famous figure of Jonah. Raphael seems to attain Mr. Santayana's "Epicurean sublime" in "The School of Athens," but in the cartoons and the later frescoes he seems to me generally grandiose and only exceptionally really heroic.

Much of Beethoven is sublime; Brahms at his best is heroic and when below his best, grandiose. Berlioz, seeking the sublime and heroic, achieved an accomplished grandiosity. Possibly the element of grandiosity in Wagner is much greater than his admirers will admit. "Carmen" seems to me an admirable example of a consistently heroic opera, albeit the heroism is of a sinister order.

Further examples the table will furnish in abundance. It may be useful in leaving the sublime to show how the broad classifications of Volkelt seem to fit as modalities within such a classification as I have suggested.

The sublime may be of an instinctive or elemental or of a reasoned and studied sort—respectively in Bunyan and Milton. It may be naïve with Homer or tend towards sentimentalism with Virgil. Objective it may be as with Dante or subjectively colored as with Browning at his rare great moments. It may with Pindar and Sophocles employ conscious emphasis, or it may skilfully use a restrained and matter-of-fact style—instances, the story of Ugolino in Dante, the death scene of Roland in the great "Chanson." Finally it may deal with the typical, as in Marlowe or with the highly characterized as in Shakespeare. In short, Volkelt's cardinal classifications seem to serve as useful subdivisions of any of mine.

Before proceeding to our other fundamental classifications it is well to insist that all the partitions are more or less pervious. Each experience of beauty freely draws from the others whatever may enrich or enhance it. Thus the sublime in all its modalities will have in it something delectable, if austerely so. It will often seek a higher reality of effect through thorough characterization. By way of foil or contrast, it may even draw upon the apparently alien riches of the comic in any or all of its varieties. But all these borrowings will be fully assimilated in a general effect of sublimity.

In classifying under the delectable—Poussin's noble word for subsuming the entire teleology of art—the major part of experiences of beauty, I am fully aware of the breadth and looseness of the category. Yet it seems to correspond to the very various nature of the material to be classified. The word implies an amenity of experience comprising a certain dignity and serenity—that "grave beauty" which Winckle-mann attributed to Greek sculpture, which Poussin himself embodied in his painting. Psychologically the delectable is experienced at less tension than the sublime and permits wider shifts of level. From the hearer or beholder it exacts less conscious effort. It readily loses tension and gravity, shading off into experiences where no effort is involved and where levels shift widely and irresponsibly. One may say that Gluck's "Orfeo" is delectable, while Lehar's "Merry Widow" is pretty, sprightly and witty, but of a much attenuated delectability. Between these extremes lie infinite modulations; of multiplying labels there would be no end. The graceful (Correggio's painting), the elegiac (Milton's *Lycidas*), the pathetic (Landor's *Rose Aylmar*), the lyrical (Shelley's *Indian Serenade*), the reflective (Wordsworth's *Tintern Abbey*), the idyllic (Goethe's *Hermann and Doro-thea*), the elegant (Horace's "O matre pulchra filia pul-chrior"), the mannered elegant (Pope's *Rape of the Lock*), the sprightly (Southey's *John Gilpin's Ride* or Fortuny's painting), the weird (Poe's *The Raven* or Coleridge's *Lay of the Ancient Mariner*)—all these and many more similar would be obvious and fairly tenable subclassifications of the delectable. Probably they would serve no really useful purpose.

By the delectable we mean what the eighteenth century (which may be said to have respectfully kicked the sublime upstairs) meant by beauty, and it is of this relatively untaxing beauty that Lord Bacon demanded that it should have "some strangeness in its proportions." It is here that the Aristotelian unexpectedness reigns, effecting swift and telling changes of psychic levels. Such tragedy as is short of the sublime (Racine's), the ordinary dramatic and, when good, the melodramatic fall comfortably under the auspices of the delectable. Some of these tentative subdivisions are presented with examples in the table at the end of the book. It will be noted that the category of the delectable is precisely Goethe's central class of serious-playful beauty (page 244), with some overlapping into his class of the playful. And his synthesis of the serious and the playful explains why there are many rhythmically related levels in the delectable whereas the sublime is experienced with small change of level.

As the sublime tends to enrich itself from the parallel varieties of beauty, so does the delectable. It will draw moderately on the sublime and at times very freely on the characteristic and the comic. Such overflow is admirably illustrated by a romantic comedy such as *As You Like It,* or by a novel like Scott's *The Antiquary*.

Again, in making of the characteristic a main variety of beauty I have Goethe's precedent. Here psychologically the tension is still less, for the appeal is less to sympathy than to understanding. The attitude of appreciation is relatively objective. When, exceptionally, the appeal to sympathy is strong, the characteristic may tend to become the sublime as in the best portraiture of Rembrandt. But in general we are dealing with a less agitated and impassioned experience in which simple curiosity tends to dominate. The true characterizer is always setting the question "What are people and things like?" adding, if philosophically minded, the further question, "How do they get that way?" Jane Austen is perhaps the high type of the pure characterizer.

Obvious subdivisions need hardly be dwelt on. One may think of characterization as generalizing,—Molière's Harpagon, or Voltaire's Le Huron; or as highly individualizing—Flaubert's Emma Bovary or Tolstoy's Anna Karenina; as magnifying, Boswell's Johnson; as caricaturing—Daumier's lawyers, Sterne's *Tristram Shandy*. And the grotesque may be regarded, according to its quality, as the heroizing or degradation of the characteristic.

Naturally the realm of the characteristic is the home of the novel and the biography as it is of much critical and descriptive art. Comedy, portrait and genre painting here belong. It is the field of most good illustration.

Apart from producing its own glories, the characteristic is the natural feeder of all the other varieties of beauty. The sublime, the delectable in all its phases, the comic will all call upon the characteristic so far as they need it, if only to increase the credibility of their effects. Of all the main varieties of beauty it has the widest legitimate overflow. Conversely, the characteristic will draw freely from all the other categories of the beautiful, will move readily in the direction of the delectable or the comic.

Psychologically the tension of the characteristic is low, being generally just that of ordinary living enhanced by art. On the other hand, it may evoke all tensions that arise from character in thought or action and, as we have already noted, pass over into the sublime. And the levels of the experience of the characteristic are as various as those of individual character itself. The maintenance of a dominating mood is less important than it is in the sublime or the delectable, for character is not always consistent and unified, indeed is often quite the contrary. Diana Vernon can do a shabby and uncharacteristic thing and still remain Diana Vernon. George Meredith must take her as she comes and not as she ought to be. In short, in the sublime there seems to be some sort of reference to an ideal fortitude and rectitude; in the delectable, a reference to an ideally pleasurable serenity; in the characteristic such reference to an ideal is ordinarily absent or merely tentative. When such reference is clear and emphatic, the characteristic is moving towards the delectable or the heroic. Thus *Marius the Epicurean* may be said to balance between the characteristic and the delectable; Plato's Socrates in *The Apology,* between the characteristic and the heroic or sublime.

The comic has been briefly discussed earlier in this chapter and here requires only a few supplementary observations. With the sublime at the extreme end of the scale of beauty, the comic has certain interesting coincidences. In both categories, great scale, magnification, plays a large part. But magnification in the sublime has inherent fitness while in the comic it is arbitrarily imposed. Good examples are the Rabelaisian giant hero of the American lumberjack, Paul Bunyan, the Gargantuan family of Rabelais himself, the giant of Jack the Giant Killer, Homer's Poly-phemus. They should be compared with Prometheus or Milton's Satan. To minimize is also a standard comic pro-cedure. In short, any great unexpected change in physical or psychical scale produces a comic effect, as an assertion of the incongruous. Beyond this, the table at the end of the book may spare me much writing and the reader super-fluous reading.

The comic naturally fortifies itself from the charac-teristic, seeks a degree of delectability, and, in the grotesque, may approach the heroic or sublime (Cyrano de Bergerac; Dr. Samuel Johnson). Psychologically the levels of the comic are highly *staccato* or intermittent. The tension is rather low and of short duration. In this, the comic is the opposite of the sublime, though psychologically the oppo-site of the sublime is less the comic than the base or the mean. The tolerance implied in the genial comic is ob-viously analogous to that magnanimity by which the sub-lime is distinguished.

Such classifications as have been roughly suggested are to be regarded merely as conveniences of thought repre-senting approximately the main orientation of the various experiences of beauty. Between these more or less artificial categories there is constant interpenetration. The true diagram would not be simply tabular. The more suggestive diagram, which with some misgivings I present as an ap-pendix, would consist of four polygonal cells, each touch-ing the others at two or three sides. The partitions are to be thought of like the sheaths of living cells, as sufficiently tight to preserve the integrity of the habitual content, yet as somewhat pervious and permitting a constant but not far-reaching osmosis. In the figure I have given the delectable and the characteristic, the classifications which most tend to overflow, three sides in contact with other categories; the comic and sublime, more self-contained categories, two sides. But the figure will suggest that something from any cell may get into any other directly or indirectly. So, while the mere approximateness of the figure is fully admitted, it may be useful to the reader.

After writing a book on esthetics, the question tardily arises, What is the use of esthetics anyway? The most obvious use is simply the exercise and gratification of intellectual curiosity. At a certain stage of development our minds challenge insatiably their own processes, wish to understand their own activities. This tendency there is no gainsaying. We simply want to know what is going on inside ourselves, and we do our best to find out. Esthetics is merely the attempt to suggest what is actually going on when we experience beauty. As a field of special study, it needs defense just as much as and no more than psychology and philosophy.

Yet I believe esthetic analysis may have a more personal usefulness. While analyzing those activities of the soul that make the sense of beauty, if only for their unexpected richness and implication, we may gain a deeper respect for these beautifying activities. Such a heightened respect and understanding may intensify and enrich our subsequent direct experiences of beauty. But we get this good only on condition of a real humility. The danger of all esthetic investigation is that we may become more interested in our own receptive processes than we are in nature, the artist, the work of art. And the danger is always present, for, after all, whatever we know about beauty—in contrast with simply experiencing it—is merely what we may learn about our own receptive life and that of others. Very great estheticians, even an Emmanuel Kant, often strike me as caring very little about art, and very much about the feelings they would have had if they cared. From his mere circumstances, the esthetic life of Kant must have been thin and poor. Profoundly impressed with the wonder of his own soul, he seems to me only superficially impressed with the wonders of art and nature. Less strenuous thinkers on esthetics, a Schopenhauer, a Santayana, give the sense of a far more rich and various experience of beauty. It is as true of esthetics as it is of direct perception of beauty, that the way to deeper knowledge and fuller experience is the way of self-abnegation.

And, in conclusion, the broader and still more searching question imposes itself, "What is the use of beauty and art?" It is, in brief, to establish a fuller and richer humanity in the lover of beauty. Such an enhancement of personality, such larger living is primarily within the sealed garden of beauty itself. The habit of living in a readier and more discriminating sympathy with the beauty of nature and art may or may not be extended into our living generally. That will depend upon our general character. From the experience of beauty we gain much that is available for everyday experiences requiring discriminating sympathy; whether we avail ourselves of it or not is another matter, concerning which beauty issues no commands. Conversely, the higher personal experiences of morality give us much that is available for our activities of beauty, but again morality does not order this extension. It is, I believe, a part of the good life to discern the parallelisms and analogies between these two fields of activity and to strive to blend them. But the blending is our personal task; the two fields do not touch intrinsically. Through our own will and wisdom they may be brought into contact. It is we who impose the synthesis, and we may or may not be great enough to do it.

Negatively, no one was ever worse off morally for an abundant experience of beauty. Positively, insofar as anyone experiences beauty, he is a better human being, lives more richly and generously wherever beauty is. Outside of this field, his moral destiny is in his own hands, and these may be feeble or strong. Thus, while many have crossed over unconsciously and blessedly from the realm of beauty to that of the good life, my practical advice to anyone who wishes to negotiate this often perilous pass, is to start from the good life.

In similar spirit Professor A. V. Whitehead has written admirably in *Adventures in Ideas*. In his words rather than in my own I may most effectively bid my reader farewell:

"It is the essence of art to be artificial, but it is its perfection to return to nature, remaining art. In short, art is the education of nature. Thus in its broadest sense art is civilization, is nothing other than the unremitting aim at the major perfections of harmony."

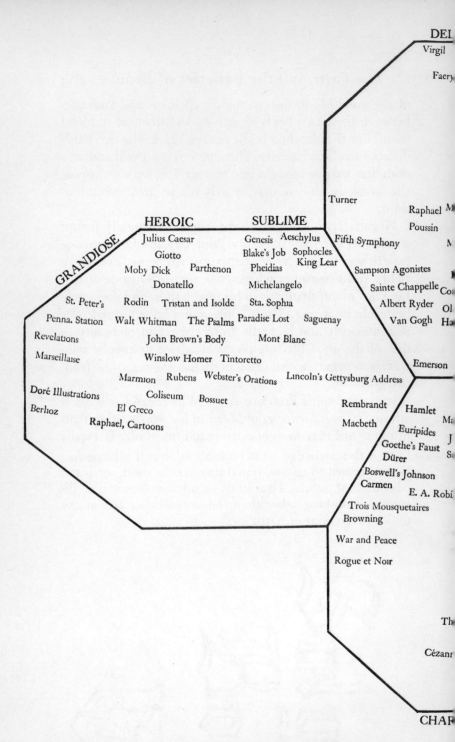

What is classified is the experience of beauty evoked by the works or scenes cited. When a title stand

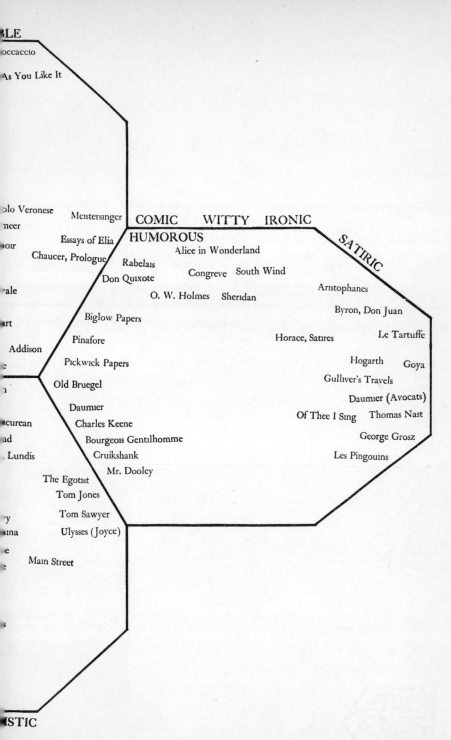

LE

occaccio

As You Like It

olo Veronese

neer   Meistersinger   COMIC   WITTY   IRONIC

oir   Essays of Elia HUMOROUS   SATIRIC

Chaucer, Prologue   Rabelais   Alice in Wonderland

ale   Don Quixote   Congreve   South Wind

rt   O. W. Holmes   Sheridan   Aristophanes

         Biglow Papers   Byron, Don Juan

Addison   Pinafore   Horace, Satires   Le Tartuffe

e   Pickwick Papers   Hogarth   Goya

n   Old Bruegel   Gulliver's Travels

curean   Daumier   Daumier (Avocats)

ad   Charles Keene   Of Thee I Sing   Thomas Nast

Lundis   Bourgeois Gentilhomme   George Grosz

         Cruikshank   Les Pingouins

      Mr. Dooley

The Egotist

Tom Jones

y   Tom Sawyer

ina   Ulysses (Joyce)

e

      Main Street

STIC

rder it has qualities of the adjoining class. Blank space is left to be filled at the reader's judgment.

BIBLIOGRAPHY

T HERE has been no attempt to record my entire reading for this book. I have listed only books which, even though I may not have quoted them, have been especially useful to me, and which I can recommend to the reader.

Aristotle, *The Poetics;* Longinus, *On the Sublime,* Loeb Classical Library. New York and London, 1932.

Barnes, Albert C., *The Art in Painting*. New York, 1925.

Basch, Victor, *Essai Critique sur l'Esthétique de Kant,* 2ᵉ ed. Paris, 1927.

Baudelaire, Charles, *Variétés Critiques*, 2 vols. Paris, Crès.

Bell, Clive, *On Enjoying Pictures*. London and New York, 1934.

Carritt, E. F., *The Theory of Beauty*. London, 1928.

Chandler, Albert R., *Beauty and Human Nature*. New York, 1934.

Cheney, Sheldon, *Expressionism in Art*. New York, 1934.

Colman, Samuel, *Nature's Harmonic Unity*. New York, 1912.

Coomaraswamy, Ananda Kentish, *The Transformation of Nature in Art*. Cambridge, Mass., 1934.

Croce, Benedetto, *Estetica*. Bari, 1908.

Delacroix, Eugène, *Œuvres Littéraires*, 2 vols. Paris, Crès.

Dewey, John, *Art as Experience*. New York, 1934.

Flaccus, L. W., *The Spirit and Substance of Art*. New York, 1931.

Fry, Roger E., *Transformations*. London, 1926.

Gauss, Christian, "Sinclair Lewis *versus* his Education," *Saturday Evening Post,* December 26, 1931, pp. 20-1, 54-6.

Goethe, J. W. von, *Schriften zur Kunst,* Bd. 33-35. Jubiläums Ausgabe.

Hambidge, Jay, *Dynamic Symmetry, the Greek Vase.* New Haven, 1920.

Hildebrandt, Karl, *Das Problem der Form.* Stuttgart, 1910.

James, Henry, *The Art of the Novel.* New York, 1924.

La Farge, John, *Considerations on Painting.* New York, 1901.

Lee, Vernon and Anstruther-Thomson, *Beauty and Ugliness.* London and New York, 1912.

Lipps, Theodor, *Grundlegung der Ästhetik,* 2 Auf. Leipzig, 1914.

————*Die Ästhetische Betrachtung und die Bildende Kunst.* Leipzig, 1906.

Listowel, William Francis Hare, Earl of, *A Critical History of Modern Aesthetics.* London, 1933.

Lowes, John L., *The Road to Xanadu.* Boston, 1927.

McMahon, A. Philip, *The Meaning of Art.* New York, 1930.

Maritain, Jacques, *Art et Scolastique.* Paris, 1927.

Ogden, C. K., Richards, I. A., and Wood, James, *The Foundations of Aesthetics.* London, 1922.

Parker, DeWitt H., *The Analysis of Beauty.* New Haven, 1926.

Richards, I. R., *Principles of Literary Criticism.* London and New York, 1925.

Santayana, George, *The Sense of Beauty.* New York, 1908.

————*The Life of Reason & Reason in Art.* New York, 1934.

Schopenhauer, Arthur, *Philosophie der Kunst,* 2 Bde. Leipzig, 1891

Simkhovitch, Vladimir, *Political Science Quarterly,* Vol. XLIX (March 1934), p. 44.

Stace, W. T., *The Meaning of Beauty.* London, 1929.

Taylor, Henry Osborn, *Human Values and Verities.* London, 1928.

Volkelt, Johannes, *System der Ästhetik,* 3 Bde. Munich, 1914.

Wilenski, R. H., *The Modern Movement in Art.* New York, 1927.

INDEX